The International Politics of Human Trafficking

Gillian Wylie

The International Politics of Human Trafficking

palgrave
macmillan

Gillian Wylie
Trinity College Dublin
Ireland

ISBN 978-1-137-37774-6 ISBN 978-1-137-37775-3 (eBook)
DOI 10.1057/978-1-137-37775-3

Library of Congress Control Number: 2016951092

Printed on acid-free paper

This Palgrave Macmillan imprint is published by Springer Nature
The registered company is Macmillan Publishers Ltd. London

Acknowledgements

I am a person who loves to collaborate, so writing a monograph has been a major challenge. However, thankfully, over the years researching human trafficking, I've been blessed by working at various times with three wonderful collaborators—Deirdre Coghlan, Penny McRedmond and Eilís Ward. What I have learned from and with each of them informs much of the thinking in this book. But besides all I have learned from them, I am really fortunate that they are my friends.

There is a wider circle of people I have met over the years who have contributed to the development of this book in many ways, through conference encounters, research projects, editorial work or just in telling conversations. I would like to thank all of the following for shaping my thinking about the international politics of human trafficking: Diana Correa Corrales, Rochelle Dalla, Louise Deegan, David Feingold, Sharron FitzGerald, Roy Huijsmans, Susann Huschke, Ronit Lentin, Eithne Luibhéid, Kathryn McGarry, Cezara Nanu, Erin O'Brien, Nicole Record, Christien van den Anker and Rachel Wechsler.

I did not foresee that shortly after I signed my contract with Palgrave I would be made head of my department. The last three years have been challenging, so I would like to thank all my wonderful administrative and academic colleagues (old and new) across the two sites of the Irish School of Ecumenics in Dublin and Belfast for all their support and encouragement: Carlo Aldrovandi, Iain Atack, Brendan Browne, Bridget Cahill, Caroline Clark, Maja Halilovic-Pastuovic, Christine Houlahan, Jude Lal Fernando, Gladys Ganiel, Linda Hogan, Dong Jin Kim, Damian Jackson, Bill McSweeney, Claudia Meium, David Mitchell, Karen Nicholson,

Brid O'Brien, Andrew Pierce, Mary Priestman, Etain Tannam, Geraldine Smyth, David Tombs and Aideen Woods. The ISE Trust, under the leadership of Salters Sterling and Dermot McCarthy, are also a source of great support. It is working with all of these people that makes coming to work a joy, despite the worries carried by any head of department.

The other joy at work is of course working with students. While writing this book, I've been involved in the supervision of several PhD students—John Agberagba, Leanne Doyle, Sue Foy, Barbara Hart, Salome Mbugua, Chiara Mizzone, Caroline Munyi, Astrid Peréz Piñán, Polycarp Ugwu and Sinéad Walsh. I'm grateful to them all for what I've learned from them about gender, feminism, women's activism, migration politics and ethics, all of which feeds into this book in various ways.

This book would not be appearing but for the help and gentle prodding of the team at Palgrave, so many thanks are due to Harriet Barker Eleanor Davey-Corrigan, Hannah Kaspar, Samantha Snedden, Sarah Roughley and Julia Willan. The other person deserving enormous thanks for ensuring this book came to fruition is my friend Trudi Brook, who offered to proofread the manuscript (even when I tried to dissuade her) and did a superb job—often late at night, if the timings on e-mails are to be believed.

The book was also nursed along by the love and kindness of my friends and family. My parents and sister, John, Marj and Karen Wylie, gave time to ensure my family was minded, as well as always asking probing questions. Inge Schmidt-Kanev and Kathrin Häselbarth, mother and sister-in-law, also came each summer to gift me time. Joe Fleming, calmest child-minder ever, kept our household sane. Finally, the biggest thanks of all are for my beloved husband and sons—Olaf, Max, Hanni and Oscar Schmidt—the inventors and enforcers of 'thoughtful Thursdays'. Without your amazing support I would not have managed this. I love you all.

Contents

CHAPTER 1

Introduction: The International Politics of Human Trafficking

The idea to write this book crystallised in my head at a very particular moment in 2012 as I was walking towards a day conference being hosted by Ireland's Department of Justice on the future direction of prostitution policy in the state. I was going to the conference because of my research interest in human trafficking—and in Ireland, as in many other places, debates on the issue have become focused around the particular question of sex trafficking and whether the 'answer' lies in how states regulate prostitution. Although just an audience member, I was dreading the day because I knew it would be a fraught event for everyone involved. There are two camps in the prostitution policy debate. Feminists who consider prostitution and sex trafficking as synonymous forms of violence against women that are always exploitative and feminists who do not equate prostitution to trafficking, arguing that sexual labour is not necessarily coerced and should be recognised as legitimate work. Their policy prescriptions are worlds apart: abolition of prostitution and criminalisation of sex buyers on one side, a legal and rights framework for sex workers on the other. When the sides clash, debates are always vehement and highly emotional, and indeed that would prove to be the case that day, with diametrically opposed claims to knowledge provoking anger and tears. Yet, approaching the event I felt puzzled by a disjuncture between the intensity of debates and energy being vested in civil society and political responses to the issue of sex trafficking and the sense that there was no clear evidence or consensus about the nature or extent of the problem. Listening to the debates, it was clear that the civil society representatives were divided on who should

G. Wylie, *The International Politics of Human Trafficking*,
DOI 10.1057/978-1-137-37775-3_1

be classed as a trafficked person or what should be done about it. Women and men with experiences of prostitution/sex work offered clashing perspectives on their understandings of their lived experiences. A police representative from Sweden promoted his country's neo-abolitionist approach, but self-defined sex workers in the room strongly condemned the impact the law has on women. The civil libertarian-inclined Minister for Justice seemed swayed by the legalisation route but appeared outnumbered by a broad pro-abolitionist political coalition that was forming. The politics were intense but also bewildering. What had brought the issue of human trafficking (particularly sex trafficking), so relatively obscure until recently, to such heated prominence and discussions at the heart of government?

Although I begin from my Irish context, this is a puzzle the spreads across international dimensions. Twenty years ago human trafficking was virtually no one's concern globally. Widespread nineteenth-century panics in colonial metropoles about the apparent trafficking in women for what the sensationalist press of the day dubbed a 'white slave trade' of forced prostitution (Soderlund 2013) gradually subsided into international bureaucratic measures. After being considered in the work of League of Nations committees and then codified in a 1949 UN Convention, by mid-twentieth century, human trafficking was largely parked in a 'hallowed, if irrelevant, position on the sidelines of the United Nations' human rights system' (Gallagher 2009, 792). Yet over the course of the last two decades human trafficking has come to be commonly referred to as 'a defining problem of the 21st century' (Shelley 2010, 58), with others claiming that 'human trafficking chains increasingly blanket the globe' (Tiano and Murphy-Aguilar 2012, 4). Human trafficking is commonly said to be the third largest form of transnational organised crime (after drugs and arms) and an industry worth tens of billions each year to criminals (UNRIC 2016). Some accounts of the significance of the problem to contemporary global peace and security are almost apocalyptic, such as Louise Shelley's analysis that trafficking will cause governmental corruption, the spread of diseases and family breakdown (Shelley 2010, 60–61). In reaction to this apparently frightening problem the last 20 years have seen the development of a large and complex edifice of international and national anti-trafficking responses. This includes the spread of anti-trafficking norms, new international and domestic legal frameworks, policing and security measures, services provided by multiple civil society organisations, slews of academic and advocacy research, generous funding streams and omnipresent cultural representations. All of this exists despite the equally commonly acknowledged problems that there is little consensus on what human trafficking is and no one is very sure how to count or counter it. This book, trying to banish my own puzzlement, explores the international politics of how we got from there to here.

Human Trafficking: The Shaky Evidence Beneath the Global Edifice

It is very common, and only honest, that many studies of human trafficking begin with the proviso that data on the extent of the problem are unreliable. The reasons for this difficulty are pragmatic and/or political. On the practical side, there are the methodological obstacles to researching 'hidden populations' or activities involving criminality (Zhang et al. 2014, 68). Accessing representative samples and negotiating with 'gatekeepers' may add to these complications (Brunovskis and Surtees 2010, 6). Lack of definitional clarity about who constitutes a 'victim of trafficking' also problematises research (Tyldum 2010, 7), as do the constraints of research ethics, which necessarily delimit research into 'vulnerable populations' (Lee 1993). However, the politics of what is being counted are even more confounding of reliable research than the practicalities when it comes to collecting data on human trafficking.

There is an internationally agreed definition of what constitutes human trafficking as found in the UN Palermo Protocol to Prevent, Suppress and Punish Trafficking in Human Beings, Especially Women and Children (UNODC 2000). That definition reads as follows,

> 'Trafficking in persons' shall mean the recruitment, transportation, transfer, harbouring or receipt of persons, by means of the threat or use of force or other forms of coercion, of abduction, of fraud, of deception, of the abuse of power or of a position of vulnerability or of the giving or receiving of payments or benefits to achieve the consent of a person having control over another person, for the purpose of exploitation. Exploitation shall include, at a minimum, the exploitation of the prostitution of others or other forms of sexual exploitation, forced labour or services, slavery or practices similar to slavery, servitude or the removal of organs...The consent of a victim of trafficking in persons to the intended exploitation set forth [above] shall be irrelevant where any of the means set forth [above] have been used.

This is obviously a convoluted definition that is hard to operationalise. It can be boiled down to human trafficking being the result of three steps—movement of a person, by an act of deceptive or coercive recruitment, which ends in their exploitation. Yet, as my introductory paragraphs above hinted, even when reduced to a simpler formula, the devil is in the interpretation. Feminists cannot achieve consensus on whether all commercial sex is a form of exploitation or whether it is possible to consent to sex work. And they are not the only ones addled by different stances on aspects of the definition. State agencies seeking to prosecute traffickers are focused on being able to connect evidence of all three elements of the definition; service providers seeking to assist people they see as exploited care less about how they got to the difficult place they are in than the exploitative situation they are facing.

My own awareness of these difficulties emerged from the research process of trying with my colleague Eilís Ward to conduct the first baseline study of sex trafficking into Ireland in 2006–07 (Ward and Wylie 2007). By interviewing service-providing non-governmental organisations (NGOs) and statutory agencies, we tried to establish some basic figures. Methodological problems were plentiful, such as incomplete records amongst NGOs or the fact that we were only counting cases known to our informants. Yet, more importantly, it became obvious that the numbers given were seen through the prism of each interviewee's position on the prostitution/sex work debates. Most NGOs took the neo-abolitionist line on the indistinguishable relationship between prostitution and sex trafficking, so all women they dealt with were by definition trafficked. Those involved in law enforcement took the narrower view that the three elements of coercion, movement and exploitation needed to be provable to constitute a countable case. The numbers were never going to add up to everyone's agreement. In the end our data were too low for the NGOs and too high for the law enforcers. Ten years on, and hopefully wiser, I would not attempt the same study again, having learned through the process that gathering trafficking data is inherently problematic and unavoidably politicised.

The need for caution about trafficking data is often noted in the literature but this does not prevent the wide circulation of some numbers that have acquired the status of common knowledge on the subject. A good example here is the headline figure from the US State Department's annual Trafficking in Persons (TiP) Report (US Department of State 2016). Over recent years this report has regularly returned the number of 700–800,000 people trafficked around the globe annually (80% of whom are women and children for sexual exploitation). Due to its provenance in the powerhouse of the State Department and its frequent repetition in government statements and numerous venues, the TiP figure gains traction. However, the methodology behind the TiP Report is frequently queried, most embarrassingly by the US Government's own Office for Accountability in its 2006 report, which noted the lack of clarity about the methods used and reliability of the data (GAO 2006 and Feingold 2010, 64). TiP data rely on reporting from US embassies throughout the world who themselves rely on estimates from local sources, and so ideological positioning along the whole chain of reporting inflects the eventual statistics. The localised politics I illustrated in relation to Ireland are passed up the global chain, while the ideological persuasion of the US administration of the day affects the slant of the data too. Under George W. Bush, for instance, who was a strong endorser of anti-prostitution activism, sex trafficking figures were privileged and wider labour exploitation statistics neglected.

Other trafficking data projects, such as the UN Office on Drugs and Crime GIFT project (Global Initiative to Fight Trafficking) (UNODC. GIFT.HUB 2016) aim to provide harder statistics by relying solely on judicial data about prosecuted cases from around the world. Yet this kind of project is questionable as well for its reliance on how effectively states police trafficking laws or how differing justice systems interpret the meaning of the law. It also leaves hanging a sense that this approach cannot capture the full extent of the problem—whatever it is defined to be.

David Feingold and his colleagues in the UNESCO Bangkok Project on trafficking data make it their goal to collect, trace back and try to identify the research methods and empirical bases of trafficking data from multiple sources around the world (UNESCO Bangkok 2009). His conclusion is that in relation to human trafficking there is plenty of 'numerical certainty' but behind that huge 'statistical doubt' due to differing definitions at work in each data set and methodological opaqueness. The numbers however tend to gain veracity by repetition (Feingold 2010, 59) or an invincibility given by the claim that 'hidden populations' can never be fully known, so whatever numbers we have must be underestimates. Carole Vance makes a telling point in her inspired reference to trafficking statistics as 'numerical vampires' that cannot be killed off (Vance 2011, 936). One explanation for the seemingly eternal life of these statistics lies in the political work the numbers do, justifying the great global anti-trafficking edifice that I will give a rough sketch of below.

Before doing so it is important to clarify that in refuting the reliability of human trafficking statistics, I am not denying that many people suffer the kinds of experiences, particularly as they migrate, that the trafficking definition tries to capture. My own position, based on research I was involved with in Ireland on trafficking for forced labour alongside my wider reading of international literature, is that the narrowness of the three-pronged trafficking definition does not capture the complex realities of people's migration stories. People may start out willingly but end up exploited, or their troubles may come as a result of their migratory status (that is, becoming 'undocumented'), rather than as a result of the work of human traffickers. Authorities dealing with harsh labour conditions may not consider the person 'exploited enough' to be considered a trafficking victim (Coghlan and Wylie 2011). Very often the circumstances that might be classed as 'trafficking' are simply 'labor migration gone horribly wrong in our globalized economy' (Chuang 2006a, 138). For these reasons I think it is more useful to use the concept of a 'continuum of experience' (Anderson and O'Connell Davidson 2002, 12) or a 'continuum of exploitation' (Anderson and Andrijasevic 2008, 140) within migration to capture all these possibilities and I do not think moral concern should be limited to only those who might be legally defined as trafficked. However, why human trafficking has come to be the cause célèbre and the category of choice for governments and NGOs in singling out particular victims who need protection or agents who ought to be prosecuted relates to political choices that will be explained in the course of this book. As will become clearer, I am interested in the political work that the concept of human trafficking does in relation to, for example, delineating 'deserving' from 'undeserving' migrants (O'Connell Davidson 2010, 245), legitimating neo-abolitionist politics or justifying the securitisation of borders.

Empirical claims about the nature and extent of trafficking seem to turn to dust when subjected to scrutiny. Common claims such as the number of trafficking victims worldwide is huge and growing or human trafficking is the third largest form of transnational crime are made with 'no substantial evidence or clear methodology behind them' (Weitzer 2014, 11). The lack of solidity to claims about trafficking ought to have provoked a 'credibility problem' by now for all the actors so engaged with the topic (Zhang et al. 2014, 66). But this seems far from the case if the immense fabric of global and local responses to the issue is anything to go by.

The Anti-trafficking Edifice Built on the Shaky Foundations

The Palermo Protocol signalled a reinvigoration of the issue of human trafficking and the start of today's global anti-trafficking edifice building. For various reasons to be discussed later, Palermo's ratification was followed by a rapid spread of the new international framework to regional and domestic polities. A few examples suffice to give a sense of the ever-growing architecture from 2000 onwards.

Every regional governance structure in the world has assimilated the global framework into their context since 2000. These include the Association of South East Asian States' (ASEAN) Declaration against Human Trafficking particularly Women and Children (2004), the African Union's (AU) Ouagadougou Plan of Action on Trafficking in Human Beings Especially Women and Children (2006) and the establishment of an Anti-Trafficking in Persons Unit within the secretariat of the Organization of American States (OAS 2007). The Council of Europe (CoE) created its own Convention on Action against the Trafficking in Human Beings (Council of Europe Convention 2005), and the EU has passed a number of anti-trafficking Directives over the last 15 years. These commitments on paper translate into policies and activities, such as the CoE's establishment of a monitoring mechanism for the implementation of its Convention or the AU's agreement with the EU to take anti-trafficking measures as part of curbing migration in exchange for development assistance.

Even at sub-regional levels there are action plans and strategies to combat trafficking. So, within the context of the African Union there are numerous examples such as the Libreville Common Platform for Action of the Sub-regional Consultation on the Development of Strategies to Fight Child Trafficking for Exploitative Labour Purposes in West and Central Africa (UNICEF 2000), the Declaration of Action against Trafficking of the Economic Community of West African States (ECOWAS 2001) and the ECOWAS and Economic Community of Central African States (ECCAS) Joint Action Plan (UNODC 2008, 76).

Descending to the nation-state level, many countries have elaborated new or amended anti-trafficking laws, developed training and enforcement procedures for police and border guards, established monitoring and reporting mechanisms (such as National Action Plans or National Rapporteurs) and funded NGOs to offer protections to designated victims. Such funding can be of immense significance, such as the $1.2 billion funnelled to anti-trafficking programmes by the US State Department between 2001 and 2011 (Weitzer 2014, 22).

NGOs working on the issue of trafficking are multitudinous. Numerous transnational networks of organisations lobby on sex trafficking, most prominently (though from diametrically opposite stances) the umbrella groups the Coalition Against Trafficking in Women (CATW) and the Global Alliance Against Traffic in Women (GAATW). Within many nation-states there are plenty of local organisations responding to the issue. For example, in a later chapter when I focus on Ireland, I will mention that there are at least 60 civil society organisations that see sex trafficking as (at least) part of their remit. NGOs concerned with labour exploitation issues are thinner on the ground but they do exist from the International Labour Organization downwards to domestic civil groups focused on support to migrant workers.

As well as the political, policing and civil society responses to human trafficking, interest in the issue has also grown exponentially in academia. There is so much research on the topic that I am painfully aware that this book does not rest on anything like the resource base that exists. Recent years have seen the foundation of new journals on the issue, such as *The Journal of Human Trafficking* (established in 2015) and the *Anti-Trafficking Review* (established 2012). Research is also undertaken by advocacy groups or on the part of governments (like the TiP Report) or international organisations (such as the UNGift report of the UNODC). But knowledge about trafficking (although always contested) is not confined to the academic or policy/advocacy worlds but is equally prevalent in everyday culture. Representations of trafficking in cinema, television, social media and journalism are widespread and consolidate a sense of the existence of a global problem needing to be addressed.

Despite all this activity and the political architecture it spawns, the basic disjuncture persists between any surety regarding empirical claims about trafficking and the sheer exuberance of interest in the issue and multiplicity of political, social and cultural responses it evokes. It seems very much the case that in relation to human trafficking, 'enormous interest is running ahead of theory and evidence' (Agustin 2007, 36 quoting Salt).

In this book I am not trying to do anything in relation to finding better evidence. I do not think this is even possible for the methodological but also ideological reasons affecting all trafficking 'evidence' that I mentioned before. Yet it is quite commonplace in human trafficking studies to admit that 'the data is contested but the problem is significant' (Shelley 2011, 4) and so find a way to carry on with discussing the problem regardless. I do not want to make that move in this book but rather focus on the politics that keeps interest in human trafficking alive despite the lack of reliable evidence. I am interested in developing a theory to account for the gap between solid evidence and intense interest and action. To borrow from my colleague Roy Huijsmans (2011), I want to answer some basic questions. Why so much focus on human trafficking? Why the interest now? And (to add my own) what are the political and human consequences of the marked interest in trafficking? To do this I will rely on constructivist accounts of international relations [inflected often by feminist International Relations (IR) and gender analysis] as my theoretical underpinning with particular reliance on a theory about why certain norms come to matter in and shape international politics.

Theorising the Lifecycle of International Norms

Constructivism as a theoretical tradition within IR is based on the ontological premise that the socio-political world is made through human action and the epistemological premise that as humans in the 'world of our making' we cannot be neutral observers of it. Chapter 2 will deal in more detail with the reasons why I find this way of seeing the world convincing, as opposed to other theoretical traditions in IR. At this point it is sufficient to say that from a constructivist viewpoint ideas, beliefs and values are as important to the shaping of international politics as material structures and interests (Reus-Smit 2005, 196). This includes norms as ideas about what constitute appropriate behaviour. Such norms can be 'regulative' in terms of defining what states ought to do and/or 'constitutive' in terms of determining what behaviour is required for states to be considered legitimate actors in the international system (Risse 2000). Examples of regulative norms in the current international system include gender equality, environmental sustainability or civilian immunity in war; constitutive norms include sovereignty or liberal democracy. However, it is sometimes hard to draw lines between the two types. Human rights for instance are both regulative in terms of what states ought to uphold and constitutive in the sense preserving them increasingly defines what it is to be a 'civilised state' in the modern world (Risse 2000, 5). The Western provenance of these prominent examples already hints that there will be power politics and persistent contention around many norms. Moreover, norms are usually made up of compounds of ideas and internally complex. As Finnemore and Sikkink note 'political scientists tend to slip into discussions of "sovereignty" or "slavery" as if they were norms, when in fact they are (or were) collections of norms and the mix of rules and practices that structure these institutions has varied significantly over time' (Finnemore and Sikkink 1998, 891). Human trafficking is no exception. Although as a means of shorthand throughout this book I refer to trafficking as a norm, I am of course implying opposition to human trafficking as an international norm. And while there may be general consensus that people ought not to deceive, coerce and exploit other humans, what each of these terms means to different actors is internally contested, as are ideas about what kind of practices and institutions ought to emerge in response. Like many norms, the anti-trafficking norm is not 'stable in terms of content' and indeed in the politically charged discursive processes around norm formation it is the case that some versions of the meaning of trafficking come to dominate while others get silenced (Krook and True 2012, 108).

Having said this, constructivists have long argued that norms, as ideals and when institutionalised, shape states' identities and interests. However, as Martha Finnemore and Kathryn Sikkink argue, this basic position leaves us with many questions, such as where norms come from, how they create political change or how we can demonstrate their causal significance (Finnemore and Sikkink 1998, 888). Offering a way to answer their own questions, the two authors outlined their classic model of the norm lifecycle. The model proposes that it is possible to trace international norm emergence to the efforts of inspired moral entrepreneurs (often, though not exclusively, civil society actors). If they successfully advocate for norm adoption and build political alliances in global forums, growing consensus around a new norm will reach a 'tipping point' at which conformity to the norm becomes essential to legitimate state behaviour. After this tipping point, the norm will 'cascade' from the global to the local, as socialisation and internalisation processes occur by which a new global norm will meet and shape domestic politics. At the 'far end' of the norm lifecycle the normative concept is so embedded that it becomes 'taken for granted' (Finnemore and Sikkink 1998).

The norm lifecycle is a helpful model and a useful framework for organising a coherent discussion of how norms evolve and come to shape international politics and state behaviour. As such I will pin the structure of this book to it. However, the norm lifecycle model has not been without its critics. For example, some have pointed out that it emphasises international politics from the bottom up, neglecting the top-down promulgation of norms (Reimann 2006, 45–68), with others arguing that states' material interests or 'hard power' (Reich 2010, 4) cannot be siphoned out of the analysis of why and how certain norms become consolidated in international political life. There is also something too rational about the lifecycle model. It does not capture battles within entrepreneurial communities over the meaning of a norm or the on-going controversy that can arise between global expectations and local views when international norms are transposed to particular contexts (Kravtsov 2009, 295–316). So, based on this critical literature, I will argue through Chap. 2 that understanding the rise of the global anti-trafficking norm makes more sense when read against a model of the norm lifecycle, which also takes points about politics inside and outside entrepreneurial communities and before and after norm adoption into account. As such I hope that this book, though primarily concerned with the international politics of human trafficking, will also contribute to theoretical debates in IR about the interplay of norms, identities and interests in the construction of international relations.

The Norm Lifecycle and the Chapters of This Book

Following the theoretical framework established in Chap. 2, the subsequent chapters of this book will move step by step through the norm lifecycle to build an answer to those puzzling questions—why trafficking, why now and with what consequences?

Chapter 3 is concerned with why human trafficking re-emerged forcefully on the international agenda from the 1990s onwards. Following Finnemore and Sikkink's first clue, this chapter identifies the moral entrepreneurs involved prior to and during the UN's adoption of the Palermo Protocol. This involves examining the genealogy of movements like the Coalition Against Trafficking in Women and the Global Alliance Against Trafficking in Women (amongst others) and demonstrating how their contradictory activism intersected with the positions of nation-state parties in international forums, particularly the negotiations leading to the UN Convention on Transnational Organized Crime and the accompanying Protocol (UNODC 2000). What is of interest here is to depict how diverse entrepreneurs framed their understanding of the problem and sought to engage political support through public discourse, appeal to moral frameworks and adept lobbying. It is also important to recognise the outcomes of entrepreneurial controversies in that certain versions of the norm came to dominate international discourses: human trafficking as being primarily about sex trafficking and the moral problem of 'the prostitution of women and children' and trafficking being simultaneously a problem of organised crime requiring a 'hard power' response. The coincidence of the rise of the trafficking norm with the end of the Cold War and the construction of new security concerns for states (Goodey 2008), suggests a material as opposed to purely altruistic interest for states in adopting anti-trafficking norms. Therefore, the chapter suggests that moral entrepreneurship alone is not the only reason for the resumption of the anti-trafficking lifecycle.

The fourth chapter examines the cascade of the global anti-trafficking norm, with an emphasis on the key role of the United States as effectively 'the global sheriff' when it comes to combating human trafficking (Chuang 2006b). Through mechanisms such as the annual TiP report and its associated rankings and sanctions, the US modifies the behaviour of other states in regard to their expected anti-trafficking standards (Gallagher 2011, 382; van Schendel et al. 2012). To an extent the punch packed by the TiP report seems to validate Simon Reich's argument that international norm adoption requires not only an acceptance of moral worthiness but also 'hard power' behind the moral pressure, particularly US sponsorship (Reich 2010). Yet, material interests alone cannot explain the reasons why the US invests so much effort on the trafficking issue. In the constructivist vein, this chapter argues that US politics are shaped by the intersection of ideals, identity and interests. Key aspects in America's self-understanding, relating, for example, to freedom and faith, explain the self-appointed and influential role of the US as a moral entrepreneur and international disciplinarian in relation to human trafficking.

Chapter 5 continues following through the norm lifecycle model, with emphasis on the socialisation processes that lead to the internalisation of norms from global to domestic politics. While pressure from the US is part of this story in relation to trafficking, other dynamics are in operation too. As the section above on the 'edifice' mentioned, many regional organisations adopted their own anti-trafficking frameworks post Palermo. Members are then socialised into these new regional-level expectations, as will be illustrated in this chapter with reference to the impact of EU Directives on member states. Yet by analysing the development of anti-trafficking policy and politics on the island of Ireland, the chapter will demonstrate once more that the lifecycle model does not capture the messiness of the political world of norm adoption. Across Ireland, vociferous civil society campaigns for neo-abolitionism draw on and bolster regional-level campaigns (such as that of the European Women's Lobby) and claim inspiration from the sex purchase laws in Nordic states. This reveals that the internalisation of international norms is not solely a top-down process but involves an intimate crossover between local mores and global expectations.

As Chaps. 3–5 work through the lifecycle of the anti-trafficking norm, one thing that becomes obvious is that concerns about sex trafficking predominate in activism and architecture. This is despite the fact that under the Palermo definition human trafficking can lead to other exploitative ends, particularly servitude, forced labour or organ removal. Chapter 6 therefore poses the question of why certain understandings of the anti-trafficking norm do not attract such zealous entrepreneurship, leading to adoption and internalisation. Focusing on the issue of labour trafficking, this chapter will explore why this element of the anti-trafficking norm has failed to emerge, cascade and internalise to any great degree. In one respect, looking at the majority and positions of NGOs engaged in these issues, it is possible to suggest that the heat and (perhaps) light generated by moral proselytism surrounding sexual exploitation is lacking in relation to labour trafficking more generally. However, there are other reasons for neglect of this facet of the anti-trafficking norm. These include the gendering of ideas about human agency, which consign women to victimhood and innocence while expecting agency and rationality of men. Men are therefore much more likely to be deemed 'smuggled migrants' (and so agents in their own irregular border crossing) than women, who are recognisable as 'trafficking victims'. Importantly, the chapter will also revert to the argument about state interests and norm acceptability. Contemporary globalisation is built on a great contradiction: the free movement of everything except people (Munck 2008). Yet, at the same time the developed world relies on immigrants from the poorer parts of the world to undertake the 3D (dirty, dangerous, demeaning) jobs of the 'liquid world' (Baumann 2004). In this contemporary capitalist context, many states are chary of agreeing to a norm of what constitutes 'decent work' or enabling more regularised migration. This chapter therefore provides analysis as to why any norm might flounder when it lacks moral sponsors and contradicts states' material interests.

Chapter 7 will bring us to the 'far end' of the norm lifecycle, at which point Finnemore and Sikkink suggest normative ideas mature and acquire the status of generally accepted common knowledge (1998). Close to

20 years on from the politics recounted in Chap. 3, the anti-trafficking norm lifecycle has evolved, and the notion that human trafficking (particularly for sexual exploitation) is an extensive and established problem needing governance has indeed achieved the status of common knowledge globally and locally. Chapter 7 will exemplify the many ways such public knowledge is constructed through media such as popular press, film and campaigns. Although common knowledge is never without its dissenters, I will argue that the most prevalent representations work to reinforce dominant discourses that trafficking is primarily about sexual exploitation and organised criminality. The consequences of such representations are the legitimisation of government responses to trafficking that prioritise border control and state security at the expense of identifying or addressing the root causes of exploitative migratory experiences in the complexities of global inequalities, contradictory globalisation practices and constrained migration possibilities (van den Anker and van Liempt 2012). As Chap. 7 ends the poignancy of this analysis will be made clear with reference to European governments' responses to the migrants coming to Europe in 2015–2016.

There are no neat beginnings or endings to norm lifecycles. Anti-trafficking ideals and activism pre-dated the 1990s, and this latest phase of the norm contains instabilities and contestation that will persist. A book must end somewhere though, so the conclusion of this one will offers some thoughts on what the chapters reveal about the international politics of human trafficking in particular and the question of why and how norms develop and impact on international politics in general.

Biases and Limitations in This Account of the Politics of Trafficking

I have said enough already to indicate that controversy about what constitutes trafficking is rife, as are debates about what might be the best responses to it. Although treating opposition to human trafficking as a norm, it is clear that this is not a case where there is a singular interpretation or stable consensus about the meaning of the term. Because I am of the opinion that researchers are not neutral observers of the socio-political world, this raises the question of where I stand on trafficking debates and how this impinges on the analysis and argument in this book.

Elsewhere I have written with my colleague Eilís Ward about how our research experiences and engagement with debates in the field led us to a position of opposition to neo-abolitionism, at a time when it was being forcefully lobbied for in Ireland. The reasons for this relate to our reading of the politics and consequences of abolitionist laws in the Nordic states and our philosophical position that we could not write off the voices of women and men in sex work who did not consider themselves to be victims. We ended up among a very small minority of Irish civil actors who opposed the proposition to criminalise the purchase of sex in Ireland as an anti-prostitution and anti-trafficking device. Taking this stand publicly was personally difficult and caused us much discomfort, but inspired by Wanda Pillow's idea of the 'reflexivity of discomfort' we drew on our experiences to think about how hegemony over public knowledge on the trafficking issue was created by civil society organisations committed to abolitionism (Ward and Wylie 2014). Something of that story is drawn on in Chap. 5 as I trace the internalisation of a global norm in a local context.

Having admitted to a position on the sex trafficking and prostitution debates, I also confess that I find the predominant focus on sex trafficking too reductive. Why the politics of sex trafficking overshadows international normative concern with forced labour more generally is the subject of Chap. 6. It is sometimes said that people approach human trafficking through different lenses. Gendered violence, migration, human rights, security, crime, law and order are commonly named amongst possible framings. If there is one lens I privilege when thinking about the trafficking issue (although not losing sight of others), it is the migration one, recognising the exploitative ends across a range of labour sectors that people on the move can experience and looking in particular at the ways state policies create migrant vulnerabilities (Anderson and Andrijasevic 2008, 142). The politics of why some of these experiences get categorised as 'human trafficking' (and others do not) by the international community and nation-states is a key concern in this book. However, one exclusive lens would be too narrow and I do also pay attention to the working out of gendered stereotypes and questions of workers' rights as they impact on the social construction of human trafficking.

Throughout this book, I try to give a faithful account of the politics of human trafficking as it plays out in a series of venues, paying attention to a multitude of actors and their roles. But in terms of the overall argument, I am building an understanding of the politics of human trafficking that is critical of neo-abolitionist agendas and also of the ways states use trafficking discourses to justify the securitisation of migration. I hope the argument convinces, but it is undeniably reflective of my own politics on the issue, and readers should consider their own positions in engagement with mine.

The longer I have worked on this book the more aware I am of the impossibility of doing justice to the scholarship on the field. One aspect that has shaken me in the last months is the realisation of both the hubris and the limits of my rather grandiose claim to be offering an analysis of 'the international politics of human trafficking'. Late in the day, I read Amita Acharya's call for a reform of IR to a genuinely global study of politics, away from the Western-centred traditions of the discipline (Acharya 2014). Although I write here with a strong awareness of the impact of global inequalities on creating the politics of trafficking and, I hope, a sensitivity to what Acharya calls 'the two way diffusion of norms' (2014, 647), I fear I have written yet another account of IR that centres on the activities of the US and Europe and relies of Western theoretical traditions. Reading works by Kamala Kempadoo (2015) and Pardis Mahdavi (2014), I realise I underplay the orientalism and racism in trafficking discourses and neglect the possibilities in post-colonial readings of international politics for explaining human trafficking. That said, I write from where I sit, trying to be alive to the power dynamics of globalisation that set so many people in motion but throw obstacles in their paths at the same time, leading to the complex experiences which some class as 'human trafficking'. I begin my exploration of the politics by which this term and its consequences have become so ubiquitous by turning now to elaborating the theoretical framework I will use for tracing the lifecycle of the anti-trafficking norm.

Bibliography

Acharya, A. (2014). Global international relations (IR) and regional worlds. *International Studies Quarterly, 58*, 647–659.

African Union (AU). (2006). Ouagadougou action plan to combat trafficking in human beings, especially women and children as adopted by the Ministerial Conference on Migration and Development. (November 22–23). http://ec.europa.eu/development/body/tmp_docs/2006/Action_plan_OUAGADOUGOU.pdf, date accessed 13 March 2016.

Agustin, L.-M. (2007). *Sex at the margins: Migration, labour markets and the rescue industry*. London: Zed Books.

Anderson, B., & Andrijasevic, R. (2008). Sex, slaves and citizens: The politics of anti-trafficking. *Soundings, 40*, 135–145.

Anderson, B., & O'Connell Davidson, J. (2002). *Trafficking—A demand led problem? A multi-country study*. Stockholm: Save the Children.

ASEAN. (2004). Association of South East Asian States (ASEAN) Declaration against human trafficking particularly women and children. (29 November 2004) https://www1.umn.edu/humanrts/research/Philippines/ASEAN%20Declaration%20Against%20Trafficking%20in%20Persons%20Particularly%20Women%20and%20Children.pdf, date accessed 13 March 2016.

Baumann, Z. (2004). *Wasted lives: Modernity and its outcasts*. Cambridge: Polity.

Brunovskis, A., & Surtees, R. (2010). Untold stories: Biases and selection effects in research with victims of trafficking for sexual exploitation. *International Migration, 48*(4), 1–38.

Chuang, J. (2006a). 'Beyond a Snapshot: Preventing Human Trafficking in the Global Economy', *Indiana Journal of Global Legal Studies, 13*(1), 137–163.

Chuang, J. (2006b). 'The United States as Global Sheriff: Using Unilateral Sanctions to Combat Human Trafficking', *Michigan Journal of International Law, 27*, 437–494.

Coghlan, D., & Wylie, G. (2011). Defining trafficking/Denying justice? Forced labour in Ireland and the consequences of trafficking discourse. *Journal of Ethnic and Migration Studies, 37*(9), 1513–1526.

Council of Europe Convention. (2005). CoE convention on action against trafficking in human beings. 16 May 2005, https://www.coe.int/t/dghl/monitoring/trafficking/Docs/Convntn/CETS197_en.asp, date accessed 26 February 2016.

ECOWAS. (2001). Declaration on the fight against trafficking in persons, 20–21 December 2001. http://www.unodc.org/pdf/crime/trafficking/Declarationr_CEDEAO.pdf, date accessed 13 March 2016.

Feingold, D. (2010). Trafficking in numbers: The social construction of human trafficking data. In P. Andreas & K. Greenhill (Eds.), *Sex, drugs, and body counts: The politics of numbers in global crime and conflict* (pp. 46–74). New York: Cornell University Press.

Finnemore, M., & Sikkink, K. (1998). International norm dynamics and political change. *International Organization, 52*(4), 887–917.

Gallagher, A. T. (2009). Human rights and human trafficking: Quagmire or firm ground? A response to James Hathaway. *Virginia Journal of International Law, 49*(4), 789–848.

Gallagher, A. T. (2011). Improving the effectiveness of international law of human trafficking: A vision for the future of the US trafficking in persons report. *Human Rights Review, 12*, 381–400.

GAO. (2006). *Better data, strategy, and reporting needed to enhance U.S. antitrafficking efforts abroad*. US Government Accountability Office. http://www.gao.gov/products/GAO-06-825.

Goodey, J. (2008). Human trafficking: Sketchy data and policy responses. *Criminology and Criminal Justice, 8*, 421–442.

Huijsmans, R. (2011). Teaching (Anti)trafficking: Some reflections drawing on the Dutch Context. Paper presented at *Incorporating Human Trafficking in*

Academic Institutions: The European experience. Organized by the Protection Project, John Hopkins University, Kloveniersburgwal 48, Oost-Indisch Huis, University of Amsterdam, 25–26 November 2011.

Kempadoo, K. (2015). The Modern-Day White (Wo)Man's Burden: Trends in anti-trafficking and anti-slavery campaigns. *Journal of Human Trafficking, 1*(1), 8–20.

Kravtsov, V. (2009). ARV treatment and AIDS Entrepreneurs in South Africa: Domestic opposition to an International Norm (1999–2004). *Global Society, 23*(3), 295–316.

Krook, M., & True, J. (2012). Rethinking the Lifecycles of International Norms: The United Nations and the Global Promotion of Gender Equality. *European Journal of International Relations, 18*(1), 103–127.

Lee, R. (1993). *Doing research on sensitive topics.* London: Sage.

Mahdavi, P. (2014). *From trafficking to terror: Constructing a global social problem.* New York: Routledge.

Munck, R. (2008). Globalisation, governance and migration: An introduction. *Third World Quarterly, 29*(7), 1227–1246.

O'Connell Davidson, J. (2010). New slavery, old binaries: Human trafficking and the borders of 'freedom'. *Global Networks, 10*(2), 244–261.

Organization of American States. (2007). Anti-trafficking in persons Section. 7 June 2007, OAS: http://www.oas.org/atip/atip_detail.asp, 13 March 2016.

Reich, S. (2010). *Global norms, American Sponsorship and the emerging patterns of world politics.* Basingstoke: Palgrave.

Reimann, K. (2006). A view from the top: International politics, norms and the worldwide growth of NGOs. *International Studies Quarterly, 50*(1), 45–68.

Reus-Smit, C. (2005). 'Constructivism'. In S. Burchill, A. Linklater, R. Devetak, J. Donnelly, M. Patterson, C. Reus-Smit and J. True (eds.), *Theories of International Relations* (3rd edn.). Basingstoke: Palgrave.

Risse, T. (2000). "Let's Argue": Communicative action in world politics. *International Organization, 54*(1), 1–39.

Shelley, L. (2010). *Human trafficking: A global perspective.* Cambridge: Cambridge University Press.

Soderlund, G. (2013). *Sex trafficking, scandal and the transformation of journalism: 1885–1917.* Chicago, Illinois: University of Chicago Press.

Tiano, S., & Murphy-Aguilar, M. (Eds.). (2012). *Borderline Slavery: Mexico, the United States and the Human Trade.* Farnham, Surry: Ashgate.

Tyldum, G. (2010). Limitations in research on human trafficking. *International Migration, 48*(5), 1–13.

UNESCO Bangkok. (2009). Trafficking and HIV AIDS Project: Data comparison sheets. http://www.unescobkk.org/culture/diversity/trafficking-hiv/projects/trafficking-statistics-project/data-comparison-sheet/, date accessed 12 March 2016.

UNICEF. (2000). Common Platform for action of the sub-regional consultation on the development of strategies to fight child trafficking for exploitative labour purposes in West and Central Africa, 22–24 February. http://www.unicef.org/media/newsnotes/platform.pdf, date accessed 13 March 2016.

UNODC. (2000). United Nations convention on Transnational organized crime and the Protocols Thereto. 15 November 2000. https://www.unodc.org/documents/treaties/UNTOC/Publications/TOC%20Convention/TOCebook-e.pdf, date accessed 12 March 2016.

UNODC. (2008). *Toolkit to combat trafficking in persons*. Vienna: UNODC.

UNODC.GIFT.HUB. (2016). Global initiative to fight human trafficking. http://www.ungift.org/knowledgehub/en/about/unodc.html, date accessed 12 March 2016.

UNRIC. (2016). United Nations Regional Information Centre for Western Europe. http://www.unric.org/en/human-trafficking, date accessed 12 March 2016.

US Department of State. (2016). Trafficking in Persons Report. http://www.state.gov/j/tip/rls/tiprpt/, date accessed 12 March 2016.

van den Anker, C., & van Liempt, I. (Eds.). (2012). *Human rights and migration: Trafficking for forced labour*. Basingstoke: Palgrave.

van Schendel, W., Lyons, L., & Ford, M. (2012). *Labour migration and human trafficking in Southeast Asia: Critical perspectives*. London: Routledge.

Vance, C. (2011). States of contradiction: Twelve ways to do nothing about trafficking while pretending to. *Social Research, 78*(3), 933–948.

Ward, E., & Wylie, G. (2007). *The Nature and extent of trafficking of women into Ireland for the purposes of sexual exploitation 2000–2006: A Report from findings*. NUI Galway: SSRC Research Papers and Reports No. 39.

Ward, E., & Wylie, G. (2014). Reflexivities of discomfort': Researching the sex trade and sex trafficking in Ireland. *European Journal of Women's Studies, 21*(3), 251–263.

Weitzer, R. (2014). New directions in human trafficking research. *Annals of the American Academy of Political and Social Sciences, 653*, 6–24.

Zhang, S., Spiller, M., Finch, B., & Qin, Y. (2014). Estimating labor trafficking among unauthorized migrant workers in San Diego. *Annals of the American Academy of Political and Social Science, 653*, 65–86.

CHAPTER 2

Norm Construction in International Politics

Introduction

The degree to which ideas, ideals or norms matter in international politics is one of the issues at the heart of the theoretical fault line between realist and constructivist IR theorists (Wendt 1999; Katzenstein 1996). Neo-realists emphasise the determining importance of states' self-preservatory interests, which are pre-ordained for them by their existence in the insecurity of international anarchy. This contrasts strongly with the constructivist view of the world as a malleable creation of human agency in which ideas and norms play a crucial role in the shaping of states' and other international actors' interests and identities. This chapter will begin with a swift rehearsal of the main contours of these debates and explain why for ontological, epistemological and empirical reasons I belong within the latter school of thought. From this position of accepting that ideas and norms are integral to the shaping of international politics, it will be possible for me over the course of this book to outline and analyse the international politics surrounding, shaping and embedding the anti-trafficking norm. However, as Finnemore and Sikkink point out, this position that norms matter still leaves many questions to answer, such as where norms come from, how they create political change or how we can demonstrate their causal significance (1998, 888). To offer a way to answer their own questions, Finnemore and Sikkink developed their model of the norm life-cycle (1998), which traces norm emergence through the lobbying efforts, most often the work of inspired civil society entrepreneurs, till the norm

G. Wylie, *The International Politics of Human Trafficking*,
DOI 10.1057/978-1-137-37775-3_2

reaches a 'tipping point' or critical mass of state endorsements, before finally achieving internalisation as a new global norm meets and shapes domestic politics and the norm becomes socialised for governments and publics as constituting 'common sense'.

This chapter will outline the lifecycle model and argue for its persistent usefulness because it does enable the identification of key agents in the political life of ideas and allow the tracing of intersecting global and local political processes that demonstrate and account for the growing influence of particular norms in international and domestic politics. By drawing attention to a step-by-step progression—from norm emergence, to tipping point, to cascade and finally internalisation—the model also provides a helpful organising device for dealing with a complex topic and so provides a sensible structure to this book [and the model has indeed already been used so by others, such as Lisbeth Segerlund (2010) in her book on the adoption of the international norm of corporate social responsibility].

The norm lifecycle model has not been without its critics, however. Amongst the critics, some have pointed out that the norm lifecycle model emphasises international politics from the bottom up, so neglecting the top-down promulgation of norms (Reimann 2006), with others arguing that states' material interests or 'hard power' (Reich 2010, 4) cannot be siphoned out of the analysis of why and how certain norms become consolidated in international political life. There is also something too rational about the lifecycle model. It does not capture the on-going controversy surrounding certain norms, which might manifest as persistent debates about the interpretation of a norm's meaning, opposition between global expectations of norm adoption and local views (Kravtsov 2009) or simply the failure of a norm to inspire or embed. I would also add that the term 'lifecycle' seems to imply a neat and recognisable start and ending. In real life, norms have to be understood as being shaped by the intellectual traces and political structures created by pre-existing norms. They then remain continually perturbed by debates, which often rumble on well past their formal adoption, in processes of argument, diffusion or even reversal, rather than simply achieving internalisation by states—or indeed citizens—as the life cycle comes to a recognisable halt.

At the close of this chapter, I will argue that the convoluted and on-going story of the political rise (or even resurrection) of the global anti-trafficking norm makes more sense when read against a model of norm lifecycle, which also takes these critical points and additional factors into account. The chapters that follow will illustrate this point by showing how each stage of the lifecycle of the anti-trafficking norm—emergence, tipping, cascade and internalisation in Finnemore and Sikkink's terms—has been the result of the entangling of the power of ideas and moral entrepreneurship with power politics and (unresolved) 'norm battles' (van Kersbergen and Verbeek 2007, 217). This nuanced reading of the politics of the norm lifecycle will eventually, as this book progresses, allow me to explain something of the mystery referred to in the introductory chapter—why on the one hand the rapid rise of the norm-shaping discourse on human trafficking has been so politically successful, to the extent that most international actors and citizens accept there is a problem that must be responded to (particularly in relation to sex trafficking), while at the same time what really constitutes that problem and how it is best responded to remain issues of on-going controversy.

Norms and the Construction of International Politics

Arguments about whether, how or why norms or ideas matter in shaping international politics do have a long history in the academic discipline of international relations. In fact, if we wanted to look at the 'pre-history', before the normal dating of the official academic pursuit of international relations to the early twentieth century, then tales of normative ideals around abolitionism of slavery or even 'white slaving' would of necessity be part of the story. However, if we begin with the traditional telling of disciplinary history in the early twentieth century, it tends to centre on a dichotomous story of tension between 'idealists' who thought and hoped that normative ideals of democracy or minority rights could assure international peace and 'realists' who analysed the primacy of realpolitik driven by state insecurity, therefore foreseeing the inevitable perpetuation of inter-state violence (Smith 2000). The pre-eminence of realist theories for much of the century subdued (though never obliterated) theoretical discussion of norms and IR for decades, almost until the century's close. Looking back at what could now be grouped as a new wave of theorising about norms and international politics (a selection of books and articles all published around the mid-1990s, which I will look at below), it is obvious that they were part of the theoretical aftershock in academic IR caused by the end of the Cold War.

Before 1989, IR was fairly set in its theoretical ways under the dominance of the neo-realist/neo-liberal paradigms. Separated only by the question of whether cooperation between states is either possible or reliable in the context of international anarchy, both the 'neo-neo' paradigms assume that states are the key actors, power politics are central, and states' interests and identities are exogenously generated by the anarchical international system. For neo-realists in particular, anarchy provides the determining feature of the system. From their perspective, states are forced to pursue self-interest and survival through self-help, competition or power balancing, given the absence of world government. In developing neo-realist theory Kenneth Waltz sought to bring the explanatory power of natural science ontology, epistemology and methodologies to IR. Working from a positivist ontology and epistemology that presumes there is a separate socio-political world 'out there' that we can coldly and objectively analyse as scientific 'armchair observers' (Tanesini 1999), Waltz aimed to distil in neo-realism the regularities and laws that governed the international political world—and he argued he had found those in the determining effects of international anarchy (Waltz 2010).

The shocking and unlooked-for end of the Cold War problematised the empirical and theoretical claims of neo-realists. The peaceable retreat of the USSR from super power, accompanied by the manifestation of 'people power' from below, shook up staid IR knowledge about who are the actors, what are state interests and why things happen as they do in the international realm. The assumed determinism of anarchy was problematised by the evidence of the impact of 'new thinking' from political elites, unexpected political choices about what constituted interests and the interaction of largely non-violent domestic upheavals with international change. Against this background the theoretical renaissance of IR began to move apace with an accelerating turn to the social from the natural sciences as the underlying epistemology. The fundamental ontological premise of emerging constructivist theory was that the international political world is a work of human agency and choice, far removed from the world of determining laws and regularities that natural scientists aim to discern in the material realm. The basic constructivist premise was ever so neatly summed up in the title of Alexander Wendt's seminal article: 'Anarchy is what states make of it' (Wendt 1992). Concomitant to this development was a pluralisation of thinking about who the actors in international politics are, with space opening for considering the roles of non-state actors—below, above and across the boundaries of nation-states—in 'making' international politics (Walker 1994; Keck and Sikkink 1998). Debates about the role of local and global civil societies in shaping international life and state actions proliferated (Anheier et al. 2001).

As Steve Smith suggested in his survey of the history of IR theory, it is not accurate or wise to present theoretical developments in IR as a series of evolving 'grand narratives' rather than a complex story of shifts and resistance, which enables a more accurate capturing of the discipline's history (Smith 2000). And indeed in confirmation of this, it can be seen that although we can discern the shapes of 'grand narratives', over the post-Cold War years the 'sociological turn' has spun on and sometimes retracted in numerous ways. Spinning on—the idea that states, their interests and their relationships are socially constructed has been viewed through ever more varied lenses. One example lies in the work of feminist IR scholars who have asked in what ways gendered norms of masculinity and femininity construct states' identities, actions and interests or in what ways and with what impact feminist movements engage international politics (Tickner and Sjoberg 2011). Retracting—the thorny question of the extent to which choice and agency are constrained by established structures, or to what extent ideas are constrained by material realities, has led to attempts to find a *via media* between social constructivist and realist theories (Wendt 1999).

It is against this theoretical ferment that a new tranche of writings about norms and international politics emerged. The end of the Cold War was, of course, seminal in loosening disciplinary thinking, but it was not the only current event of the 1980s and then the post-Cold War period, which seemed to be running contra realist expectation. In her book on norms in international politics, Audie Klotz puzzled over the decisions made by many states to impose sanctions on South Africa despite the costs to them in strategic or economic terms. The African Front Line States bordering South Africa paid a very heavy price in terms of economic development and military losses for their determined isolating of South Africa. Even the US, contravening the neo-liberalism of Reaganism and its strategic interests in Southern Africa, eventually adopted sanctions. In Klotz's analysis these self-denying policies can only be understood in relation to the centrality of norms in shaping states identities and interests. In these cases the norms of racial equality and/or pan-Africanism fomented in civil and political societies and, touching nerves of identity and morality, trumped the material self-interests of the sanctions imposing states (Klotz 1999).

Other writers in the first 'norm wave' started their analyses from similar observations of states acting against their conventionally understood self-interests (of protecting sovereignty and security by accumulating and projecting power) to engage in what could be considered 'odd' international behaviour. Finnemore discussed this in relation to humanitarian intervention where states engaged in military intervention against their strategic interests and the sacrosanct norm of sovereignty in the name of other norms of human rights or common humanity (Finnemore 1996). Similarly, Richard Price considered the success of the campaign to ban landmines as proving a 'hard case' for those who argue that ideas and values matter in international politics because in this case he argues that civil society norm entrepreneurs successfully challenged states' monopoly on defining 'military security' (Price 1998). They, and other writers of the same period, came to the conclusion that norms mattered in explaining state behaviour (see Nadelmann 1990; Risse 2000) because in a socially constructed world 'norms shape interests…and interests shape action' (Finnemore 1996) and 'norms construct states with specific identities' (Katzenstein 1996).

For these authors, norms as ideas about appropriate behaviour are understood to play a dual role—both regulative and constitutive—in shaping states' behaviour. On the one hand, accepted norms come to regulate what states can or cannot do; on the other, they have a constitutive function in relation to how states understand their identities and interests. Risse exemplifies this dual role in reference to the norm of human rights. As he elaborates, while human rights can protect citizens from states by regulating governmental behaviour, adherence to human rights standards also becomes part of constituting a state's identity as being a 'civilised state' (Risse 2000, 5).

To my mind, the basic premises of the theorists making the general 'sociological turn' and those developing it in a new wave of writing about the normative shaping of international politics make eminent sense. I share the fundamental ontological starting point that the social and political worlds are not analogous to the natural or material world and the epistemological standpoint that we cannot be neutral observers of a world in which we are intimately implicated. Therefore, I concur that the history, current ordering and on-going politics of the international system are the creation of human action and are not pre-ordained by 'the anarchical system'. What seem to be laws or inevitabilities are the ingrained outcomes of practices, habits and choices rather than the natural order, and they are therefore changeable. My own PhD studies in the field of international politics happened in those immediate post-Cold War years, and my thesis topic about transnational peace movements and the end of the Cold War gave me a chance to undertake an empirical engagement with these kinds of ontological and epistemological claims. My studies focused on a particular reading of the Cold War, and the consequent activism associated with it, which was developed by the pan-European peace movements of the 1980s, particularly the UK-based European Nuclear Disarmament (END). The intellectual underpinning of this movement was an analysis that the Cold War was a set of political practices and habits, which legitimated Superpower domination in the domestic and international interests of both the USA and the USSR. In other words, the Cold War provided the 'other' that both the USA and the USSR needed, in contrast to the realist reading which suggested that their domination stemmed from their existence as two overweening powers forced into inevitable balance of power by international anarchy. From this analysis, END activists also argued that citizen activists could delegitimise the Cold War and reimagine international relations through practicing 'détente from below' through citizen contacts across the East-West divide (Kaldor 1991; Meyer and Marullo 1992). My own empirical study of END and its relations with Polish independent movements (Wylie 1999) showed how fraught such 'détente from below' could be with Eastern and Western European social movements clashing over political and normative priorities and their contending interpretations of ideas such as human rights, freedom and peace. Yet at the same time I also concurred with those who argued that domestic dissent and changing international politics were intertwined, that 'new thinking' from above and below (particularly Gorbachev's adoption of ideals of *glasnost* and *perestroika*) was part of the unsettling of Cold War rhetoric and realities and that dissidents in both East and West did engage in domestic and transnational civic activism, which was part of reimagining the international, challenging the inevitability of Cold War and contributing to its peaceful end.

Having said this I could not wholeheartedly agree that 'détente from below' caused the end of the Cold War as some of its most enthusiastic proponents proclaimed. For one reason, the relationships across the East-West divide were not always as flourishing as the Western peace activists claimed, but also these movements did exist in a situation of extreme power inequality between themselves and other actors in the international system, and a more complex account of the end of the Cold War would need to take into account growing material power imbalances between East and West, the economic woes of the Soviet bloc and elite bargaining to name but a few factors. In other words, my point of view would be that this is not a world where everything can be made anew simply by the power of moral entrepreneurship because the material reality of the world has profound effects on the choices made by actors (Schonberg 2009, 11). Pre-existing material and military power structures, historical norms and practices around social categories such as gender, race or class, and varying interpretations of interest create a global material reality within which states and others act, but also meet their limits. In other words, and in a nutshell, I accept Marx's famous statement that, 'men make their own history, but they do not make it as they please; they do not make it under self-selected circumstances, but under circumstances existing already, given and transmitted from the past. The tradition of all dead generations weighs like a nightmare on the brains of the living' (Marx 1852).

Asserting that norms and ideals matter, but the extent to which they do is shaped by the material realities their proponents encounter, slightly distances me from the apparently more straightforward claim made in the first wave of norm writing in IR that 'norms shape identities and interests' (Katzenstein 1996). The degree to which norms matter (encompassed in the question, 'ideas all the way down?' Wendt 1999) has remained open for debate, and the interaction of norms and material realities does need disentangling. This is one of several critical points evident in a 'second wave' of norm writing, which will become clearer when I discuss more contemporary norm analysis in IR further below.

Accepting, however, the basic premise that norms do matter in the complex construction of state identities and interests, several follow-up questions arise. As Finnemore and Sikkink point out, their position that 'norms matter' still leaves many questions needing answers, such as where norms come from, how they change and how they create change and how we can know that they make a difference in politics (Finnemore and Sikkink 1998, 888). Their ideas about how to answer these questions are outlined next.

The Norm Life Cycle

In their influential article *International Norm Dynamics and Political Change*, Martha Finnemore and Katherine Sikkink (1998) suggested that the process by which new norms became politically salient and eventually embedded in international and domestic political life could be mapped through a lifecycle model. Their suggestion was that this cycle had three stages: norm emergence, norm cascade and norm internalisation.

At stage one of the lifecycle, Finnemore and Sikkink pinpoint a crucial role for people they called 'norm entrepreneurs' in norm emergence. Norm entrepreneurs, who could be individuals, non-governmental or even governmental organisations, are people driven by altruism, empathy or ideational commitment (Finnemore and Sikkink 1998, 899) whose mission is to convince a critical mass of states and public opinion that a norm matters. To do this entrepreneurs seek access to international platforms upon which they can present their case, framing the issues as they want them to be understood by states. With the zeal of 'moral proselytisers', norm entrepreneurs will seek to shape their audience's understanding of an issue. Through the language chosen, the use of expertise and 'facts' or the dramatising of their concerns, they engage in the 'management of meaning' surrounding a norm (1998, 897–900). Significantly, given the focus of this book, they also suggest that norms that 'prohibit bodily harm for innocent or vulnerable groups' are 'most likely to find transnational support' (1998, 907). The importance of this insight in terms of the framing of anti-trafficking norms will be returned to in later chapters.

Stage two of the lifecycle—norm cascade—occurs when, through their persuasiveness, norm entrepreneurs begin to garner enough state supporters for the norm to reach a 'tipping point'. Finnemore and Sikkink are aware that an exact science to measure a 'tipping point' is impossible, but they estimate it can roughly be said to happen when a third of the states in an international body adopt an ideal (1998, 901). Thereafter, peer pressure, the desire of states to be identified as behaving legitimately and the on-going work of entrepreneurs, mixed in with the threat of disciplinary sanctions, begins to produce widespread norm adoption and compliance. By the cascade's end, the new ideal has reached stage three by which it has become 'taken for granted' in domestic and global politics (1998, 903). This 'taken-for-grantedness' is made manifest in the development of international and national laws, bureaucracies and institutions around the new norm that all embrace and enact new 'standards of appropriateness', which are 'no longer seen as controversial' (Segerlund 2010, 27–30). Alongside this formal validation of norms, social recognition and 'cultural validation' also develop, the first through repeated interaction on the issue between states and the second through the development of shared meanings surrounding the norm (Wiener 2008).

Norms are elusive—as ideals, standards, values, they are intangible and immaterial. As Wiener suggests they form an 'invisible constitution of politics' and therefore elude easy analysis or measurement. The virtue of Finnemore and Sikkink's model is that it makes the imperceptible visible. As they claim, the model is one way in which norm researchers can show precisely how 'the ought becomes is' (Finnemore and Sikkink 1998, 911). The lifecycle model leads to the identification of real people with their ideals, strategies and practices and draws attention to the ways in which they achieve influence with states to the extent that eventually they tip their ideals through the international system. The model also highlights the practices and techniques that will further the 'tipping' (peer pressure, desire for legitimacy and so on) and shows the symptoms by which normalisation can be detected (for example, new laws or common knowledge).

Writing before the publication of *International Norm Dynamics and Political Change* but working with reference to Martha Finnemore's earlier work, Richard Price's research on the landmines ban is a neat exemplification of the stages of norm life as captured in the model (Price 1998). Price focused on the campaign to ban landmines, and his work demonstrated the key role of identifiable moral entrepreneurs, who formed international networks, accessed appropriate platforms and identified state allies, to push through the eventual international ban. Central to their success was the campaign's framing of the issue. The use of statistics to 'create a new social issue' was one central plank of this, as was the use of the personal stories of amputees to illustrate the indiscriminate effects of landmines on civilian populations long after conflict. Besides this powerful human framing, Price also suggests that the campaign's use of research studies of mines and military effectiveness put militaries on the back foot, forcing them to defend the dubious military utility of landmines, and this was key to their success. By use of 'social pedagogy' involving information, persuasion, shame and discipline, the landmines campaigners 'taught' states to see their interests and identities differently on this issue. Citing Finnemore he writes 'states are receptive to being taught about what is appropriate by outsiders' (Price 1998, 617) and as tipping occurs other states become keen to be identified as 'responsible international citizens' through adopting the issue (1998, 635).

Neat and helpful though it is in focusing attention on tangible actors, processes and outcomes to make the invisible constitution of politics visible, the model inevitably carries the burdens (like neo-realism, ironically) of trying to impose neatness on the messy realities of international politics.

It loses sight of the raggedy beginnings and ends of lifecycles and the intense contestation surrounding many norms. It overestimates the willingness of states to be taught and the mixed motives that might lead states to accept 'an ought becoming an is'. These—and other lines of criticism—are discernible in what can be grouped as a second wave of norm writing that followed a decade after the first.

The Second Wave: Norms Matter, But...

The first wave of writing about norms and IR—and the capturing of the dynamics of norm formation in the lifecycle model—were certainly refreshing for a discipline so long ensconced in the notion that in global political life only states in the anarchical system matter and that the system has a way of imprinting on those states what their interests and identities have to be. The constructivist turn interposed the idea that states are actors composed of malleable identities and interests and, in relationship with other non-state actors, they are the agents of the fate of the international system. As indicated above, the constructivist turn has borne much fruit, and theoretical plurality is now well established in IR as an academic field. However, the 'turn' has not been without its moments of conceptual 'rewind', particularly around questions of the degrees to which ideas matter or power politics still predominates with material realities constraining value-based behaviour. A further set of queries also hover over the degree to which norms—even when widely cited by international actors—straightforwardly shape state identities and interests or whether they often remain controversial, subject to dispute over meanings, interpretations and resulting practices in international politics. These complicating questions, amongst others, can be seen in a 'second wave' of more contemporary writing about norms and international relations.

To be fair to those writing in the early days about norms and IR, there was an awareness that these kinds of questions would arise. In the preface to his key edited collection, *The Culture of National Security*, Peter Katzenstein reveals that he made space for a 'critical' chapter 12, despite the quiet urging of some contributors that he drop it. Rather he defended its inclusion on the grounds that it would enable a self-critical discussion of acknowledged weaknesses in the book's analyses (Katzenstein 1996, xiv). In fact, controversial chapter 12, by Paul Kowert and Jeffrey Legro, did not dispute that norms mattered or that their study held promise for making sense of the gaps in understanding state behaviour, which definitely problematised the 'neo-neo' accounts offered by realism and liberalism (Kowert and Legro 1996, 468). However, they argued that scholars still needed to pay more attention to the sources of norms, the 'embarrassment' or ubiquity of norms (leading to questions about why some become influential and others not or why some prompt change, others continuity) and their relationship to the material world (Kowert and Legro 1996, 469 and 483–490). Legro soon followed up these generic critical points in his comparative, empirical study of norms and warfare. Arguing against the tendency in norm writing to focus only on 'the norm that worked' (Legro 1997, 33), he showed how of three different norms on constraint on military usage agreed in the inter-war years (bans on U-boat warfare on merchant ships, aerial bombing of cities and the use of chemical weapons), only one (the latter) constrained state behaviour in the Second World War. From this evidence he suggests that states' strategic interests in combination with their bureaucratic and military organisational cultures often—but importantly not always—overwhelm normative prohibitions in time of war. Equally, in Martha Finnemore's writing there is a foretaste of some of the critical points to come. Although the life-cycle model seems to imply a straightforward path for ideas assiduously promoted by moral entrepreneurs through the international system, she was aware of the necessity of paying attention to both a norm's precursors and the controversy norms may attract, writing that it is better to think of norms as part of a 'fabric of inter-woven norms', which may be subject to 'continued contestation' (Finnemore 1996, 161 & 160). And in a footnote to the issue of power politics lurking in the wings of their model, Finnemore and Sikkink heed that norms may be socialised by means of political might rather than moral value, if they become widely accepted because they are 'sponsored by the international hegemon' (Finnemore and Sikkink 1998, footnote 85).

Some of the seeds sewn in these more 'self-critical' reflections have come to fruition in a second wave of norm studies. Over many empirical studies covering, amongst other issues, the rules of war loot, sexual violence and war, gender mainstreaming, commercial whaling, environmental standards, HIV-AIDS, EU subsidiarity, EU constitution making, corporate social responsibility and so on, a number of authors have reiterated the idea that norms matter in international relations but not without recognising the politics that surround them—without and within, before and after. While earlier studies of norms may have overstated the global scope and consensus on norms and failed to disentangle how material and social power fuse (Reich 2010, 23–24), this current round of scholarship raises and addresses these issues in various ways.

Power 'Without' (The Impact of Material Power)

As Jennifer Bailey has pointed out, in much IR writing about norms, the role given to human agency is striking (Bailey 2008, 291). Individual entrepreneurs and their networks are made visible and seen to be effective in their framing, lobbying and persuading. Yet, while the world is teeming with such transnational activism, not all the norms being advocated will fly, or fly in the directions their advocates imagine. Bailey's own study of anti-whaling activism details the slow accruing of support over decades for a moratorium on commercial whaling, as an alliance of environmentalists, conservationists and scientists beavered away to produce a tipping point. Yet, the norm entrepreneurs may have won battles but not the war, because the tipping point swayed back, and whaling has once again been on the increase in recent years. A fundamental cause of this reversal is that Norway and Japan, with strong material, commercial interests in whaling, cannot be persuaded to adopt the norm and have found ways to re-frame their activities (as 'scientific' or 'aboriginal' whaling) to legitimate their persistence (Bailey 2008). Numerous ideals similarly run into the international sands: prohibitions on the use of particular weapons, securing universal agreement on banning child soldiering, promoting anti-retroviral drugs (ARVs) against HIV, establishing the International Criminal Court, the Tobin tax or carbon-reducing environmental agreements are among many examples. The most straightforward rationale for explaining these norm 'failures' is the contradiction between them and the 'realistically' understood strategic, military or economic interests of the states that do not sign up.

Conversely when norms do fly, again the question of whether their adoption owes more to meeting the interests of powerful states than the moral weight of entrepreneurs' arguments bears consideration. In a study of the long cycle of changing international norms surrounding the plunder of artworks in war, Wayne Sandholtz argues that the norms that have held sway have done so because of the support of the key international powers of the contrasting periods he studies (Napoleonic France and Britain/US post World War II) rather than the achievement of universal moral consensus (Sandholtz 2008). Likewise, apparent normative consensus at the international level can dissipate at the local, if domestic governmental opposition is fierce—as is recounted in case studies of the tension between the South African government and the international push for ARVs as a response to the HIV AIDS crisis (Kravtsov 2009). On the basis of this case study, Kravtsov warns that there is 'danger (in) assuming too much causal power for entrepreneurs' (Kravtsov 2009, 311). And whether it is the entrepreneurs or the mighty backers who have the causal power is a question echoed by Simon Reich in his writings on norms and IR. In his book he argues that while the work of civil society entrepreneurs may be vital to getting issues onto international agendas, in the end material capabilities are necessary to ensure norms are implemented. And in his opinion this boils down in the current international balance of power to 'American commitment to resource implementation' (Reich 2010, 49), exemplified in his book by the norms that so deeply affected international politics in the 2000s: the Bush administration's adoption of pre-emption and prevention for the War on Terror (and also interestingly the anti-trafficking norm, which was assiduously promoted by a series of US administrations, of which more in Chaps. 3 and 4).

The point encompassed by all these examples is that the 'striking emphasis on agency' can lead those tracing norm lifecycles to neglect existing power structures. In the norm lifecycle model, the agency of non-state actors is privileged without enough heed being paid to their context in international political structures in the forms of the existing power distribution, the international structures created by pre-existing norms and sovereign calculations of interest made on strategic, military or economic grounds. The lesson of this is that, in effect, students of norms in IR have to avoid their tendency to 'ignore the material world' (Sørensen 2008, 10).

Having said this, it is important to recognise that structure and agency are not dichotomous but are mutually constitutive. Analysing EU climate policy as shaped by 'green' normative commitments alongside pragmatic interests in energy security and the economic gains to be had from being at the forefront of new technologies, van Schaik and Schunz suggest that 'in social reality norms and interests can—and often do—coexist as determinants of actor's policy choices' (Schaik and Schunz 2012, 171).

As in the tradition started by Katzenstein and his contributors, there is a need to recognise the degree to which norms are part of the constitution of identities and interests, but equally there is a need to write into the norm lifecycle a greater appreciation of the complex interplay between structure and agency, creating a means to analyse more effectively instances of norm failure or diverse norm interpretation, as well as explaining those instances where norms demonstrably become internalised in international political life.

Politics 'Within' (The Instability of Norm Contestation)

The whaling, ARV and pre-emption examples mentioned above are also indicative of another key theme in more contemporary norm writing in IR: a greater awareness of how contested most norms are. First wave writers were not unaware that norms could be contentious, but the lifecycle model with its 'actors with ideas to socialisation to internalisation' pathway does not seem capable of capturing what in effect can often be intense 'norm battles' surrounding ideals that gain currency (van Kersbergen and Verbeek 2007, 218) or answer questions about the politics of norm neglect in other cases.

In their critical engagement with the norm lifecycle model, Mona Krook and Jacqui True find it odd that against the inherent dynamism of the model (which involves plenty of action in terms of norm creation, socialisation, diffusion) there is a tendency to understand norms themselves as static 'things'—as stable formulations of ideas and principles (Krook and True 2012, 104). Instead, they argue that this stability is illusory, given the political contestation surrounding norm entrepreneurship and the differing interpretations that actors in the system attach to norms at whatever stage of the lifecycle they reach. Krook and True even go so far as to use language such as 'bloody processes' (quoting Epstein) and 'silencing' of certain views by others (Krook and True 2012, 108) to give a sense of the degree of contest that can surround the politicking amidst entrepreneurs and between them and the other actors in the lifecycle more widely. They illustrate this in relation to their case study of gender norms at the UN.

In their article, Krook and True point out that in the politicking, not all norms will gain salience (2012, 111). This is a point taken up by Charli Carpenter in her work, when she asks why, despite increasing international concern about the impact of sexual violence in warfare and child soldiering, there has been no campaign for the rights of children born of war rape. In order to understand the silences around issues, which, like 'war babies', have rich potential to provoke normative action, Carpenter argues that it is necessary to study the internal politics of advocacy networks. In doing so she notes that 'gatekeepers' play a vital role in determining what issues matter, taking active part in 'turf wars' to protect their dominance on certain issues and keeping a pragmatic eye to 'organisational survival' as much as normative commitments (Carpenter 2007, 114–116).

'Norm battle' may also persist well after formal norm adoption into international and domestic laws or practices, so complicating the end point in the lifecycle, which assumes 'internalisation' and the associated 'taken-for-grantedness' of a new norm in domestic and international politics. This persistent instability of norms is picked up in several EU-related studies, as authors point out that even once new norms are promulgated within the system—such as constitutionalism, conditionality or subsidiarity—their meaning and implementation differ depending on individual interpretations and structural contexts into which they are being woven. Weiner's study of *The Invisible Constitution of Politics* in the EU provides empirical evidence from interviews with European and national bureaucrats of the varying degrees to which norms acquire different 'meanings in use' depending on the emotional, cultural and political responses they provoke amongst those implementing new EU norms (Wiener 2008, 6 and 17). Addressing the particular case of EU subsidiarity, van Kersenberg and Verbeek suggest that despite common political purpose behind the promulgation of the idea (that is, addressing concerns about the balance of power and responsibilities between the EU centre and the sovereign members), the vagueness of the norm has implied that 'norm battle' continues post-adoption and as yet subsidiarity has achieved 'no common meaning' (van Kersenberg and Verbeek 2007, 225).

Writing at a time between the two waves of norm literature, Thomas Risse suggested that norms do eventually acquire 'taken-for-grantedness', which can be assumed to mean the end point of the lifecycle model has been reached. However, he acknowledges that this will only happen after a period of argument through which reasoned consensus will emerge. Although he notes that there are those who resist the power of rational argument till 'blue in the face', he expected that 'true reasoning' would prevail (Risse 2000). The histories of many of the norms discussed above suggest too much expectation is being placed by Risse on the possibilities of 'civilised' argument and, even where contestation leads to norm adoption, what the principles subscribed to mean and how they might come to shape the identities and actions of the states adopting them remain unsettled by the politics of interpretation and interests. All of the above implies an intense political messiness, which the parsimony of the lifecycle model cannot capture.

Before and After

The section above has already touched on another critical issue with the lifecycle model: the idea implicit in the term 'lifecycle' that there are discernible beginnings and ends. Although already raised, these aspects are worth elaborating on in a couple of further respects. As well as leaving rumbles of controversy and unresolved interpretations, the internalisation of norms at cycles 'end' can produce unpredictable or distressing consequences for many of the entrepreneurs who championed the cause. As an example, Janet Halley and her interlocutors write about the increasing effectiveness of feminist advocates in international fora dealing with sexual violence in war and human trafficking. Such is the efficacy of their lobbying (in changing the laws of war to include gender-based crime, among other things) that Halley defines these entrepreneurs as involved in a practice of 'governance feminism' now discernible in the international system (Halley et al. 2006). Yet, the consequences of success can be contrary to hopes and expectations. In her discussion of the impact of the new laws surrounding rape as a war crime in the International Criminal Tribunal on the former Yugoslavia (ICTY), Halley argues that the interpretation of the norm that sex in the context of conflict can never be consensual reifies ethnic divides by determining that no inter-ethnic sexual relationships could be freely chosen (Halley et al. 2006, 384). Ironically, the radical feminist impact on international law ends up redrawing other boundaries in unlooked for ways. Halley's colleagues subject feminist lobbying on sex trafficking to the same analysis, and their thoughts will be returned to in later chapters.

Finally, to end with the beginning (which is not very logical but perhaps in line with my analytical aim to suggest that the logic of the lifecycle model is too neat), norms do not emerge *ex nihilo*. As flagged by Carpenter (2007), there is a political process that gatekeepers engage in to decide 'what matters;' they in turn are influenced by the long-cycles of pre-existing norms and the laws and practices they have spawned. Which norms get brought to the surface in international debate will also depend on the gatekeeping of international organisations like the UN. Increasingly, these bodies have themselves adopted the norm of enabling civil society participation in line with their commitments to spreading global democracy and liberalism (Reimann 2006). However, not all norm entrepreneurs will be considered by the institutions of global governance as legitimate to speak, depending on their concurrence with liberal/democratic norms and 'civilised' lobbying practices. Openness from the top-down to civil society actors by the emergence of 'global patrons of civil society' may also have the effect of 'mainstreaming' and so siphoning the radicalism out of moral entrepreneurs, effectively turning them into service providers for UN programmes (Reimann 2006, 48–52).

The Norm Lifecycle in the Light of the Critique

Models are meant to be parsimonious and clear, and heaping on too much complexity sinks that purpose. In the case of the norm lifecycle the elegance of the model directs attention to specific actors, their political activities and their interactions with states, tracing their actions and outcomes in order to discern a dynamic route through which norms are created, socialised and internalised. What the many critical insights above amount to however is the complicating and politicising of all these stages. The critics introduce the idea that the creation and proselytisation of norms is the result of prior political choices by moral entrepreneurs, shaped in many degrees by the norms that pre-exist them and that almost surely entails the silencing of other normative projects or interpretations of values. Other critics add the political dimension pointing out that socialisation of norms happens within structures of prevailing political power balances, where material interests shape norm adoption (just as norm adoption shapes interests). Others query the degrees of straightforward socialisation, internalisation or eventual 'taken-for-grantedness' by highlighting on-going disputes, contrary framings and competing interpretations surrounding norms. Engaging with the lifecycle model the critics problematise the unity of normative ideas, attend to the realities of contestation, challenge the presumed trajectory that norms will follow a progressive circle from inception to completion and recognise the often-unexpected consequences of norm adoption. Without losing sight of the helpful pinpointing of agents, processes and outcomes that employing the lifecycle model enables, to understand the rise and impact of norms in international politics, it is necessary to analyse them with an awareness of all these complicating factors.

The Complex and Incomplete Lifecycle of the Anti-Trafficking Norm

In the introduction to this book the spectacular rise of the anti-trafficking norm was outlined. In line with Finnemore and Sikkink's model, it is not hard to identify a number of civil society moral entrepreneurs, particularly in the global women's movement, who advocated the norm, used international platforms to further their aims and framed the issue in particular ways. As the next chapter will show, it could be argued that their presence at the international negotiations that were key to the socialisation of states on the issue produced a tipping point in the UN, through the elaboration of the Transnational Organised Crime Convention and Palermo Protocol of 2000 (UNODC 2000). Since then the norm has cascaded from the international to the domestic, with states worldwide adopting anti-trafficking legislation and action plans. So extensive and well established is the contemporary global and local anti-trafficking architecture that it can be said that the norm has been internalised and is taken for granted—not just by moral entrepreneurs, governments and international organisations, but it has also achieved the status of widespread common knowledge amongst 'ordinary' people.

The bare bones of the story of the rise of the anti-trafficking norm can to some extent therefore be analytically pinned down through reference to the lifecycle model, and so the following chapters will continue to use the model as a trajectory for the book. But pinning the analysis to this skeleton shows that this alone cannot give an adequate accounting of the international politics of the anti-human trafficking norm. For one thing, the norm, particularly as it relates to trafficking for sexual exploitation, is extremely contested amongst moral entrepreneurs, while another aspect of the norm (the prohibition on labour trafficking) has been consigned to the political doldrums. Whether its cascade owes more to the political clout of the US than the socialisation skills of the moral proselytisers is also debatable. The complex relationship between ideals and material interests needs disentangling in order to account for US sponsorship of the anti-sex trafficking norm. On-going contestation and problems in interpreting what it means to oppose human trafficking are also prevalent in the post-adoption phase everywhere. And the strange consequences of the apparent successful incorporation of feminist agendas into international and domestic political life, as states ally themselves with the cause to bolster their border regimes rather than enhance migrants' rights, are becoming clearer. In the chapters that follow, this complex interweaving of the 'fabric of norms' (Finnemore 1996, 161) with power politics, material interests, moral contestation, unresolved dilemmas and unintended consequences will be explored to produce a more nuanced account of the rise of the anti-trafficking norm in particular—and the political life of ideas in international politics more generally.

Bibliography

Anheier, H., Glasius, M., & Kaldor, M. (2001). *Global Civil Society 2001*. Oxford: Oxford University Press.

Bailey, J. (2008). Arrested development: The fight to end commercial Whaling as a case of failed norm change. *European Journal of International Relations, 14*(2), 289–378.

Carpenter, C. (2007). Setting the Advocacy Agenda: Theorizing issue emergence and non-emergence in Transnational Advocacy Networks. *International Studies Quarterly, 51*, 99–120.

Finnemore, M. (1996). Constituting norms of humanitarian intervention. In P. Katzenstein (Ed.), *The Culture of National Security: Norms and Identity in World Politics* (pp. 153–186). New York: Columbia University Press.

Finnemore, M., & Sikkink, K. (1998). International norm dynamics and political change. *International Organization, 52*(4), 887–917.

Halley, J., Kotiswaran, P., Shamir, H., & Thomas, C. (2006). From the International to the local in feminist legal responses to rape, prostitution, sex work and sex trafficking: Four studies in contemporary governance feminism. *Harvard Journal of Law and Gender, 29*, 335–423.

Kaldor, M. (1991). *Europe from below: An East-West dialogue*. London: Verso.

Katzenstein, P. (1996). *The Culture of National Security: Norms and Identity in World Politics*. New York: Colombia University Press.

Keck, M., & Sikkink, K. (1998). *Activists beyond borders: Advocacy Networks in International Politics*. Ithaca, New York: Cornell University Press.

Klotz, A. (1999). *Norms in international relations: The struggle against apartheid*. Ithaca, New York: Cornell University Press.

Kowert, P., & Legro, J. (1996). Norms, identity and their limits: A theoretical reprise. In P. Katzenstein (Ed.), *The Culture of National Security* (pp. 451–497). New York: Columbia University Press.

Kravtsov, V. (2009). ARV treatment and AIDS Entrepreneurs in South Africa: Domestic opposition to an International Norm (1999–2004). *Global Society, 23*(3), 295–316.

Krook, M., & True, J. (2012). Rethinking the Lifecycles of International Norms: The United Nations and the Global Promotion of Gender Equality. *European Journal of International Relations, 18*(1), 103–127.

Legro, J. (1997). Which norms matters? Revisiting the failure of internationalism. *International Organization, 51*(1), 31–63.

Marx, K. (1852). The Eighteenth Brumaire of Louis Bonaparte. https://www.marxists.org/archive/marx/works/1852/18th-brumaire/ch01.htm, date accessed 7 January 2015.

Meyer, D., & Marullo, S. (1992). Grassroots mobilization and international politics: Peace protest and the end of the cold war. *Research in Social Movements: Conflict and Change, 14*, 99–140.

Nadelmann, E. (1990). Global prohibition regimes: The emergence of norms in international society. *International Organization, 44*(4), 479–525.
Price, R. (1998). Reversing the gun sights: International Civil Society Targets Landmines. *International Organization, 52*(3), 613–644.
Reich, S. (2010). *Global norms, American Sponsorship and the emerging patterns of world politics.* Basingstoke: Palgrave.
Reimann, K. (2006). A view from the top: International politics, norms and the worldwide growth of NGOs. *International Studies Quarterly, 50*(1), 45–68.
Risse, T. (2000). "Let's Argue": Communicative action in world politics. *International Organization, 54*(1), 1–39.
Sandholtz, W. (2008). Dynamics of International Norm Change: Rules against Wartime Plunder. *European Journal of International Relations, 14*(2), 101–131.
Schonberg, K. (2009). *Constructing 21st century U.S. Foreign Policy: Identity, Ideology, and America's World Role in a New Era.* Basingstoke: Palgrave MacMillan.
Segerlund, L. (2010). *Making corporate social responsibility a global concern: Norm construction in a globalizing world.* Farnham, Surrey: Ashgate Publishing.
Smith, S. (2000). The discipline of international relations: Still an American social science? *British Journal of Politics and International Relations, 2*(3), 374–402.
Sørensen, G. (2008). The case for combining material forces and ideas in the study of IR. *European Journal of International Relations, 14*(1), 5–32.
Tanesini, A. (1999). *An introduction to feminist epistemologies.* Oxford: Blackwell.
Tickner, J. A., & Sjoberg, L. (2011). *Feminism and International Relations: Conversations about the past, present and future.* Abingdon, Oxon: Routledge.
UNODC. (2000). United Nations convention on Transnational organized crime and the Protocols Thereto. 15 November 2000. https://www.unodc.org/documents/treaties/UNTOC/Publications/TOC%20Convention/TOCebook-e.pdf, date accessed 12 March 2016.
van Kersbergen, K., & Verbeek, B. (2007). The politics of international norms: EU subsidiarity and the imperfect competence regime of the European Union. *European Journal of International Relations, 13*(2), 217–238.
van Schaik, L., & Schunz, S. (2012). Explaining EU activism and impact in global climate politics: Is the union a norm- or interest-driven actor? *Journal of Common Market Studies, 50*(1), 169–186.
Walker, R. (1994). Social Movements/World Politics. *Millennium: Journal of International Politics, 23*(3), 669–700.
Waltz, K. (2010). *Theory of international politics.* Longrove, IL: Waveland Press.
Wendt, A. (1992). Anarchy is what states make of it: The social construction of power politics. *International Organization, 46*(2), 391–425.
Wendt, A. (1999). *Social theory of international politics.* Cambridge: Cambridge University Press.
Wiener, A. (2008). *The invisible constitution of politics: Contested norms and international encounters.* Cambridge: Cambridge University Press.
Wylie, G. (1999). Social movements and international change: The case of 'Détente from Below'. *International Journal of Peace Research, 4*(2), 61–82.

CHAPTER 3

Norm Emergence: Entrepreneurs, Interests and the Palermo Protocol

Introduction

To begin at Finnemore and Sikkink's beginning, the norm lifecycle starts with efforts made by moral entrepreneurs to promote normative change and so influence states' identities and interests. As this chapter will show, re-ignited interest in the issue of human trafficking in the 1990s did indeed owe much to the advocacy work of identifiable moral entrepreneurs, most prominently women's NGOs and social movements, as they interacted in transnational networks and lobbied for change. However, it is important to recognise that this was a *re-ignition* of anti-trafficking ideals, not a normative change ex nihilo. As the first section below recounts, there is a pre-history to contemporary anti-trafficking norm entrepreneurship, particularly between the 1880s and 1940s, which left important traces on the shape of the norm for the late twentieth century.

Undeniably post 1949 there were several quieter decades before the issue was resurrected with great gusto at the twentieth century's end. As this chapter will explore, transnational women's advocacy work on trafficking built up through a series of international forums and conventions on women's issues dating back to the 1970s and intensifying around the UN's Beijing Conference in the 1990s. In terms of new international political and legal developments, the influence of anti-trafficking advocacy efforts can be seen during the short but productive round of 11 UN ad hoc committee meetings at the UN Commission on Crime Prevention and Criminal Justice in Vienna from 1999 to 2000. This produced

G. Wylie, *The International Politics of Human Trafficking*,
DOI 10.1057/978-1-137-37775-3_3

the UN Convention on Transnational Organised Crime, including the Optional Palermo Protocol to Prevent, Suppress and Punish Trafficking in Persons, Especially Women and Children, which is the key international anti-trafficking framework for these times (UNODC 2000).

Looked at in this light, as Simon Reich suggests, the emergence of the anti-trafficking norm does indeed seem to represent a success for entrepreneurial sponsorship of a norm from the bottom up rather than the top down (Reich 2010, 182). However, as I will suggest below, it seems to me that his telling of this bottom-up process, while convincing in many respects, is a strangely bloodless one because he assumes a degree of normative consensus within the anti-trafficking networks. In the previous chapter, I noted the point made by several authors that norms are not often static or consensual. Bearing this in mind, I will argue that Reich does not capture the intense contestation that arose between different norm entrepreneurs about how to define and oppose trafficking in the UN context. This chapter pays attention to these rifts, tracing their provenance in contending entrepreneurs' ideologies and the resultant highly emotional 'norm battles', which characterised the lobbying around the Palermo negotiations. Accounts of the intense disagreements between lobbyists at the Palermo negotiations are readily available, as activists on both sides have written up their first-hand experiences. Therefore, as well as citing from these accounts to make the point concerning norm battles and instability, I also add something new to the existent material by offering a genealogy of the drafts of the Protocol leading up to its final version. Arguably the marks of these entrepreneurs' ideological influence and their norm battles can be followed through the mutating wording of the drafts to the outcome, which in the end produced a highly compromised document: one that still remains open to diverging interpretations and produces myriad political consequences to this day.

In the last chapter when discussing the norm lifecycle, I also drew on the 'second wave' of norm writing in International Relations to suggest that the adoption of norms by nation-states is not usually the outcome of moral persuasion alone. Therefore, while emphasising that contentious norm entrepreneurship from below was undoubtedly part of the reason for the resurrection of global anti-trafficking politics in the late twentieth century, my analysis at this chapter's end will re-join Reich's in his insistence that the readiness of states to develop and endorse the Palermo Protocol lies not only in the effects of moral persuasion but also needs to be seen as equally firmly rooted in realising states' material interests.

Reich's particular emphasis is on US interests, which I will focus on in Chap. 4 in respect to norm cascade. However, along with the US, other states can also be seen as pursuing their material interests through anti-trafficking norms, particularly as they relate to managing the insecurities of the Post Cold war era and the shoring up of their borders against the disruptions of globalisation. The importance of this dynamic in giving political 'life' to anti-trafficking norms and laws in the context of the UN negotiations will form the latter part of the discussion in this chapter.

Politics Before: The Pre-history of the Anti-trafficking Norm

Despite the heading of this chapter, it would be more accurate to say that anti-human trafficking norms and politics *re*-emerged forcefully in international politics in the 1990s, in many ways echoing the politics of the 1890s. As one illustration of this, Stephanie Limoncelli gives her readers the sense that we are caught in a time warp with the opening quotes in her book on the politics of trafficking (Limoncelli 2010, 1). Those quotes—activists' words denouncing the traffic in women—are over a century old yet sound freshly familiar and contemporary as in the example below,

> There is a regular trade in young girls who are bought and sold, imported and exported...and in a very large number of cases the movement (is) under stress of fear or fraud, often minors incapable of consent. (Limoncelli 2010, 1 quoting P. Bunting)

Trafficking in women and children for sexual exploitation was indeed an early *cause celebre* for the emergent local and transnational women's movements of the nineteenth century. As Margaret Keck and Kathryn Sikkink point out, it was then one of the 'less controversial' issues for early women's activists to promote publicly, dealing as it did in emotive claims about morality and the abuse of vulnerable female bodies rather than the tougher political question of demand for women's suffrage, over which women's activists themselves were divided concerning how far to push in the early days of the movement (Keck and Sikkink 1998, 52).

Energetic transnational norm entrepreneurship around prostitution and sex trafficking was very evident in the late nineteenth century. For example, Josephine Butler of the International Abolitionist Federation was involved in relentless peripatetic efforts to promote the cause by building activist networks, running social projects and lobbying (Jordan 2007). The Women's Christian Temperance Union was a key contributor to early abolitionism amongst other issues and one of their leaders, Mary Cheavitt, undertook an 8-year global tour to establish branches around the world (Coleman 2008). Their particular abolitionist concern was opposition to the efforts of European states to regulate prostitution (both at home and in their colonies) through imposed brothel registration and compulsory, intrusive sexual health checks for the women involved. These first abolitionists were therefore primarily concerned with abolishing state regulation of prostitution but also with abolishing the sexual double standards, which they saw as ensuring the social condemnation of women involved in prostitution without turning public scorn on the buyers and organisers of the sex trade. These abolitionist normative ideals were hotly contested by men and women who were pro-regulation on medical, military or 'moral purity' grounds, most notably transnationally organised in the International Bureau for the Suppression of the White Slave Traffic (later the International Bureau for the Suppression of the Traffic in Women and Children). The titular concern with 'white slave traffic' reveals that the International Bureau was particularly agitated by reports of the time that white women and girls were being trafficked into prostitution in Europe and the colonies.

Many of these 'white slavery' reports were the products of a new media development, the rise of investigative journalism. As Gretchen Soderlund points out, the histories of humanitarian campaigns against sex trafficking and investigative journalism share an intertwined history (to this day), with the latter practice abetting the cultural construction of sex trafficking as a violation of vulnerable and innocent women and children (Soderlund 2011). There were several celebrated exposés of sex trafficking via this new art of 'revelatory' investigative journalism. W.T. Stead's *The Maiden Tribute of Modern Babylon* (Stead 1885) was perhaps the most famous and then infamous of these pieces, drawing mass public attention (through what were later revealed in court to be dubious investigative techniques) to an alleged trade in young girls throughout London (Soderlund 2013, 54–60).

In terms of political impact, the International Abolitionist Federation had notable policy success in Britain with the repeal of the Contagious Diseases Act (which mandated health checks on women) in 1886 and in The Netherlands and its colonies where regulation was also abandoned. Overall, however, the International Bureau's activities and policy proposals tended to meet with more governmental approval around Europe because most states wished to maintain control over their domestic prostitution regimes, women's migration and sexual relations in their colonies (Limoncelli 2010, 145).

The persuasive powers of these lobbies moved from domestic to international venues with the passing of the first International Agreement for the Suppression of the White Slave Traffic in 1904 (amended in 1910) and ensured that concern to implement anti-trafficking measures was written into the remit of the League of Nations after World War I. In a progressive move, the League of Nations engineered a move away from the racialised rhetoric of 'the white slave' trade with the 1921 re-titling and reformulating of the International Convention for the Suppression of the Traffic in Women and Children (Legg 2012, 657). Interestingly, the early political advantage of the regulationists gave way over years of lobbying and research within the committee system of the League of Nations to a more pro-abolitionist position. In 1927 the League Committee decided that reports from member states indicated that there was a link between regulation and sex trafficking and so subsequent international conventions reflected this different tenor. The 1933 Convention, augmenting the 1904, 1910 and 1921 agreements, eliminated the possibility of consent to prostitution (Legg 2012), so condoning a key abolitionist principle, and the subsequent 1949 UN Convention reiterated this definitively abolitionist tone. A shift in title for this iteration of the Convention (as the Convention for the Suppression of the Traffic in Persons and of the Exploitation of the Prostitution of Others) signalled a move away from a focus on women and children only to a nominal regard for 'persons' more neutrally but the overriding concern of the document remained with sexual exploitation of women and children and the punishment of:

> any person who, to gratify the passions of another:
> (1) Procures, entices or leads away, for purposes of prostitution, another person, even with the consent of that person;
> (2) Exploits the prostitution of another person, even with the consent of that person.

The continued central equation of trafficking with prostitution and the refusal to countenance the notion of consent to prostitution are thus both made abundantly clear in the Convention's script (UN 1949).

The short section above cannot do justice to the fascinating history of the first transnational movements against trafficking culminating in the 1949 UN Convention. The authors of the books and articles referred to above do provide a much more comprehensive account and they make for enthralling reading. What is interesting for the purposes of this book is that echoes of the past are easily discernible in contemporary anti-trafficking discourses and current 'norm battles' are still being fought on the terrain shaped by them.

An obvious legacy of the work described above is that trafficking was first and foremost understood as intrinsically linked to the sexual exploitation of women and children. This was the shared understanding of all the norm entrepreneurs—abolitionists and regulationists—described above. Within the early women's movement in general there was a keenness to engage with the moral and emotive issue of women's vulnerability to sexual exploitation but an absolute reluctance to take on issues of class, 'wage slavery' and labour exploitation more widely (Keck and Sikkink 1998, 76). That there was some conceptual shifting over the decades to allow for a widening of possible victimhood to include 'persons' more generally is signalled in the title of the 1949 Convention. Yet this broadening was not reflected in the subsequent text, which still focused on the prostitution of women and girls. Indeed, as Kristina Hahn points out, any UN declarations between the 1949 Convention and the late 1990s that mention human trafficking have taken the stance that it is always primarily associated with prostitution, for example the Convention on the Elimination of all Forms of Discrimination Against Women (CEDAW 1979, part 1, article 6), with one exception being the Declaration on Violence against Women in 1994 that did make a distinction between 'voluntary' and 'forced' prostitution. However, as she says, this one exception did not mean that the 'old' understanding had been abandoned (Hahn 2010, 226). So, entering a new wave of anti-trafficking politics in the late twentieth century, the assumption that trafficking is fundamentally about the sexual exploitation of women and girls was (and remains) the deeply engrained starting point for public and policy makers alike and whether conceptual stretch to develop a normative focus on men as well as women or labour exploitation more generally is possible or desirable remains part of the new round of debate.

Norm contestation is also a clear part of the history of the anti-trafficking movement. The strongly opposing views of the Federation and the Bureau and their differing policy impacts in varied arenas and over time are testament to that. As will be described further below, the core issues that divided them are somewhat different from those that form the contours of norm contestation in contemporary trafficking debates. Today's 'neo'-abolitionists focus on abolishing prostitution by criminalising men's demand for prostitution rather than by abolishing state regulation and their chief opponents are not those who would use the state to regulate the lives of women in the sex trade in pursuit of moral and medical purity but rather those who would seek to establish the rights of those who undertake sex work to do so. Yet aspects of the older normative divides persist—particularly around whether consent to prostitution is something that is either really possible or morally permissible. The abolitionist tone that evolved in the later League of Nations and early UN documents set a historical normative precedent that lends strength to the one side of this debate who can look back on 1949 as an 'abolitionist victory' (Marcovich 2002, 9), while likewise, this pre-existing legal landscape creates something of an uphill struggle for those seeking normative change in a different direction.

A third echo from the past is found in the intersection of state interests and anti-trafficking norms. In trying to make sense of why nineteenth-/early twentieth-century governments took up the sex trafficking issue in domestic legislation and as parties to international agreements, Stephanie Limoncelli's insightful analysis points to the furthering of states' interests through these frameworks. Whether it was regulating a healthy 'supply' of women in prostitution for militaries, governing brothels to ensure racial segregation in colonies or endorsing abolitionist activities aimed at warning women of the dangers of travel into the unknown, they all played into imperial governments' endeavours to control borders, territories and colonial relationships, as well as women's sexuality and movement (Limoncelli 2010). It may not be the conscious intent of anti-trafficking norm entrepreneurs, but when their efforts coincide with states' interests in the regulation of migration and sexuality, this can produce the unlooked for consequence of enabling more intrusive state regulation of women's lives rather than less. For example, nineteenth-century states' clamp down on 'white slavery' often constrained the movement of women deemed vulnerable to sexual exploitation, and this is a dynamic that can still be seen at play in contemporary anti-trafficking politics and policies.

A final echo from the past is the central role of the media in constructing public conceptions of trafficking. Early investigative journalism, through the work of Stead and others of his ilk, created the view that trafficking was synonymous with prostitution and conjured up the imagery of 'sexual enslavement, captive innocents and mercenary villains' (Soderlund 2011, 193 & 198) that persists in trafficking reportage to this day. Never mind that claims about 'the horror of white slavery' have been definitely debunked over the decades (Doezema 2010), the predominant imagery of sex trafficking created through nineteenth-century media prevails to this day and shapes taken-for-granted common knowledge of what constitutes human trafficking. As will be discussed in later chapters, through looking at contemporary investigative journalism such as the work of Victor Malarek (2004), the tropes establish 100 years ago do recycle. This widespread imagery, focusing on the innocent female victims of evil goons, does lend weight to abolitionist normative agendas and at the same time problematises attempts to broaden concepts of trafficking, to acknowledge the complexity of the contemporary global sex trade or to sway normative engagement with the issue to questions of labour or migration more generally.

In at least these four ways, the hallmarks and consequences of the first round of anti-trafficking activism have undoubtedly shaped the existing legal framework, cultural constructions and normative debates that provide the formative background to the latest manifestation of the international politics of human trafficking, to which I now return.

Norm Entrepreneurs and the Road to Palermo

Between the foundation of the UN and the 1970s there was something of a lull in global agitation around human trafficking. The lack of international interest or action on trafficking is partially understandable against the Cold War background. Cold War politics dominated the global realm both practically and ideologically. In practical terms, human movement between global East and West was highly restricted by militarised boundaries. Moreover, as recounted above, trafficking was seen as a 'women's issue' and ideologically such issues became one more political football between the Superpowers with, for example, the Soviets claiming to have 'ended women's oppression' through equality and work (Harrington 2011, 565), including socialism's supposed banishment of the spectre of sexual exploitation for women. Felicia Gaer also suggests that there was a general consignment of 'women's issues' in the UN to questions of economic development in its early years, after the decision was made to separate the Commission on the Status of Women from the UN Human Rights machinery back in the 1940s (Gaer 2009, 62). For all of these reasons the trafficking issue was not a prominent one for a number of decades.

From the late 1970s onwards, however, feminists began to challenge this separation of women's issues from human rights and sought to reframe issues of violence against women within this framework. This activism can be detected in processes outside and inside the formal organisations of international politics. As Sanja Milivojevic and Sharon Pickering recount, women's civil society activists held international conferences on the trafficking issue in the 1980s, including a 'Global Workshop to Organize against Traffic in Women' in Rotterdam in 1983. Divisions between feminists became obvious at that meeting, leading to a separate feminist-abolitionist international conference on 'Trafficking in Women' in 1988 (Milivojevic and Pickering 2013, 590).

Within the formal fora of the United Nations, spaces for reframing women's concerns also became available from the 1970s onwards, picking up momentum post-Cold War. There were a number of UN conferences on women (Mexico 1975, Copenhagen 1980, Nairobi 1985, Beijing 1995 and on Human Rights in Vienna 1993) during which state delegations increasingly interacted with NGO-populated parallel forums. This effected a gradual shift in the prevalent UN emphasis on 'women's issues' as 'women and development' towards women's rights and the issue of violence against women. In this period feminist thinkers and activists developed critiques of the supposed universality of human rights, which in effect neglected to name and protect the particularities of women's rights and pushed against what they saw as a limited conceptualisation of violence against women to broaden the concept to include 'cultural violence' such as Female Genital Mutilation (FGM) and sexual violence as a war crime (Gaer 2009, 63). The creation of a reporting mechanism for member states to the CEDAW committee, and that committee's willingness to accept shadow reports from NGOs, also created another pressure point for women's movements to do the 'creative cultural work' of defining issues and shaming states to comply with women's rights in order to acquire 'civilised status' (Merry 2003, 949). One such issue raised through the CEDAW reporting mechanism, as well as at Beijing and Vienna, was trafficking in women (2003, 973). Sally Engle Merry's analysis of the impact of shadow CEDAW reporting on states is reminiscent of the argument put forward by IR's norm scholars and made in Chap. 1 that norms begin to shape states' identities and interests when norm conformance comes to be seen as a hallmark of international legitimacy.

The involvement of feminist activists in shaping international agendas by using UN fora, international legal instruments and domestic political and bureaucratic structures to redefine women's rights as human rights and politicise the nature and extent of violence against women, including such specific issues as opposing FGM, promoting gender mainstreaming or defining rape as a weapon of war, became so marked and successful over the last decades of the twentieth century that Janet Halley uses the term 'governance feminism' to capture this intrusion of feminists and their ideas into international (and also domestic) politics. Although, in her opinion, feminists still prefer to understand themselves as the underdogs, marginalised from state power, which they see as the province of men, Halley believes that this is nowadays tantamount to a disingenuous refusal by feminists to admit to their own 'will to power' and indeed the success they have had in institutionalising themselves and their ideas in bureaucracies and polities. Feminists have strategised and become indispensible, 'by positing themselves as experts on women, sexuality, motherhood etc., feminists walk the halls of power' (Halley 2008, 22).

There is evidence that feminists did walk the halls of power at the Vienna ad hoc committee in its rapid series of meetings to create the UN Convention on Transnational Organized Crime and its associated Protocols (the Protocols on Human Trafficking, Human Smuggling and Illicit Trafficking in Firearms). As will be illustrated below the evidence is written in to the evolution of the Protocol and the accounts of those who were there. What is equally clear however is that when feminists walk the halls of power they are not all walking in the same direction.

The Ad Hoc Committee, Moral Entrepreneurs and Norm Battles

Post Cold War, the issue of transnational organised crime moved up the UN agenda and its status as a priority theme for the UN Committee on Crime Prevention and Control was thoroughly established at a World Ministerial Conference in 1994, which produced the Naples Political Declaration and Global Action Plan against Transnational Organized Crime (UN Audio-Visual Library 2013). Interestingly, at this stage the Naples Declaration singled out drug trafficking as particularly heinous and there was only passing concern for 'trafficking in minors and aliens... coerced labour and prostitution', which were deemed 'relatively low risk' compared to drug trafficking (Report of the Secretary General 1994, 24).

Part of the plan in the Nice Declaration was that the UN should elaborate an appropriate Convention to deal with the issue and so in 1998 the UN General Assembly established an open-ended inter-governmental ad hoc committee from within its Crime Commission, charged with elaborating a UN Convention on Transnational Organized Crime. The ad hoc committee held its first meeting in Vienna in January 1999 and completed its work in July 2000, with the Convention and three Protocols (on human trafficking, on smuggling of migrants and on trafficking in firearms) open for signing from winter of that year.

As has become normal practice at such UN forums (Reimann 2006), accredited civil society organisations formed a shadowing presence at these meetings. Amongst the many lobbyists on the human trafficking issue were the Coalition Against Trafficking in Women, Soroptimist International, Equality Now, the Global Alliance Against Traffic in Women, La Strada International and the International Human Rights Law Group. Behind the NGOs actually present at the negotiations was also a Greek chorus of multiple supportive organisations who became signatories to submissions made by the leading NGOs (Gallagher 2001, 1002). As Gallagher points out, such intense NGO excitement around the UN Crime Commission's meetings was an unusual occurrence (Gallagher 2001, 1001).

Simon Reich (2010) suggests that the development of the Palermo Protocol (and simultaneously the US's domestic anti-trafficking law) represents 'a rare success story', in the words of his chapter's sub-title, for these norm entrepreneurs, singling out the effectiveness of the Global Alliance Against Traffic in Women (GAATW), the Polaris Project and an alliance of US feminists movements and Christian evangelicals. He believes that GAATW in particular, with its Bangkok base and its transnational network, brought an important perspective from the global South into the negotiations, which found ready Northern partners in its work to define trafficking. While Reich may have a point about the general influence of these civil society entrepreneurs, what he does not spot is the vivid tensions and divisions between many of them.

As the UN Crime Commission engaged with the issue of trafficking, those concerned to lobby from very different perspectives grouped into two coalitions to push their agendas. The first to form was the Human Rights Caucus (HRC), with groups such as GAATW at its core and the Network of Sex Work Projects at its periphery, and later a second coalition equally sought to take up the human rights label as the International Human Rights Network (IHRN) with the Coalition Against Trafficking in Women at its core (Saunders 2005). Ironically, the determination of both these groups to appropriate the language and label of human rights promoters for themselves does not signal any closeness between them but rather hints at their diametrically opposed views on how to define and address trafficking. Their differences lay (and still lie) principally in their understandings of prostitution/sex work, the relationship of prostitution to trafficking and the agency of women within prostitution and/or trafficking. For one side, the HRC, human rights meant the rights to exercise agency and to migrate and work safely, in any sector including the sex industry. But for the IHRN prostitution was understood as a form of violence against women and therefore a human rights violation and so they worked to vindicate women's rights not to be sexually exploited in any broadly understood way. Such is the vehemence of the differences between these positions that there have been long-standing 'sex wars' between their protagonists (which pre- and post-date Palermo), leading to the dispiriting situation of 'feminists seeing each other as the biggest problem around' (Chapkis 1997, 4). This intra-feminist division was replicated at the ad hoc committee in Vienna. In order to understand these differences some further introduction to the central moral entrepreneurs, their back stories and their ideological positions is required.

The International Human Rights Network

At the heart of the International Human Rights Network in Vienna was the US-based Coalition Against Trafficking in Women (CATW). Founded in 1990 in the aftermath of the 'Conference on Trafficking in Women' mentioned above (Milivojevic and Pickering 2013), it owes much of its origins to the feminist abolitionist movements against prostitution and pornography that emerged in the US in the 1970s and 1980s. Although CATW works from this historical and philosophical base in the US, it has entered into coalition with NGOs throughout the world sharing in its basic analysis and policies. Therefore it can count amongst its membership individual organisations and coalitions in Mali, the Philippines, Mexico, Venezuela, Georgia, Japan and India (inter alia) (CATW 2016).

From the outset this movement defined prostitution and pornography as always and integrally harmful to women and children and consequently engaged in campaigning for the abolition of both these practices. The movement consciously links itself back to historical precursors in earlier abolitionism, celebrating the work of women such as Josephine

Butler and holding to the tenets of the 1949 UN Convention (Marcovich 2002). However, the more contemporary theoretical touchstone for this stance is found primarily in the writings of Kathleen Barry. According to Barry's structuralist analysis, the prostitution of women's sexuality is the outcome of the exploitative exercise by men of patriarchal power over women (Barry 1979 and 1995). This bald analysis of patriarchy as *the* overarching social reality makes Barry the archetypal 'power feminist' in Janet Halley's term, that is, those feminists who think 'everything about the relationship of males to females manifests domination and subordination' and 'characterize male sexuality as a vast social problem' (Halley 2006, 33–57 and 27). As such, contemporary neo-abolitionists associate themselves with a policy position that advocates abolishing prostitution by decriminalising the women who sell sex while criminalising those who organise commercial sex ('pimps') and those who buy sex (male clients). CATW shares this position with a number of other feminist national and transnational NGOs who were part of the IHRN, such as Equality Now and the European Women's Lobby (who will feature strongly in Chap. 5). Intriguingly, however, it is equally a position that allies these feminists with many evangelical Christians and the Christian evangelical lobby surrounding trafficking will be discussed in the next chapter.

One consequence of this understanding of all prostitution as the 'paradigmatic expression of male domination over women' and a 'system of gender-based totalitarianism' (Leidholdt 2004, 172) is that those of IHRN's persuasion refused (and continue to refuse) to draw a distinguishing line between prostitution and trafficking in women and children. In this reading all women in prostitution are trafficked, whether within states or across borders, in the sense that they are being moved, bought and sold by those controlling the sex industry for exploitation by men (Raymond 1998; Leidholdt 2004).

In telling the history of CATW it is striking that Dorchen Leidholdt, a prominent CATW activist, constructs a story about the Coalition that positions it from the outset in the intra-feminist 'sex wars'. She recounts that when she and others responded to violence against women in prostitution by campaigning against sexual exploitation in the 1970s, they were met on the streets by other feminists who argued that the violence could only be halted by recognising prostitution as a legitimate form of work. This has proven to be the dispute that has wound its way through all of Leidholdt's campaigning career to date, since she is continually pitched against those who seek to counter trafficking by legalising sex work (of which more below). In her account this constant friction with other feminists has left her with 'battle scars' (Leidholdt, n/d).

CATW and its allies in the IHRN at the Vienna negotiations were steeped in a determination to counter any argument or policy that would legitimate prostitution and thus, in their view, the trafficking of women and children. Its actions were geared to defining trafficking and prostitution as inseparable forms of violence against women and furthering abolitionism, and as such it had to battle other women who thought (and think) otherwise.

The Human Rights Caucus

The key moral entrepreneurs in the Human Rights Caucus included the International Human Rights Law Group, Human Rights Watch and the Global Alliance Against Trafficking in Women (importantly they also co-operated with a 'silent partner' in their coalition, the Network of Sex Work Projects, whose silence will be explained further below). The alternative theoretical perspective linking these groups lies in their foundational assumptions, which emphasise human agency rather than the structuralist analysis of the other coalition. Although those in the HRC recognised the constraints of structure that may lead to women's involvement in sex work, including poverty, gender inequality and global restrictions on migration for work, they emphasise that women migrating for work, including sex work, should be understood as 'courageous, enterprising and determined' agents (GAATW 2015) making rational choices. Rather than being dupes of their own 'false consciousness' (as CATW would explain away any woman who claimed to choose sex work), from this perspective it is possible to distinguish between consensual and non-consensual sex work. Not all prostitution is forced or is tantamount to trafficking in women.

GAATW can stand as an example of this way of thinking and its normative and policy implications. GAATW was founded in Thailand in 1994 and now has a global membership that stretches from there to India, the Philippines, Colombia, Germany, Poland and the US (again inter alia) (GAATW 2015). In GAATW's perspective trafficking has to be seen in the context of women's engagement in labour migration for various types of employment. The restrictions placed almost universally by states in the global North on migration possibilities for poorer women imply that many will opt for moving irregularly with dependence on third party facilitators and in that process cross the grey lines between consent and coercion, smuggling and trafficking, work and exploitation. In this context some women moving for sex work will end up entrapped or some women irregularly migrating will end up being forcibly sexually exploited. What is notable from this standpoint is that trafficking and prostitution and prostitution and exploitation are definitely not conflated. Rather, from this perspective, sex work constitutes a rational choice made by many women and so migration for non-coerced sex work cannot be considered to be trafficking. On this basis GAATW's efforts are directed at lobbying for safeguards for the human rights of migrant women workers (GAATW Bangkok Call 2002) and the legalisation of prostitution/sex work as a means of protecting those who work voluntarily in this sector. Such legalisation would, according to this perspective, also allow for easier detection and protection for those who are illegally trafficked or enslaved. GAATW was an influential presence at the UN Beijing Conference where there were 'terrible fights' between themselves and the abolitionists (Lal 2010, 29) before its entry into the Vienna process and its involvement in the HRC.

Within the HRC, the 'silent partner' of the Network of Sex Work Projects was an influential discussant, although an unofficial one. NSWP lobbyists, advocating for the rights of female, male and transgender sex workers, were of the view that the very promulgation of a new trafficking protocol was an unnecessary and negative international development, given their analysis that all preceding international agreements on the issue of prostitution were inevitably detrimental to sex workers. As outlined above, for example, the preceding 1949 UN Convention, though not widely ratified, was an abolitionist document, which conflated prostitution and trafficking by defining both as 'incompatible with human dignity' and encouraging state parties to 'protect' and repatriate travelling women where exploitation was suspected (UN 1949). Fearing the reiteration of such legacies, NSWP fundamentally did not support the development of the new Protocol and therefore did not officially sign up to any of the statements from the HRC, although they engaged in developing its thinking (Doezema 2005, 75).

While enjoying collaborative relations with those in the HRC, activists associated with the NSWP perspective were incensed by those from CATW and the IHRN whom they saw as portraying trafficked women and sex workers as the weak, helpless victims of patriarchy or 'crude, unfettered capitalism' (Doezema 2001, 18 and 30). This sin is compounded by the accusation that CATW women are white, middle class, non-sex working

Western women who cannot comprehend or presume to speak for the circumstances of Third World women (Kempadoo and Doezema 1998, 11–12). As a consequence of their powerful positioning these Western women infantilise and exoticise Third World women, instead of seeing them as rational agents who make decisions about economic strategies, which can include sex work and/or chancing illegal migration. All of this ends in the virulent condemnation of women like Kathleen Barry and those who seek to abolish prostitution/sex work as modern day Victorian colonisers.

In Chap. 1 I asserted, referring to authors such as Krook and True (2012), that norms are not the static objects they appear to be in the lifecycle model, but instead they are often the sites of agitated contestation and on-going, profoundly differing interpretations amongst norm entrepreneurs at all stages of the lifecycle. The sketches of the key anti-trafficking agitators above suggest the normative fault lines that pre-dated the Vienna negotiations and thoroughly dogged them. The basic issue of defining trafficking, whether trafficking is primarily an issue of the sexual exploitation of women and children as opposed to other forms of work, who could be understood as victims of trafficking and the related questions of possibilities of consent and necessities of coercion, created drawn-out, difficult negotiations for all involved. All the NGO norm entrepreneurs, whilst not party to the official talks, did their utmost to persuade state delegations of their respective viewpoints by verbal lobbying, submitting position papers, seeking allies in the UN system and bringing in ever 'larger numbers of representatives to have greater impact' (Ditmore and Wijers 2003). Interestingly, several UN agencies [including the Office of the High Commissioner for Human Rights (OHCHR), the UN High Commission for Refugees (UNHCR) and the International Organization for Migration (IOM)] were equally keen to make interventions on the emerging texts of the Protocols, impinging as they did on their bailiwicks of migration, human rights and refugee issues (Gallagher 2001, 985).

Key actors on both advocacy sides record their memories of difficult and emotional negotiations (Raymond 2002; Ditmore and Wijers 2003; Doezema 2005), where so much time was spent on arguing about defining trafficking that certain aspects that might have created points of collaborative potential (most importantly protections for trafficking victims) unfortunately slipped from their grasp as time ran out (Ditmore and Wijers 2003, 80). Intriguingly both coalitions claim a degree of victory for their lobbying efforts in affecting the shape of the Palermo Protocol.

The GAATW website, for instance, credits the role of the Human Rights Caucus with the important recognition of force and coercion as necessary to the trafficking definition and also the opening up of the Protocol to include other forms of trafficking in human beings. From the IHRN/CATW side the fact that the Protocol maintains the 1949 emphasis on the exploitation of women and children for prostitution and the recognition of demand for sexual exploitation as a key concern are seen as victories, with the Protocol read as 'the first international instrument that mentions the demand that creates all forms of exploitation that leads to trafficking' (Ekberg 2004, 1202; Raymond 2004).

How such a compromise document, inevitably full of 'very ambiguous...meanings' (Stoyanova 2013, 66), emerged, and the influence of the lobbyists on the debates can be discerned from a genealogy of the Protocol's drafts across the 11 sessions of the ad hoc Committee in Vienna. Analysis of these successive papers shows the shifting sands around the ideas and words that eventually found their way into the Palermo Protocol and the accompanying Protocol on the Smuggling of Migrants by Land, Sea and Air.

The Evolution of the Palermo Protocol and the Traces of Norm Contestation

Looking back into the records of the UN Crime Commission, it appears that human trafficking came on to the agenda of this particular UN body rather later than in other UN forums. As evidenced in the 1994 Nice Declaration, 'trafficking' in its 1990s remit was related primarily to drugs but also to guns and cars. Trafficking in stolen cars featured on its agenda right up to 1997—but as the proposal to create the new UN Convention on Transnational Organized Crime (UNCTOC) developed and the ad hoc committee was established, rather bizarrely cars vanished and women and children appeared.

In 1997 there was evidence that the Crime Commission was aware of the growing salience of issues of violence against women, stemming from the lively debates and 'governance feminism' successes cited above, particularly the Beijing Platform for Action, and the subsequent infiltration of concerns with violence against women and trafficking to the UN agenda more widely. The issue can be seen trickling into the Crime Commission's agenda through the record of its meetings. At its 1997 meeting women were defined as vulnerable to domestic violence while children were seen as potential trafficking victims. The only mention specifically of trafficking in women was made in the chair's closing remarks (UN Crime Commission 1997, 136). The idea had evidently rooted though and by 1998 when the ad hoc committee was charged with elaborating the Organized Crime Convention and its Protocols, they were to cover matters under the following headings: 'trafficking in women and children,' 'trafficking in firearms' and 'illegal trafficking in and transporting of migrants by sea' (UN Crime Commission 1998, iv).

There is at least one point within these headings that suggests an initial lack of conceptual clarity around what was being defined and legislated against. In the first header trafficking was clearly associated with a crime against women and children [and hence by the implication of the existing anti-trafficking Convention (UN 1949) understood to be about trafficking for sexual exploitation]. Then curiously in the third sub-heading trafficking is prefixed by the word 'illegal' in relation to the movement of migrants by sea. This surely begs questions about the lack of the word 'illegal' to qualify trafficking in the first header but its inclusion along with the gender neutral word 'migrants' in the third. I suggest these headings were signals of the confusion to come over how to define trafficking, its victims, its purposes and issues of consent, but it also suggests an underpinning gendering of trafficking, with the innocent sex-trafficked victims assumed to be women and children and the 'illegal trafficked' by implication assumed to be men. Later on in the ad hoc committee's deliberations the third header was differentiated from trafficking and re-conceptualised as 'smuggling', understood to be a crime against state borders committed knowingly by the 'illegal' migrant and the paid smuggler. So human trafficking through this process of differentiation came to signify people who were not culpable in states' eyes for their movement or exploitation but were 'victims' of a crime. In the real world of complex migratory journeys and regimes, this trafficking/smuggling distinction has proven very hard to maintain. However this semantic dichotomy has its effects. For example, the continuing association of trafficking with women and children (somewhat modified but perennial nonetheless) has the effect of gendering the 'innocent' trafficked victim female while the 'illegal' smuggled migrant is thereby male, assumed to be the masculine agents of their own travels and travails. This is an issue that continues to dog attempts to create moral entrepreneurship and norm socialisation around trafficking for forced labour, to which I will return in Chap. 6.

So from this outset, in gendered terms, it was assumed that 'women and children are particularly vulnerable to the crime of illegal trafficking' (UN Crime Commission 1998, 28). This was a position very much supported by the IHRN. Given their basic radical feminist premise that all women are subordinate to all men and that they should therefore be 'carrying a brief for women' (Halley 2006, 18), they were wary of any attempts to broaden the frame of trafficking victims to include men and boys, or indeed to define trafficking for any purposes other than sexual exploitation. For the HRC, with their concern first for women but also for all migrants facing constraints, the possibility of trafficking occurring to people in general and for purposes other than sex was apparent.

If one looks at the papers from the ad hoc committee meetings, it is clear this was a point of contention for the state negotiators as well as the NGO blocks, as two definitional options were kept on the table till the fifth revision of the text of what became the Palermo Protocol. One early definition, sponsored by Argentina, was only focused on trafficking in women and children for 'illicit acts' because they were defined as 'more vulnerable' to victimisation, whereas the US sponsored version suggested 'trafficking in persons' for the purposes of sexual exploitation or forced labour (UNODC second session 1999). The compromise agreed by the fourth session of the committee was a general agreement on 'trafficking in persons, but especially women and children' (UNODC fourth session 1999), which is the wording that eventually made it into the title of the Palermo Protocol. Compromise too was reached over the purposes with sexual exploitation and exploitation of the prostitution of others being joined by labour, slavery and trafficking for organs. In this sense a broadening of the purposes of human trafficking was achieved (an HRC aim) but somehow the implication that this was a crime where women and children were most likely the victims for sexually exploitative purposes was preserved and privileged (an IHRN aim).

The compromises emerging around other hotly contested issues within the negotiations can also be traced through the drafts in relation to the issues of the relationship of prostitution to trafficking and consent to them both. Again the Argentinian opening position was abolitionist in tone. Picking up from 1949, this option proposed that trafficking involved 'transporting a woman or facilitating her entry into another state' for 'illicit purpose' including prostitution, *even with the consent of that person* (UNODC second session 1999). For other delegations, however, trafficking had to be related to non-consensual exploitation and prostitution was not accepted as being by definition coercive. At the ninth session 'several delegations expressed that it was essential to distinguish victims of prostitution from those who chose to engage' (akin to the HRC position) (UNODC ninth session 2000). Once again the playing out of these debates led to a highly compromised final outcome. The well-known, convoluted Palermo definition of trafficking lays out the act, means and purposes of trafficking (movement by deception or coercion for exploitative ends) but then clause 3b overrides consent even for adults when any of the defined means have been used. For IHRN clause 3b is read as a victory as it negates consent, which in their view is impossible anyway given the inherent exploitation of prostitution (CATW 2001, 8). For the other side the reading is in the opposite direction. Because consent is negated if *any of the means* have been used, it is only then that trafficking happens—when 'force, deception, coercion or abuse of vulnerability' occurs and not in any situation of 'sexual exploitation'. Mary Robinson, in her capacity as UN High Commissioner for Human Rights, wrote in an informal note to the ad hoc committee warning that leaving such imprecise and emotive phrases as 'sexual exploitation' undefined in relation to adults would lead to interpretation and implementation difficulties for the Protocol (UNODC informal note 1999). Yet in the end several such terms were left undefined in another compromise to get the deal done.

Looking back over the drafts of the Palermo Protocol, it is possible to trace the stories of contending normative positions argued out between states and NGOs on who counts as trafficked, what exploitative end trafficking is for and whether prostitution can be consensual. Compromises along the way are evident and left both lobbying sides claiming victory—at the price of unending ambiguity and also arguably at the price of allowing states to get away with taking the focus off victims' rights (Ditmore and Wijers 2003) and facilitating some contrastingly weak and draconian provisions further into the Protocol, which arguably enabled states to further their own very material interests.

The Genealogy of State Interests in the Palermo Protocol

There were 11 meetings of the ad hoc committee on the trafficking protocol between 1999 and 2000, each lasting a week or more. Not surprisingly, the first draft of what would become the Palermo Protocol was much briefer than the final document would be. Interestingly the 'growth' area between the first and final versions can be seen most prevalently in the addition of articles on law enforcement, border control and regulating international travel documents. Due to the fact that it sits within the framework of the UN Convention on Transnational Organized Crime, inevitably from the outset the Protocol contained provisions on law enforcement and combatting organised crime. But the first version only contained a brief draft article 5 on co-operation to check documents, to ensure that those carrying false ones were not trafficking victims and to share information on trafficking routes, and so on (UNODC first session 1999). By the later versions presented to the 9th and 11th sessions of the ad hoc committee, additional articles had been added. Article 7 (previously 5), reiterated the suggested law enforcement provisions already mentioned but a new article 8 introduced the necessity of state parties taking measures to 'strengthen, to the extent possible, border control', to include the inspection of vehicles and reiterating the importance of 'carrier liabilities' with regard to enhancing border controls. Article 9 then adds another layer of concern around checking the legitimacy of international travel documents (UNODC 9th session, 2000 and 11th session, 2000). In this genealogy, from early to later versions, traces of the concern contemporary states have with border control in response to various categories of 'irregular' migration became ever more present as the drafts progressed. As forewarned by High Commissioner Robinson in her informal note to the ad hoc committee, the 'fact that national anti-trafficking measures have been used in some situations to discriminate against women and other groups in a manner that amounts to a denial of their basic right to leave a country and to migrate legally' was in danger of becoming a disturbing consequence of the ever increasing border security measures incorporated into successive versions of the Palermo Protocol (UNODC fourth session informal note, 1999).

While strengthening the border control aspects of the Protocol through negotiations, the other genealogical trace that tells of state's material interests was the eventual agreement to leave the protections aspects of the Protocol very weak. Just how much obligation states should have towards identified victims was a perennial debate in the ad hoc committee meetings. Between meetings and versions there are different listings of what duties of care or allocation of rights state parties should have for suspected victims of trafficking. Through several versions the square bracketing of keywords gives an indication of the matters under debate. For example, at the sixth ad hoc committee meeting, delegates debated whether or not to remove the brackets from the sentence; 'State parties…in appropriate cases and to the extent possible, shall [consider]…' whether identified trafficking victims should have access to temporary and/or permanent residency entitlements' (UNODC sixth session, 1999). By the ninth session the decision was taken to remove the square brackets and leave the fateful word 'consider' in, thus weakening any residency obligations to victims. The footnotes to this final wording (version 6 at footnote 28) explain, 'most delegates were concerned that the Protocol might inadvertently become a means of illicit migration if State parties were obliged to adopt legislation permitting victims to remain' (UNODC ninth session, 2000). This example over the residency question was not the only issue where the final version was to imply that state parties should only 'consider' or 'endeavour' to take measures 'where appropriate'. That weak language permeates the final document in relation to all victim protections and rights.

Anti-Trafficking Norms and Material Interests

These elements of the Palermo Protocol indicate that the re-emergence of the anti-trafficking norm cannot be understood solely as a consequence of the intense activism of moral entrepreneurs. The border security clauses and weak human rights protections are reminders that this Protocol was never intended as a human rights document, but rather that sovereignty and security issues were the true driving force behind the UN Convention on Transnational Organized Crime and its Protocols (Gallagher 2001, 976). These documents are therefore intelligible as part of state responses to the insecurities of the post-Cold War world, the fear of unruly human movement associated with globalisation and the desire to categorise and control migration.

Absent the Cold War, a series of new security threats have been identified by states and international organisations as necessitating responses. As mentioned above, the new Convention's roots date back to the UN's Naples Declaration of 1994, which spelled out the threat transnational organised crime was seen to pose to state security, democratic accountability and the global economy as networks of organised crime flourished in the context of post-Cold War instability, globalisation and new information technologies (Betti 2003, 155). That context too was understood as the progenitor of another alleged threat to state and 'societal security'—migration itself—understood as a threat because it might lead to the over-running or dilution of a host society by outsiders (Buzan et al.

1998, 121). This understanding of migration as a security threat has only been compounded in the post 9/11 world, where suspicions surrounding the movement of many people around the globe has been heightened, provoking increased use of force, surveillance and profiling of travellers at borders (Bigo 2014). Responding to these new security threats has provoked states to both co-operate more (for example, in common border control through FRONTEX in the EU) and to try to maintain mouldering borders and sovereign integrity in the face of globalisation's great contradiction, that contradiction being the radical openness of borders to capital, goods and cultural influences alongside the paradoxical closure of borders against certain categories of people as states seek to prevent migration and seek political legitimacy with their populations through the politics of border control (Munck 2008, 1227). It is easy to see where the UN Convention on TNOC and the phrasing of the Palermo Protocol as a border control instrument with its parsimonious protections for identified victims fit into realising these re-oriented state security concerns of the post Cold War world. Perversely, the anti-trafficking norm so hard fought for and over by women's NGOs becomes a way through which 'legislators have sought solutions that concurrently serve their national security interests and reinforce state sovereignty' (Foester 2009, 152). In this context, those NGOs like the IHRN that argue for greater state interventions to prevent trafficking end up in cahoots with the 'criminal justice approach' (Hahn 2010, 233) that resonated so well with the state parties at the negotiations rather than the HRC approach of arguing for states' openness to migration.

In the politics of border control, human trafficking serves another aspect of state interests—as an aspect of the classification of desired and undesired migrants. The Trafficking Protocol is part of a Convention that includes the Protocol on the Smuggling of Migrants by Land, Sea and Air. As I pointed out earlier, this twofold division related to a sense that there was 'illegal' migrant trafficking and trafficking in 'innocent' women and children. Semantic confusion was (not very successfully) resolved by redefining 'illegal migrant trafficking' as smuggling. What this division does is to suggest that there are migrants who are criminal and culpable of illegal movement and there are others who are innocent (the trafficked—deceived, coerced, moved, exploited through no fault of their own). These innocent might be deemed worthy of some state protections but the others are not and are dispensable. The concepts of trafficking and smuggling therefore are integral to the state's classification of migrants, as 'deserving' or 'undeserving' of inclusion and protection (Anderson and O'Connell Davidson 2002, 17). The innocent and vulnerable are usually imagined as women and children and men as smuggled. Thus 'innocent' women and children's bodies are used to draw borderlines and legitimate migrant exclusion in the contemporary world (Buss et al. 2005). States' material interests in border maintenance, crime prevention and migrant classification can all be read into the Palermo Protocol, mingling there uneasily alongside the concerns to prevent exploitation (however it is understood) of the diverse moral entrepreneurs who proselytised so vigorously for its adoption. The genealogy of the Palermo Protocol does provide illustration of the ways in which social and material power fuse in norm emergence (Reich 2010, 23–24).

Conclusion: Norm Emergence and the Palermo Protocol

Finnemore and Sikkink's model of the lifecycle of norms in international politics begins at the point of norm emergence, their point being that moral entrepreneurs advocate for an ideal using international platforms, creating transnational networks and alliances, persuading, framing, offering their expertise, managing the meaning of ideas—to socialise states into adopting a norm, to the point where states begin to see adherence to that norm as part of their identity and something that it is in their interest to promote. In this chapter, I have looked at the work of several such actors, showing how their energetic activism affected the emergence of the idea that trafficking (particularly in women and children) was a contemporary global problem that needed addressed. The marks of their interpretations of the issue are there in the successive drafts of the Protocol and their advocacy efforts are recorded in their own memoirs of events.

Yet, the story of the anti-trafficking norm and the eventual Palermo Protocol is equally testimony to the critical points raised about the lifecycle model in the previous chapter. Chapter 2 raised the problems of identifying beginnings and ends to lifecycles and also the necessity of analysing the politics 'within' and 'without' norm construction and both these points are amply illustrated by the material in this chapter. The anti-trafficking norm had its precursors, particularly in the international imprints of white slavery activism and the abolitionism of the 1949 Convention, which both set the predominant way of seeing (trafficking is about the sexual exploitation of women and children) and problematised the debates. The tendency to understand trafficking as being about 'women and children' was challenged at Palermo by the move to 'trafficking in persons', yet the tenacious references to 'especially women and children' has inflected the concept ever since, leaving it predominantly associated with the indefinable 'sexual exploitation'. Moral entrepreneurship on trafficking also had its new beginnings in the politics of the post-Cold War era and the platforms at which women's place in the new international order was being re-thought and very much argued over. The contention of preceding 'sex wars' and arguments so evident in forums like Beijing wound their way into the normative debates around Palermo, where fraught and emotive debates over definition, consent, coercion and exploitation were prevalent. These negotiations provide strong evidence that norms are not stable things and are in fact highly contested and open to interpretation—which knows no end, despite the setting into legal words of a trafficking definition in 2000. Moreover, interpretations of Palermo, as they cascade into international and domestic laws, may generate unforeseen and unwanted consequences (such as further state restrictions on women's migration), which the norm entrepreneurs did not foresee or perhaps are even indifferent to as a means of furthering the greater cause (Halley et al. 2006, 420). This, it turns out, is an occupational hazard for successful norm entrepreneurs, such as the 'governance feminists', whose several victories over the 1990s have ironically produced enhanced state control over women's lives.

Another aspect of norm lifecycle, which the Palermo story helpfully exemplifies, is that the emergence of a norm is not solely a bottom-up process whereby states get socialised to an idea by civil society activism. The motivation to adopt the anti-trafficking norm was equally driven by states' rethinking of their positions and concerns post-Cold War—particularly new 'threats' such as transnational organised crime and 'illegal' migration, as can be seen dating back to the Naples Declaration of 1994 and the discussions at the UN Crime Commission. Moreover while states may have partially aimed for the international legitimacy that accompanies norm sponsorship, particularly those opposing violations of vulnerable human bodies such as trafficking, their material interests were much to the fore in engaging with Palermo. It was not moral suasion alone that led to the re-emergence of the anti-trafficking norm but a politics 'within' and 'without' the idea.

This intriguing interplay of how norms shape identities and interests, and vice versa, is traceable in the Palermo negotiations. As I turn now to the next stage of the norm lifecycle, norm cascade, this same entangling of the moral and the material can be seen in the actions of the anti-trafficking norm's crucial international promoter, the United States of America.

Bibliography

Anderson, B., & O'Connell Davidson, J. (2002). *Trafficking—A demand led problem? A multi-country study*. Stockholm: Save the Children.

Barry, K. (1979). *Female sexual slavery*. New York: New York University Press.

Barry, K. (1995). *The prostitution of sexuality: The global exploitation of women*. New York: New York University Press.

Betti, S. (2003). New prospects for inter-state co-operation in criminal matters: The Palermo convention. *International Criminal Law Review, 3*, 151–167.

Bigo, D. (2014). The (in)securitization practices of the three Universes of EU Border Control: Military/Navy—Border Guards/Police—database analysts. *Security Dialogue, 45*(3), 209–225.

Buss, D., Fletcher, R., Monk, D., Monro, S., & Phillips, O. (2005). Introduction to sexual movements and gendered boundaries: Legal negotiations of the global and the local. *Social and Legal Studies, 14*(5), 5–15.

Buzan, B., Waever, O., & de Wilde, J. (1998). *Security: A new framework for analysis*. Boulder: Lynne Reinner.

CATW. (2001). Coalition Report—Coalition Against Trafficking in Women Annual Report 2001. http://www.catwinternational.org/Content/Documents/Reports/ReportOct2001.pdf, date accessed 10 February 2016.

CATW. (2016). Coalition against trafficking in women: Who we are: Mission. http://www.catwinternational.org/WhoWeAre/Mission, date accessed 5 January 2016.

CEDAW. (1979). Convention on the elimination of all forms of discrimination against women. http://www.un.org/womenwatch/daw/cedaw/text/econvention.htm#article6, date accessed 11 February 2016.

Chapkis, W. (1997). *Live Sex Acts: Women performing erotic labour*. London: Taylor and Francis.

Coleman, J. (2008). Apprehending possibilities: Tracing the emergence of feminist consciousness in nineteenth-century New Zealand. *Women's Studies International Forum, 31*, 464–473.

Ditmore, M., & Wijers, M. (2003). The negotiations on the UN Protocol on trafficking in persons: Moving the focus from morality to actual conditions. *Nemesis, 4*, 79–88.

Doezema, J. (2001). Ouch! Western Feminists' 'Wounded Attachment' to the 'Third World Prostitute". *Feminist Review, 67*(1), 16–38.

Doezema, J. (2005). Now you see her, Now you don't: Sex workers at the UN Trafficking Protocol negotiation. *Social and Legal Studies, 14*, 61–89.

Doezema, J. (2010). *Sex slaves and discourse masters: The construction of trafficking*. London: Zed Books.

Ekberg, G. (2004). The Swedish Law that prohibits the purchase of sexual services best practices for prevention of prostitution and trafficking in human beings. *Violence Against Women, 10*(10), 1187–1218.

Foester. (2009). Contested bodies: Sex trafficking NGOs and transnational politics. *International Feminist Journal of Politics, 11*(2), 151–173.

GAATW. (2015). GAATW—The history of GAATW. http://www.gaatw.org/about-us/history/156-about-us/history/438-the-roots-of-gaatw, date accessed 30 January 2015.

GAATW Bangkok Call. (2002). Bangkok call for justice for women migrant workers. http://www.gaatw.org/publications/bangkok_call4justice.pdf, date accessed 30 January 2015.

Gaer, F. (2009). Women, International Law and International Institutions: The case of the United Nations. *Women's Studies International Forum, 32*, 60–66.

Gallagher, A. T. (2001). Human rights and the new UN protocols on trafficking and migrant smuggling: A preliminary analysis. *Human Rights Quarterly, 23*, 975–1004.

Hahn, K. (2010). NGOs power of advocacy: The construction of identities in UN counter-trafficking policies. In J. Steffek & K. Hahn (Eds.), *Evaluating Transnational NGOs: Legitimacy, accountability, representation* (pp. 220–244). Basingstoke: Palgrave.

Halley, J. (2008). *Split decisions: How and why to take a break from feminism*. Princeton: Princeton University Press.

Halley, J., Kotiswaran, P., Shamir, H., & Thomas, C. (2006). From the International to the local in feminist legal responses to rape, prostitution, sex work and sex trafficking: Four studies in contemporary governance feminism. *Harvard Journal of Law and Gender, 29*, 335–423.

Harrington, C. (2011). Resolution 1325 and Post-Cold War Feminist Politics. *International Feminist Journal of Politics, 13*(4), 557–575.

Jordan, J. (2007). *Josephine Butler*. London: Bloomsbury Academic.

Keck, M., & Sikkink, K. (1998). *Activists beyond borders: Advocacy Networks in International Politics*. Ithaca, New York: Cornell University Press.

Kempadoo, K., & Doezema, J. (1998). *Global sex workers: Rights, resistance, and redefinition*. Abingdon, Oxon: Psychology Press/Routledge.

Krook, M., & True, J. (2012). Rethinking the Lifecycles of International Norms: The United Nations and the Global Promotion of Gender Equality. *European Journal of International Relations, 18*(1), 103–127.

Lal, J., McGuire, K., Stewart, A., Zaborowska, M., & Pas, J. (2010). Recasting global feminisms: Toward a comparative historical approach to women's activism and feminist scholarship. *Feminist Studies, 36*(1), 13–39.

Legg, S. (2012). The life of individuals as well as of Nations': International law and the league of nations' anti-trafficking governmentalities. *Leiden Journal of International Law, 25*, 647–664.
Leidholdt, D. (2004). Prostitution and trafficking in women: An intimate relationship. *Journal of Trauma Practice, 2*(3–4), 167–183.
Limoncelli, S. (2010). *The politics of trafficking: The first international movement to combat the sexual exploitation of women.* Stanford, CA: Stanford University Press.
Malarek, V. (2004). *The Natashas: The new global sex trade.* Toronto: Viking Books.
Marcovich, M. (2002). Guide to the UN Convention of 2 December 1949 for the suppression of the traffic in persons and of the exploitation of the prostitution of others. http://www.catwinternational.org/Content/Images/Article/119/attachment.pdf, date accessed 27 February 2015.
Merry, S. E. (2003). Constructing a global law-violence against women and the human rights system. *Law and Social Enquiry, 28*(4), 941–977.
Milivojevic, S., & Pickering, S. (2013). Trafficking in people, 20 years on: Sex, migration and crime in the global anti-trafficking discourse and the rise of the 'Global Trafficking Complex'. *Current Issues in Criminal Justice, 25*(2), 585–604.
Munck, R. (2008). Globalisation, governance and migration: An introduction. *Third World Quarterly, 29*(7), 1227–1246.
Raymond, J. (1998). Demand and the debate: NGO Stonewalling at Beijing and *Beyond*. http://www.catwlac.org/en/wp-content/uploads/2013/10/Demand_and_the_Debate.pdf, date accessed 30 January 2015.
Raymond, J. (2002). The New UN Trafficking Protocol. *Women's Studies International Forum, 25*(5), 491–502.
Raymond, J. (2004). Prostitution on demand: Legalizing the buyers as sexual consumers. *Violence Against Women, 10*(10), 1156–1186.
Reich, S. (2010). *Global norms, American Sponsorship and the emerging patterns of world politics.* Basingstoke: Palgrave.
Reimann, K. (2006). A view from the top: International politics, norms and the worldwide growth of NGOs. *International Studies Quarterly, 50*(1), 45–68.
Report of the Secretary General. (1994). Progress made in the implementation of General Assembly resolutions 46/152, 47/91 and 48/103 (A/49/593, 31 October 1994), http://www.un.org/law/avl/, date accessed 11 March 2015.
Saunders, P. (2005). Traffic violations: Determining the meaning of violence in sexual trafficking versus sex work. *Journal of interpersonal Violence, 20*(3), 343–360.
Soderlund, G. (2011). The rhetoric of revelation: Sex trafficking and journalistic expose. *Humanity: An International Journal of Human Rights, Humanitarianism and Development, 2*(2), 193–211.
Soderlund, G. (2013). *Sex trafficking, scandal and the transformation of journalism: 1885–1917.* Chicago, Illinois: University of Chicago Press.

Stead, W. T. (1885) The Maiden Tribute of the Modern Babylon. http://www.attackingthedevil.co.uk/pmg/tribute/, 27 February 2015.

Stoyanova, V. (2013). The crisis of a definition: Human trafficking in Bulgarian Law. *Amsterdam Law Forum*, 5(1), 64–79.

UN. (1949). Convention for the suppression of the traffic in persons and of the exploitation of the prostitution of others. http://www.ohchr.org/Documents/ProfessionalInterest/trafficpersons.pdf, date accessed 27 February 2015.

UN Crime Commission (1997) Report on the Sixth Session (28 April-9 May 1997). Economic and Social Council Official Records, 1997, Supplement No.10, V.97 23882(E).

UN Crime Commission (1998) Report on the Seventh Session (21-30 April 1998). Economic and Social Council Official Records, 1998, Supplement No.10, E/1998/30 E/CN.15/1998/11.

UN. (2013). UN Audio-Visual Library of International Law. http://legal.un.org/avl/ha/unctoc/unctoc.html, date accessed 11 February 2016.

UNODC. (2000). United Nations convention on Transnational organized crime and the Protocols Thereto. 15 November 2000. https://www.unodc.org/documents/treaties/UNTOC/Publications/TOC%20Convention/TOCebook-e.pdf, date accessed 12 March 2016.

UNODC Fourth Session. (1999). Ad Hoc Committee on the Elaboration of a Convention against Transnational Organized Crime, June-July 28–9, 1999. https://www.unodc.org/unodc/en/treaties/CTOC/background/session4.html, date accessed 10 February 2016.

UNODC Fourth Session Informal Note. (1999). Informal Note by the High Commissioner for Human Rights to Fourth session of the Ad Hoc Committee on the Elaboration of a Convention against Transnational Organized Crime, June-July 28–9, 1999. https://www.unodc.org/unodc/en/treaties/CTOC/background/session4.html, date accessed 10 February 2016

UNODC Ninth Session. (2000). Ad Hoc Committee on the Elaboration of a Convention against Transnational Organized Crime, February–March 21–3, 2000. https://www.unodc.org/unodc/en/treaties/CTOC/background/session9.html, date accessed 10 February 2016.

UNODC Second Session. (1999). Ad Hoc Committee on the Elaboration of a Convention against Transnational Organized Crime Vienna, 8–12 March 1999, Proposals and Contributions Received from Governments. https://www.unodc.org/unodc/en/treaties/CTOC/background/Session2.html, date accessed 10 February 2016.

UNODC Sixth Session. (1999). Sixth session of the Ad Hoc Committee on the Elaboration of a Convention against Transnational Organized Crime (A/AC.254/4/Add.3/Rev.4). https://www.unodc.org/unodc/en/treaties/CTOC/background/session6.html, date accessed 11 February 11 2016.

CHAPTER 4

Norm Cascade and the Hegemon

Introduction

Following the logical progression of the norm life cycle model, this chapter moves from the emergence (or resurrection) of a norm through the moral impress of contending civil society entrepreneurs to the second stage: norm cascade. According to Martha Finnemore and Kathryn Sikkink's model, cascade is the stage at which there is rapid uptake of norm adoption by nation-states. They suggest that this occurs after a 'tipping point' is reached at which a truly substantial number of nation-states endorse a new normative framework in international forums (Finnemore and Sikkink 1998, 901). Much of the concern in their paper is to explain why states get caught up in the cascade and they consider a number of potential causes, ranging from desires for international legitimacy, endorsement of state identity or esteem to material self-interest.

In this chapter on the cascade of the anti-trafficking norm, I will suggest that a key element behind the cascade of this norm is a process of 'hegemonic socialisation' (Finnemore and Sikkink 1998, 906), as driven by the US. This is not to suggest, however, a straightforward 'power politics' explanation of the rapid international endorsement of the Palermo Protocol. As I will argue below, the US has undoubtedly put its mighty weight behind the anti-trafficking cause but the reasons it has done so are as much to do with certain expressions of American identity as much as material self-interest.

G. Wylie, *The International Politics of Human Trafficking*,
DOI 10.1057/978-1-137-37775-3_4

Norm Cascades and Why They Happen

Stage two of the norm lifecycle is 'cascade', which follows on from a 'tipping point'. In their original article, Finnemore and Sikkink draw on a number of empirical studies to estimate that tipping points for norm adoption tend to occur when roughly one third of the world's states sign up (1998, 901). Following this critical point, a new norm gathers such pace that desistance by those not ratifying becomes futile and a norm cascade occurs, leading to widespread norm adoption and socialisation. Pressure for adoption at this stage comes more from the international arena downwards, so that even states not experiencing any domestic pressure to support the norm decide to ratify (1998, 902). The language I am using in these paragraphs is suggestive of an inevitable and natural process, for example 'gathering pace', 'futile resistance' and even the terms 'cascade' and 'tipping point' themselves carry naturalistic or physical connotations. That is not what Finnemore and Sikkink wish to convey in their discussion of this stage of the lifecycle, as they are clearly puzzling out the issue of why norms cascade and why increasing numbers of parties conform. Essentially, the heart of their discussion relies on the constructivist claim that states conform because the growing number of ratifications affirms that to be considered a legitimate member of international society, adoption of this norm becomes necessary. After a tipping point, the norm is seen to redefine what is considered appropriate behaviour for an entity called 'state' and therefore legitimate belonging in the international system and esteem from other states rests on joining the cascade (1998, 902–3). Finnemore and Sikkink do return to the issue later in the paper and again weigh up whether state behaviour results from choice or is determined by the structure of the international system, therefore resulting from material self-interest or interests pressed onto weaker states by a hegemonic power. They hold all these potential explanations in tension, but in the end they suggest that 'socialization is the dominant mechanism of norm cascade' and that this socialization occurs through the work of states or other moral entrepreneurs to 'praise or censure...reinforced by material sanctions and incentives' (Finnemore and Sikkink 1998, 902).

From a distant perspective, the progress of the anti-trafficking norm seems to fit this predicted cascade pattern. When it opened for signing in Palermo in December 2000 the Protocol already attracted more than the required one-third tipping point, with 80 signatories. Thereafter a process of accumulating signings and ratifications occurred, so that at the time of writing the number of parties to the Protocol stands at 169 (UN Treaty Collection 2000). And as the next chapter will show with a focus on Europe, these ratifications have not been without effect in terms of provoking the elaboration of regional European anti-trafficking architecture and the domestication of anti-trafficking norms in EU member states. But can it be concluded that this trajectory occurs solely as a consequence of anti-trafficking moral entrepreneurs or UN diplomats whose work effectively sets in train a political logic and momentum that leads a norm to cascade through the international system to local contexts? Clearly a comparison to other international normative frameworks, such as the UN International Convention on the Rights of All Migrant Workers and their Families, which although created in 1990 still only has 38 signatories at this time (UN Treaty Collection 1990), suggests that norm cascade is not a case of inevitable perpetual motion despite the naturalistic image the word 'cascade' creates. I would therefore assert that to go with the flow of the lifecycle as implied by the cascade metaphor does not capture the political realities driving or resisting all norm cascades in general, and this one in particular. As I noted in Chap. 2, Finnemore and Sikkink are not blind to the potentially crucial role a hegemonic power can play in promoting norm adoption (Finnemore and Sikkink 1998, footnote 85), a point very much elaborated by others such Simon Reich in his work (2010). As this chapter will show, the USA does play the part of hegemonic norm promoter in relation to anti-trafficking activism to the extent that Janie Chuang astutely dubs America the 'global sheriff' when it comes to human trafficking (Chuang 2006b). But why recent US administrations have been so particularly exercised by this issue in comparison to others is intriguing. Why for example did George W. Bush devote one third of a 2003 address to the UN to it (UN webcast 2003), and why has a particular understanding of the trafficking problem (as trafficking of women and children for sexual exploitation) come to predominate in US policy and actions? Such predominance does require explanation.

In what follows I will argue that while the trafficking issue could be seen as just another way to flex international political muscle or promote US interests, succeeding administrations' adherence to the anti-trafficking cause requires an understanding of the US not just as a power player but also as a moral entrepreneur in international relations. It also requires an understanding of the way in which international norm generation works from the 'inside out' in international relations rather than just from international organisations 'out and down' to states and their domestic politics.

As will be shown below, anti-trafficking activism inside the US was happening at the same time as the international norm formation process in the UN and involved the crossover of several civil society actors in the two arenas.

This chapter will therefore offer an analysis of how and why the US has put its hegemonic power into pushing forward the anti-trafficking cascade. To do this I first need to establish a social constructivist and gendered reading of the US as an actor in global politics, to provide the theoretical basis for understanding why anti-(sex) trafficking activism has become important in the constitution of US identity and interests in international relations.

The United States and International Politics

The previous chapter suggested that the simultaneous international renewal of interest in the issue of human trafficking as contemporaneous with the end of the Cold War was not just a coincidence of timing. The defrosting of Cold War boundaries and the accompanying perception of new insecurities in the globalising world pushed inter-related issues like organised crime, border control, migration and human trafficking up the international agenda. The end of the Cold War also had a profound effect on the US, leaving it to all appearances as the political and ideological hegemon of the international system, experiencing what Charles Krauthammer characterised as its 'unipolar moment' (Krauthammer 1990/91). While the intervening years have complicated claims to sole great power status, with the rise of economic contenders in the BRICs (Brazil, Russia, India and China) and signs of weakness in the aftermath of contentious and messy international interventions, there is still no disputing that the US is a global power in terms of military might and reach, economic and cultural influence and political clout. In these senses, realist theory with its emphasis on state pursuit of self-interest and national security in the anarchical international order seems in some respects to offer adequate account of US post Cold War politics. Even despite the apparent blow to neo-realist accounts of international politics, which came with the unexpectedly peaceful retreat of the Soviet Union from balance of power politics, a theorist such as Michael Mastanduno can still claim that 'it would be imprudent to follow the advice of realism's harshest critics and abandon the core paradigm' (Mastanduno 1997, 51). To bolster his claim he points to the policies pursued by post Cold War US administrations to uphold US primacy in international affairs, whether that be by keeping potential challenger states in check, leading the expansion of NATO or aggressively promoting the conditions for US economic dominance. From an International Relations theory point of view, therefore, it might still be possible to see US foreign policy as shaped by the inevitable and comprehensible self-promoting political actions of a state that finds itself the sole hegemon in an anarchic world. Yet, there is much about the US as an international political actor that cannot be comprehended as stemming solely from material interest, hard power and the logic of anarchy, whatever (neo)-realists would contend. For example, further examination of a theme such as the 'War on Terror', which dominated US policy from 2001 under President Bush, suggests US foreign policies are not always to be understood within the framing of rational great power calculus. Post 9/11 the George W. Bush administration opted to respond by declaring a global war on a tactic (terror) involving the pursuit of several ill-assorted 'evil' regimes associated with it. This was accompanied by an express desire to produce 'regime change' towards liberalism and democracy, often legitimated by discourses of liberating Third World women from gendered oppression (Risley 2015, 219; Russo 2006). All of this is indicative of a great power driven by its ideals and identity as much as rational interest calculation. Acknowledging that the roots of US actions often lie in these immaterial considerations, that is 'the importance of the power of ideas in shaping and delimiting the exercise of more familiar forms of political and economic power' (Schulman 2014, xii), makes more sense within social constructivist and feminist theoretical readings of US international politics. These accounts stress the importance of beliefs and values, including gendered ones, in shaping state identities and interests rather than the role of exogenous determinants such as international anarchy.

While the Bush administration during the War on Terror phase may provide the most glaring example of international engagement driven by notions of globalising American ideals, this is a trope that makes its appearance regularly in US foreign policy. Since its foundation by colonising religious dissidents from Europe, an identifiable 'Civil Religion' has shaped American politics and identity. This 'religion' presupposes that America is to be a place where certain transcendental ideals can be realised, most notably freedom, prosperity, individual dignity and limited government. American 'Civil Religion' is not necessarily Christian and does not automatically imply that the US has a mission to spread its values beyond its borders (Amstutz 2014, 18–19). Yet neither secularisation nor the official separation of church and state has ever diminished the imprint of a 'Christian presumption of American politics' (Jakobsen and Bernstein 2009, 4) or the sense of being a 'city on the hill' possessing principles of universal relevance for the international system. The intersection of Civil Religious ideals with national interests is very much at play in the formation of US interaction with the world. For instance, the imprint of Civil Religion, often combined with an evangelical Christian faith, can be traced in the policies pursued by US Presidents and administrations over recent decades (Amstutz 2014, 28). In similar vein to Mark Amstutz, David Gelernter refers to this civil religion as 'Americanism' and traces its foundations to the Puritans, with their Christian creed, pursuit of freedom and sense of building a 'promised land', which would be an example to all. He defines Americanism as 'the belief that their nation is morally superior and closer to God' and suggests that this lends Americans 'an energy which makes (them) willing to prescribe freedom, equality and democracy even for a place like Afghanistan' (Gelernter 2005, 41–42).

Gelernter's reference to Afghanistan and equality draws attention to an intriguing twist in contemporary US international interventions, which, among other things, are explicitly legitimated in gendered terms. The War on Terror, for example, frequently found legitimation in liberal discourses of gender equality, with the need to 'liberate' oppressed women frequently featuring in government rhetoric. A prime example of this was First Lady Laura Bush's radio broadcast to the nation in support of the Afghan invasion on the grounds that it was a 'fight for the rights and dignity of women' (Los Angeles Times 2001; C-SPAN 2014). This points to the importance of gendered ideas as a motivating factor in US identity and foreign policy, involving a peculiar mixing of liberal notions of equality with the role of Western militaries as masculine 'saviours' of oppressed 'other' women (Nayak 2006). Arguably, as pointed out by Amy Risley (2015, 227), these gendered discourses concerning rescue and saviours also appear as motivating ideals in relation to US anti-trafficking activism.

Below the political elite level it is also noteworthy that domestic influences on the formation of US policies are manifold. Since de Tocqueville's early nineteenth-century account of *Democracy in America* (2003) onwards, it has been recognised that America's system of government allows plenty of space for civil society contention. Space aplenty does not, of course, mean equality of resources, access or influence and, as will be detailed below in the case of anti-trafficking activism, an intriguing coalition of religious, feminist and anti-slavery advocates is key to the formation of domestic and international policy on the issue.

Religious constituencies, particularly evangelical Christian ones, exercised markedly increasing political influence in American domestic and international politics through the latter twentieth century. Evangelical Christians were fairly a-political in the first half of the twentieth century; however in the 1950s their leadership made an overt move away from a sole focus on Biblical Fundamentalism and made a conscientious decision to re-engage with social and political questions. This gathered pace in the 1970s around prominent 'culture war' questions in American society relating to abortion and sexuality but it eventually took on a more internationalist hue in the 1990s over concerns initially for 'persecuted churches' abroad but later for a number of carefully selected issues, including human trafficking (Piehl 2014, 148 and Amstutz 2014). Since then evangelical Christians have become evermore influential actors in American politics with the institutionalisation of their policy influence made concrete in the Bush and Obama years. First under Bush and continuing under Obama, official space for them as favoured civil society partners for government opened up. G.W. Bush created the Office of Faith Based and Community Initiatives, which segued into the Office of Faith Based and Neighborhood Partnerships under Obama. Under both presidencies these offices have become important sources of policy formation and disbursement of public funds (Marsden 2012).

Although mostly avowedly secular, feminist NGOs have also grown as an influential US lobby since the emergence of second wave feminism in the 1970s, when they too were prominent in relation to the 'culture wars' over abortion and pornography. Feminist concerns also internationalised in the context of the developments of the 1970s onwards [the creation of the Convention on the Elimination all Forms of Discrimination Against Women (CEDAW), the Beijing Platform for Action, and so on], including revived concern over the issue of human trafficking as recounted in the last chapter. Despite the persistent feminist self-identity as marginalised outsiders, the feminist 'will to power' (Halley 2008, 22) has been obvious in US politics for a few decades and a generation of women politicians is now more prominent, distinguished by their pasts in liberal equality and feminist politics. As will be explained further below, a curious combination of feminist and faith-based organisations has been a potent force in shaping the US human trafficking response, finding common cause despite their many differences of analysis and advocacy on almost every other issue.

In this section I have suggested that the international political involvement of the USA is forged in the interface of interests and ideals and given impetus by the interpretation of global concerns by interacting political elites and domestic NGOs. As Jakobsen and Bernstein suggest, those NGOs that gain political alliance and favour become 'particularly important site(s) for transnational influence' (Jakobsen and Bernstein 2009, 21). In these intersections it is possible to see how local and global identities and interests influence one another, with the role of domestic NGOs and faith groups shaping the international agenda of the nation-state. Global politics works not only, as Realists expect, from the outside through the pressures of the anarchic international system (Halley 2008) on the state, but from the inside out. In what follows I will suggest that this nexus can be traced in accounting for the self-definition of the US government as a global disciplinarian and moral entrepreneur on the issue of human trafficking. A short account of the US policy and activism in relation to human trafficking features in the next section, as springboard to an analysis exploring the complex intersection of interests, ideals and identities that have inspired successive US administrations to promote, domestically and globally, particular versions of the anti-trafficking cause.

The Trafficking Victims Protection Act (2000) and Its Reauthorisations

In the previous chapter the US did already feature as a key promoter and discussant at the UN conferences culminating in the Palermo Protocol. One of the driving reasons behind US activism in this UN forum was the parallel domestic political process, which was leading to the passage of the Trafficking Victims Protection Act in the US within the same time frame (the TVPA of 2000). As hinted above the passage of the TVPA, and its regular reauthorisations since 2000, does owe much to the activities of religious and feminist NGOs. Discussion of these actors and their varying motivations will follow later in the chapter but as the TVPA forms the legal basis for the US's anti-trafficking policies, architecture and initiatives, its key elements will be discussed first. As will be seen, its various transformations through different reauthorisations are also highly indicative of the changing political landscape over the years since 2000 and the changing conceptualisations of trafficking that have accompanied these political shifts.

The TVPA 2000 opens with a preamble that reasserts commonly circulated assertions about the nature and extent of human trafficking (TVPA 2000). The well-rehearsed 700,000 victims internationally, of whom 50,000 are trafficked into the USA predominantly for sexual exploitation, association with transnational organised crime and enormous profiteering, are all repeated in the opening paragraphs of the law. These openers are reiterated as fact, even though the probity of these assertions is not secure, as I made clear in the introduction to this book. Their function in the TVPA preamble though is to legitimise the necessity of a new US law to prosecute and prevent human trafficking.

As is clear from the previous chapter, definitions of human trafficking are always hotly contested and this Act is no exception. The definition written into the TVPA also bears the imprint of some of the familiar, turbulent debates concerning labour and sex, force and consent. There are plenty of compromises indicative of these fault lines evident in the wording of the TVPA. In the first place, the Act is ostensibly concerned with preventing and prosecuting all forms of trafficking but ends up, as the Palermo Protocol does, in 'symbolically privileg(ing) trafficking for forced commercial sex' of women and girls (Peters 2013, 222). The fact that the original TVPA of 2000 was part of a broader umbrella act encompassing also the Violence Against Women Act of 2000 is indicative of the overarching framework within which trafficking is understood (VAWA 2000). The coercion and consent issue is also fluffed in the 2000 Act. Sex trafficking is broadly defined as 'the recruitment, harboring, transportation, provision, or obtaining of a person for the purpose of a commercial sex act', which implies 'any sex act on account of which anything of value is given to or received by any person' (TVPA 2000, Section 103, points 9 and 3). Yet, these definitions (which would imply that all commercial sex equals trafficking) are not used to determine the heart of the crime, with the actual punishable offence being the 'severe form of trafficking' where coercion, force and fraud must be shown to have happened (TVPA 2000, Section 103, point 8).

As well as setting out to punish trafficking into the US and provide some supports to identified victims, the TVPA 2000 also established the Interagency Taskforce to Combat and Monitor Trafficking and clarified the international reach of the new policy, setting the US to work with the international community to combat trafficking, including working with or eventually penalising those countries (through humanitarian aid sanctions, for example) deemed to be 'recalcitrant' on the issue (TVPA 2000, Section 102, point 24).

The first elaboration of the TVPA was a Clinton era policy. Democrat ideas were therefore uppermost in this earliest iteration of the TVPA, so the intent was to maintain a focus on labour exploitation issues more broadly (Peters 2013, 228). However, the Act bears the same imprint as the US contributions to the Palermo debate do, i.e. a tension between this concern to define trafficking inclusively (that is, not just about sex trafficking and avoiding conflating prostitution and trafficking), while still evincing a primary concern for the victimhood of women and children in relation to sexual exploitation. This definitional tension has played out in the Act's subsequent reauthorisations, with differing emphasis on what 'matters' in relation to trafficking following different administrations and the waxing and waning influence of particular civil society actors.

Since 2000 the Act has been 'reauthorised' on several occasions (2003, 2005, 2008 and 2013) and its conceptualisation of human trafficking and accompanying policy prescriptions has morphed each time to a degree in line with the ideological preferences of administrations. Under Bush, for example, the position that trafficking and prostitution are integral to each other became accepted and anti-trafficking NGOs in receipt of government funds had to agree to a 'prostitution pledge' whereby they committed not to fund anything that could be deemed supportive of prostitution (TVPA 2003 Reauthorization, Section 7 G1). Under Obama's Democrat administration emphasis shifted again to a broader conceptualisation of the problem to include labour exploitation more generally, though the sex trafficking issue remains to the fore. Despite these definitional tensions (and the politics and ideologies behind them will be analysed further below), one thing is certain; building from the TVPA the US now possesses a byzantine anti-trafficking architecture, which manifests itself in many ways at home and abroad.

With regard to domestic politics, although the TVPA is a Federal Act its enactment has localised repercussions, with most US states subsequently passing laws against human trafficking. In research investigating how well prepared local law enforcement agencies were to deal with trafficking under new laws, Amy Farrell and co-authors found that only 18 per cent of the local police authorities questioned had started to implement trafficking training but most had investigated the crime. Therefore, in order to enhance anti-trafficking policing, the federal authorities funded the creation of 42 multi-agency law enforcement task forces (Farrell et al. 2008, 4 and 8).

With regard to the federal level, Kevin Bales and Ron Soodalter conclude that there is now 'no shortage of agencies addressing human trafficking' (2010, 220) and Alese Wooditch concurs that each reauthorisation of the Act has 'expanded jurisdiction of federal law in the area' (2011, 472). The range of federal government agencies now embroiled in anti-trafficking activism includes the Department of Health and Social Services, which is tasked with disbursing government funds to support anti-trafficking service providers, the FBI's Civil Rights Unit (CRU) in relation to crime investigation and Immigration and Customs Enforcement. Such is the political impetus behind anti-trafficking actions that Bales and Soodalter suggest that the FBI's CRU has downgraded investigation of other crimes concerning violation of civil rights and hate crimes to prioritise the 'rising trafficking agenda' (Bales and Soodalter 2010, 220–238). The TVPA also allowed for the creation of protective T-visas for those identified as victims of trafficking. Over the decade from 2002, the number of T-visas issued to individual victims of trafficking was 3309 (immigration.com, 2012) although the quota for T-visas allows for 5000 to be issued per year. As Carole Vance suggests this very limited number of visas issued is indicative of the tension between showing compassion to exploited migrants and the politics of migration control that makes US officials unwilling to be generous in their approach to identifying victims or giving them leave to remain (Vance 2011, 937). While these domestic political developments are intrinsically interesting as further evidence of the ways in which anti-trafficking architecture has burgeoned in recent years, for the purposes of this book it is the activism of the US State Department, with its inevitable international repercussions, which is of most interest in terms of hegemonic global norm promotion.

The Office to Monitor and Combat Trafficking and the Trafficking in Persons Report

After the original passing of the TVPA the Office to Monitor and Combat Trafficking in Persons (OMCTP) was established in the State Department and over the years its activities have become ever more expansive and its associated ambassadors and reports have proven influential with successive administrations. Ambassador John Miller, for example, who directed the Office for much of the Bush Administration, drew on his evangelical Christian worldview to prioritise the sex trafficking issue and champion abolitionism and the Prostitution Pledge (O'Brien et al. 2013, 42).

A central activity for the Office is the annual production of the Trafficking in Persons Report (TiP Reports 2001–2015), an ever-fatter yearly compendium and report card of anti-trafficking statistics and assessment of states' performances on the trafficking issue around the world. The question mark dangling over the statistics in the TiP Report was already discussed in the introductory chapter of this book, so what is of more immediate interest here are the political implications of the TiP report, which has evolved to include a ranking of foreign governments' zeal and action in relation to trafficking. The TiP report categorises states worldwide into three 'tiers': those found to be fully compliant with anti-trafficking legal norms, prosecutions, prevention and protection; those who are on the 'right' road; and those deemed unacceptable in their anti-trafficking efforts. There are associated sanctions and aid implications for governments deemed to be in the doldrums of tier 3 or the sinking sand of the tier 2 'watch list'.

The general principle behind the tier categorisation is supposed to be the creation of incentives to ensure that countries around the world take the human trafficking issue seriously and act accordingly. However, critical voices persistently note the politics behind the process. Tier 3 countries repeatedly resemble a list of the US's 'most wanted'. For example Cuba, Iran, Venezuela, Myanmar, North Korea and Syria are predictably included in tier 3, while many US allies with poor human rights record and/or acknowledged problems with practices such as bonded labour remain forever in the tier 2 watch list without enduring what would be a deserved demotion according to the criteria (Wooditch 2011, 477). Other states appear to modify their behaviour and take on expected US anti-trafficking standards under pressure of a threatened dismal TiP Report. Anne Gallagher gives three examples—Nigeria, Malaysia and Australia—where this influence seems to have been at play (Gallagher 2011, 387). This politics of overseeing, reporting, grading, naming and shaming and punishing or rewarding the efforts of other countries is one reason that Janie Chuang has given the US the moniker of 'global sheriff' on the trafficking issue (Chuang 2006b).

From one perspective it would seem that the US anti-trafficking effort could be read quite straightforwardly from a neo-realist theoretical position as a hegemonic flexing of political muscle. It is just another issue that gives the US the opportunity to direct global affairs by appointing itself as 'supervisor and arbiter of a complex international issue' (Gallagher 2011, 382) and so serves its own interests in relation to disciplining friends and foes alike in the post Cold War global alignment. In the same way that the annual reporting to the US Congress on the human rights record of other states is part of American 'baiting and switching' to ensure compliant behaviour from other nation-states in the international system (Mertus 2004), so human trafficking has become another tool to achieve this aim.

From a neo-realist perspective it could also be argued that the anti-trafficking agenda enables the US to protect its own interests in a world of changing security threats. When security threats are seen to come from globalised disruptions associated with porous borders, transgressing people and international organised crime, the fight against human trafficking becomes central to realising classic state interests. To cite Luis CdeBaca, Ambassador at the OMCTP under Obama,

> We have made combating trafficking in persons a priority in domestic and foreign policy because doing so is in our country's strategic interest. Trafficking in persons is a crime that threatens the rule of law. It feeds the vulnerability of marginalized populations, creating further instability and damaging communities. It corrupts the labor markets and global supply chains that are essential to a thriving global economy. (CdeBaca 2013)

This concern at the federal level also translates to the local level as governors of states that experience high levels of irregular migration use concern over trafficking rhetoric to justify militarised responses to shore up the borders, as in the use of the National Guard in Texas to prevent human trafficking by reinforcing the border (Wofford 2014). Amy Farrell and Stephanie Fahy equally note how the rhetoric of repulsing trafficking has shifted from a human rights framing to one that prioritises national security in the US (Farrell and Fahy 2009, 618).

So far, so conventional—it could be said that the US has clear self-interests related to international and domestic security and order that can be achieved through the prioritisation of human trafficking as a policy concern. By engaging in global activism on the issue the US is able once again to enact, in Madeline Albright's words, the role of the 'indispensable power' in global affairs without which nothing would get done (Slaughter 2007, xvi) and that has the might to set the perimeters of what gets done and which states get globally lauded or reviled. And yet there is something about the passion that recent administrations have brought to this issue in comparison to all other potential 'good causes' or security concerns that makes the bleak calculation of interests or exercise of hegemony seem too parsimonious an explanation of why the US invests so heavily in anti-trafficking activism. It is intriguing, for instance, that in addressing the UN in 2003, as well as speaking on the obvious burning questions around Iraq and Afghanistan, President Bush dwelt at length on what he termed the 'humanitarian crisis' and 'special evil' of trafficking, particularly trafficking of teenage girls for sexual exploitation (UN webcast 2003). I think that to understand the underpinning of US anti-trafficking activism there is a need to comprehend the predominant elaborations of 'the problem' and the 'evil' associated with it, which strike chords with notions of US identity and ideals and which intersect with contestation in political and civil society about many things but most particularly: freedom, feminism and faith. In order to understand why the US has occupied the role of global sheriff on the issue of human trafficking, comprehending a concern with imposing global law and order is only part of the equation. The US seems to be engaged not just in muscle flexing but in a 'moral crusade' against trafficking (Weitzer 2010, 62) and the reason for this brings us back to the intersection of interests with ideals and identity opened up earlier in this chapter, particularly as they concern a combustible combination of responses to slavery, religion, sex and gender in US civil and political societies.

Anti-trafficking and US Moral Crusading

Interestingly it can be said that there was no big groundswell of American public concern and interest around human trafficking in the 1990s; therefore the impetus for the first TVPA came from policymakers and those civil society actors bent on 'educating' them (Stolz 2007, 325). Some public impact was made in the late 1990s through journalistic accounts of sex trafficking, most strikingly via Michael Specter's New York Times front page exposé concerning 'contraband women', that is the naive Slavic women allegedly sold into sexual slavery by their thousands every day across Eastern Europe and the Middle East according to the report (Specter 1998). Similar reportage appeared later in the New York Times magazine written by Peter Landesman (2004), which moved the focus to sex trafficking into the USA, and by Nicholas Kristof, a prolific contributor and continuing blogger on the issue (among many examples see Kristof 2009, 2014). Such reports were cited as evidence of the trafficking problem by people giving testimony to the Congressional Hearings that prefigured the emergence of the TVPA in 2000 and its subsequent reauthorisations (in 2003, 2005, 2008 and 2013).

There have been several rounds of Congressional Hearings on human trafficking, and certain politicians associated with the evangelical right were key to establishing these hearings and determining who testified. Pre-TVPA (2000), Congressional committees chaired by Republicans Representative Chris Smith and Senator Sam Brownback considered the issues and while the first round heard submissions that considered broad definitions of trafficking and were both pro- and anti-abolitionist, the view by the time of the 2003 TVPA reauthorisation hearing under the Bush administration had swayed to a predominance of Christian and radical feminist views. Therefore key issues under consideration included the conflation of trafficking with prostitution and the adoption of measures for sex purchase demand reduction. The politicians sponsoring the Hearings and the civil society actors representing the issue to them tended to frame the issue as predominantly one of sex trafficking, using disturbing personal testimonies or compilations of 'real-life' cases to persuade the politicians of the necessity of anti-trafficking legislation (O'Brien et al. 2013, 60–61).

Looking at the list of those invited to testify to the 2003 reauthorisation hearings, it is possible to identify a number of diverse civil society leaders and organisations who have been obvious drivers of the main tenor of the US's anti-trafficking activism at home and abroad (Committee on Government Reform 2004). Most notably there are those associated with 'anti-slavery' activism, those coming from a 'faith-based' perspective and radical feminists. Obviously these are organisations that often have more to divide than unite them (particularly the last two). However, anti-trafficking activism has produced intriguing bedfellows, each of whom refer to their own readings of American identity and beliefs to inspire their association with this cause and enable their unusual willingness to work with one another.

Writing about 'the idea of America', Anne-Marie Slaughter suggests that liberty is part of the bedrock of American identity and a source of America's activism in relation to the rest of the world. For the Founding Fathers the pursuit of religious and political freedom was a fundamental concern. Given this context, slavery constitutes America's 'original sin' (Slaughter 2007, 27), with the originating ideal of liberty corrupted by revelations of the on-going practice of human bondage in America. It is problematic to conflate the terms slavery and trafficking because slavery refers to defined legal ownership of a person, but one clear strand in US anti-trafficking activism is rooted in response to horror at the idea of the persistence of slavery inside contemporary America or globally.

Key figures associated with anti-trafficking activism use the concept of slavery to frame the problem and so touch public chords in America's sense of being a nation required to continue to deal with the acknowledged original sin. As Bales and Soodalter extol, 'we can be the generation to end this nation long affliction' (2010, 16). In the work of prominent activists like Kevin Bales or David Batstone (2010) the sense of revelation and revulsion that slavery could still exist inside the America that fought its demons over the issue in the nineteenth century is a continual refrain. Bales, for instance, who is the person most closely associated with the 'global slavery index' (2014), writes in a book addressed to a popular American audience of the need to be alive to the existence of 'the slave next door' (Bales and Soodalter 2010). Using the concept of slavery tallies with American readers' sense of history and identity, indicating that although slavery is now no longer public or legal, it persists in the private spheres of ordinary America and good citizens need to be watchful for it. Bales and Soodalter build up a sense of a hidden but pervasive menace: 'it turns out there are slaves all around us' they suggest, citing case studies of exploitation in American and global homes, farms and brothels (Bales and Soodalter 2010, 13).

The anti-slavery framing of trafficking activism has notable adherents in the Obama administration's approach to the issue. Luis CdeBaca, ambassador at the OMCTP, who has an academic history in slavery studies and legal activism, has taken up the slavery lens in his work at the State Department, as witnessed in the Department's collaboration with the 'slavery footprint' project for tracing exploitation in global supply chains (slaveryfootprint.org, 2016). The slavery footprint idea does draw attention to the structural causes of contemporary exploitation by identifying slavery in global supply chains, although it does this without offering a fundamental critique of neo-liberal capitalism. Rather the website helps to point consumers towards the 'good brands' that are slavery free.

Bales and Batstone's writings are also not devoid of analysis of the systemic causes of contemporary slave-like conditions at home or abroad, and they do give some prominence to discussions of issues such as poverty or border closures. However, the overwhelming tenor of their writings, which are aimed at the mass market, is to build 'a sense of embattlement (that) these things are happening everywhere, all the time, right now' (Castelli 2005, 328) and so inspire civil and political activism. To do this they focus on individual case studies that emphasise stories of bad traffickers, nice but naive trafficked people and, most prominently, good agents of the state and NGOs/non-profits who are the heroes of the cases they describe. The language of 'folk devils', 'evil', 'slaveholders' and 'monsters in our midst' is used to label those defined as traffickers by these activists (Bales and Sodalter 2010; Batstone 2010). This personalising of the exemplary cases and lauding of the state or NGO agents of liberation leads to a response to trafficking that emphasises the importance of 'good Americans' rescuing victims, supporting the liberators and chasing out the (probably foreign) bad guys. The 'sheriff' in the white hat, bolstered by the associated goodness of opposition to slavery, rides into town. And, as most victims are assumed to be female, the gendered liberator trope at play in other manifestations of US domestic and foreign policy resurfaces as a motivator of anti-trafficking activism.

The necessity of rescuing victims (physically but also spiritually) is also one touchstone for another key anti-trafficking civil society constituency—Evangelical Christians who have made human trafficking one of their central concerns over the last decades. As mentioned above, there is academic consensus that the influence of evangelical lobbyists has grown in recent American politics, most conspicuously but not exclusively over the course of the George W. Bush administration. Official endorsement of the increasing public space for Christian evangelical activists was clear in the establishment under G.W. Bush of the Office for Faith Based and Community Initiatives, which remained in place though renamed under Obama (Marsden 2012).

Earlier in the twentieth century Evangelical Christians' political involvement on issues of international affairs was quite limited. Primacy in evangelical socio-political action was placed on internal 'culture war' questions in America: abortion, family values, sexuality and pornography. A slow turn to more international issues was instigated with concern over 'persecuted churches' in the developing world in the 1980s and 1990s (Zimmerman 2011, 572; Castelli 2005) and it is only in the last decades that sex trafficking has become one of the select number of global concerns that evangelicals enthusiastically mobilise around (Amstutz 2014). To an extent the campaign around the 'persecuted church' in places such as China, Vietnam and Sudan, presaged more recent activism around trafficking. The persecuted church campaign connects to current concerns with sex trafficking in that both extol the need to defend Christian 'family' values, the first in the context of defending Christian communities and their norms of family life and the latter in terms of preserving 'monogamous marriage' (Zimmerman 2011, 574), 'right' sexual relationships, rescuing vulnerable womanhood and preventing the corruption of manhood (as either traffickers or buyers of sex). Likewise the centrality of religious freedom is a common theme to both these campaigns. This may seem an obvious theme in contexts of religious persecution but it can be stretched to the concern with sex trafficking too. As Yvonne Zimmerman explains in her account of the theological underpinnings of anti-trafficking activism, sex trafficking is frequently termed 'evil' by evangelical commentators, including Bush. When evangelicals use this term it carries self-consciously theological meaning. Trafficking is understood as 'evil' because it enslaves and the enslaved person is not free to choose in many ways, including being free to choose to follow Christ (Zimmerman 2010 and 2013). In a final parallel, the evangelical campaign for the persecuted church also used tactics Elizabeth Castelli refers to as 'graphic synecdoche', i.e. the relaying of anecdotes of atrocious acts of violence as a tactic of mobilisation. These same tactics later re-emerged in evangelical contributions on sex trafficking (Castelli 2005, 326), for example, in the use of personal testimony of trafficking victims in US Congressional Hearings (O'Brien et al. 2013).

Clearly it is the issue of trafficking for sexual exploitation, not trafficking for labour or other exploitative ends, that almost exclusively exercises the evangelical community. As noted above this relates to evangelical concerns with righteous sexual relationships. Consequently they have hitched their policy analysis and prescriptions to the necessity of abolishing prostitution. The norm of the heterosexual family legitimised by marriage is at the heart of evangelical expectations of relationships and 'errant' people, whether 'fallen' women or men who buy sex, are therefore in need of rescuing (the former) or punishing/rehabilitating (the latter). Evangelical non-profit organisations therefore had no qualms about advocating and endorsing the 2003 TVPA 'prostitution pledge', which was then linked to eligibility for anti-trafficking funding. Indeed, many evangelically funded anti-trafficking initiatives emphasise 'rescue' raids on brothels and further abolitionist initiatives to reduce/punish demand (for example the International Justice Mission; see ijm.org, 2016).

Much of the funding channelled for anti-trafficking activism through the Office for Faith Based and Community Initiatives has been awarded to Christian organisations for dispersal. Prominent recipients have been the US Catholic Bishops and the Salvation Army. Mention of the Catholic Bishops is a reminder that not all Christian actors in the anti-trafficking arena are Protestant evangelicals or that all evangelicals are the same, sociologically or theologically. Some of those at the more liberal end of the evangelical spectrum, for example Jim Wallis of the Sojourners community, would be equally seized by the necessity of opposing human trafficking but giving more cognizance to the global structural factors that cause exploitative conditions. However, these voices form a minority view within evangelical circles, where a common core focus would be on individuals and the necessity of individual salvation as the foundations for wider social change to follow (Piehl 2014; Wall 2014).

Key evangelical campaigners on sex trafficking, such as Gary Haugen of IJM and Linda Smith of Shared Hope International, were prominent voices at the TVPA Congressional Hearings. They were brought in to testify on the invites of chairing politicians such as Sam Brownback and Chris Smith, who shared the evangelical worldview. These views, matched by the views of radical feminist advocates, were particularly influential in moving the TVPA focus to sex trafficking and abolitionism at the 2003 re-authorisation hearings (Stolz 2007, 319–20).

Opposition to prostitution and the commitment to end demand for prostitution are the connecting points enabling the unlikely alliance between evangelical activists and those radical feminists who form the third non-governmental constituency prominent as lobbyists for the successive authorisations of the TVPA. As outlined in Chap. 2, US-based lobbyists are key players in the Coalition Against Trafficking in Women (CATW) and it was involved in both the Palermo Process and the Congressional Hearings leading to anti-trafficking legislative initiatives and subsequent policy actions. CATW's ideas underpinning feminist abolitionism and their linking of prostitution and sex trafficking were discussed in the previous chapter. Domestic pressure for anti-trafficking legislation from feminists shares the same roots in the campaigns for women's human rights and against violence against women that emerged in the 1990s from Beijing and the Vienna Human Rights conference (Soderlund 2005, 70). The neo-abolitionist position was forcefully put to US Congressional hearings. For example, Janet Raymond (CATW co-executive director) argued at the crucial 2003 TVPA re-authorisation hearings, which tightened up the emphasis on sexual exploitation and demand reduction in the TVPA, that prostitution is 'inherently harmful and dehumanizing'. She warned that if organisations that support the legalisation of prostitution received state funding this would contravene the National Security Presidential Directive on Combating Trafficking in Persons, which directed that grants should only be to those who understand prostitution as harmful (Committee on Government Reform 2004, 58). The same radical feminist approach demonised clients as 'folk devils' and 'either ignored or denounced as apologists for traffickers' anyone trying to raise counter discourses to the neo-abolitionist stance (Weitzer 2010, 64 and 72).

Counter voices do exist in US civil, political and academic society. There are feminists who raise concerns about the harmful consequences of abolitionism and the ways in which it increases state power over women's bodies and lives. This can be read in for example the public interjections of scholars such as Elizabeth Bernstein on 'carceral feminism' (Bernstein 2010) or Janet Halley on 'governance feminism' (Halley 2008). Sealing Cheng also contributes an international perspective to this when she demonstrates how an alliance between the US and Korean governments to clamp down on trafficking leads to a 'politics of protection', with only women dubbed as virtuous and innocent deemed worthy of state protections (Cheng 2011, 1643). However, given their convergence with the politics of the Bush administration and the views of influential policy makers, it was the unexpected alliance of evangelical Christians and abolitionist feminists, intertwining with discourses about modern forms of slavery, that created the prevailing conceptualisation of trafficking as being about sexual exploitation and requiring an abolitionist response, through the Bush years and even beyond (Jakobsen and Bernstein 2009, 23). These strange political bedfellows—evangelicals and feminists—have been drawn together by what Jacqueline Berman refers to as a converging 'essentialist construction of womanhood' (Berman 2005–06, 280) with evangelicals presupposing the all women are called to family life and radical feminists presupposing that all women are oppressed by all men.

The pages above have focused on the key political players, civil society organisations and media outlets, which were and continue to be key influencers of dominant framings of trafficking and policy responses in the US context. To the actors already named could be added references to institutes, such as the Polaris Project and the Protection Project, which draw together academic researchers, advocates and policy actors engaged on the issue of trafficking. Add some celebrities keen to pose as experts and to appear the 'celebrity-as-rescuer-of-victim' into this potent mix of activists (Haynes 2014, 25) and it is possible to see why trafficking has become a key domestic and international policy issue for successive recent US administrations. While there was an initial openness to defining trafficking broadly under the Clinton administration and a return of more attention to labour trafficking occurred under Obama at the OMCTP and in the TiP reports, there is no doubt about which activists and which framing of trafficking have been most influential at home and abroad. It is a framing that has multiple consequences for people crossing borders, NGOs seeking funding and other nation-states seeking to avoid the ignominy of a poor TiP report.

Conclusion

In this chapter I have argued that the United States has played a central role in the global cascade of the anti-trafficking norm. Evidence of that can be found in the global reach and influence of the Trafficking Victims Protection Act(s), the Office to Monitor and Combat Trafficking in Persons (OMCTP) and the annual Trafficking in Persons reports. Each of these entities is the basis of an intricate anti-trafficking apparatus, which observes and disciplines allies and foes alike. Janie Chuang was inspired when she named the US the 'global sheriff' on the issue (Chuang 2006b). No other country has taken this global role onto itself, or has the power to ensure compliance from others with its definition of adequate anti-trafficking policies.

In this respect the 'sheriff' role is emblematic of US 'hard power'. The US maintains its hegemonic ability to try to impose order in international anarchy. Yet, sheriff is an intriguing metaphor because while it summons up a masculine figure of authority associated with imposing law and order, this is also a figure associated with imposition of 'moral law'. The sheriff wears the white hat and quells the 'baddies'. The Bush administration provided the most overt example of this rationale for engagement with the sex trafficking issue. Bush's words to the UN, that trafficking constituted a 'special evil in the abuse and exploitation of the most innocent and vulnerable' (UN webcast 2003), is indicative of his own ideological, even theological understanding, of what is at stake in trafficking. The strong engagement of successive US administrations on the human trafficking issue is a consequence of powerful currents in US civil and political society, which seek to discipline sexuality at home and abroad.

In this chapter I have explored why the anti-trafficking norm cascaded in the international system after the Palermo Protocol. Rather than being the inevitable outcome of a surge of signings provoked only by a tipping point being reached, I have argued that the global spread of anti-trafficking architecture is also the consequence of the commitment of the hegemonic world power to the cause. It is important to acknowledge the way that material power intersects with ideals in the diffusion of norms. Yet US activism, particularly around the sex trafficking issue, is not only a consequence of the ability to exercise global power. Inspired by domestic political activism, US moral entrepreneurship is driven by notions intrinsic to US foreign policy, whereby America's identity and ideals in the world are imbued with particular conceptualisations of freedom, faith and feminism.

Bibliography

Amstutz, M. (2014). *Evangelicals and American Foreign Policy*. Oxford: Oxford University Press.

Bales, K., & Soodalter, R. (2010). *The slave next door: Human trafficking and slavery in America today*. Berkley: University of California Press.

Batstone, D. (2010). *Not for sale: The return of the global slave trade and how we can fight it*. New York: Harper Collins.

Berman, J. (2005–06). The left, the right, and the prostitute: The making of U.S. Antitrafficking in Persons Policy. *Tulane Journal of International and Comparative Law, 14*, 269–293.

Bernstein, E. (2010). Militarized humanitarianism meets Carceral Feminism: The politics of sex, rights, and freedom in contemporary anti-trafficking campaigns. *Signs, 36*(1), 45–72.

C-SPAN. (2014). *Laura Bush on Women's Rights in Afghanistan*. 30 January 2014, https://www.youtube.com/watch?v=A_40s4ENOQ4, date accessed 23 March 2016.

Castelli, E. (2005). Praying for the Persecuted Church: US Christian Activism in the Global Arena. *Journal of Human Rights, 4*(3), 321–351.

Cheng, S. (2011). Sexual protection, citizenship and nationhood: Prostituted women and migrant wives in South Korea. *Journal of Ethnic and Migration Studies, 37*(10), 1627–1648.

Chuang, J. (2006b). 'The United States as Global Sheriff: Using Unilateral Sanctions to Combat Human Trafficking', *Michigan Journal of International Law, 27*, 437–494.

Committee on Government Reform. (2004). *The ongoing tragedy of international slavery and human trafficking: An over-view*. House of Representatives One Hundred Eighth Congress First Session October 29, 2003 Serial No. 108–137, Hearing before the Subcommittee on Human Rights and Wellness of the Committee on Government Reform (Washington DC: US Government Printing Office).

deTocqueville, A. (2003). *Democracy in America*. London: Penguin.

Farrell, A., & Fahy, S. (2009). The problem of human trafficking in the U.S.: Public frames and policy responses. *Journal of Criminal Justice, 37*, 617–626.

Farrell, A., McDevitt, J., & Fahy, S. (2008). *Understanding and improving law enforcement responses to human trafficking*. Report prepared for the National

Institute of Justice, 810 7th Street, NW Washington, DC, 20531, prepared by The Institute on Race and Justice at Northeastern University.
Finnemore, M., & Sikkink, K. (1998). International norm dynamics and political change. *International Organization, 52*(4), 887–917.
Gallagher, A. T. (2011). Improving the effectiveness of international law of human trafficking: A vision for the future of the US trafficking in persons report. *Human Rights Review, 12*, 381–400.
Gelernter, D. (2005). Americanism and its enemies. *Commentary, 119*, 41–48.
Global Slavery Index. (2014). *Global Slavery index 2014*. Walk Free Foundation, http://www.globalslaveryindex.org/, date accessed 21 February 2016.
Halley, J. (2008). *Split decisions: How and why to take a break from feminism*. Princeton: Princeton University Press.
Haynes, D. (2014). The celebritization of human trafficking. *ANNALS AAPSS, 653*, 25–45.
immigration.com. (2012). USCIS issues statistics on T and U visas for fiscal years 2002–2012. http://www.immigration.com/news/t-visa/uscis-issues-statistics-t-and-u-visas-fiscal-years-2002-2012, date accessed 21 February 2016.
Jakobsen, J., & Bernstein, E. (2009). *Religion, Politics and Gender Equality Country Report: USA*. United Nations Research Institute for Social Development and Heinrich Böll Stiftung, Final Research Report prepared for the project Religion, Politics and Gender Equality. Geneva: UNRISD and Berlin: Heinrich Böll Stiftung.
Krauthammer, C. (1990/91). The unipolar moment. *Foreign Affairs, 70*(1), 23–33.
Kristof, N. (2009, January 1). On the ground: Your comments on my slavery column. *New York Times*, http://kristof.blogs.nytimes.com/category/human-trafficking/page/2/, date accessed 21 February 2016.
Kristof, N. (2014, January 10) On the ground: Google+ hangout on human trafficking. *New York Times*. http://kristof.blogs.nytimes.com/category/human-trafficking/, date accessed 21 February 2016.
La Strada International (2016a) Home Page, La Strada International, http://lastradainternational.org/, date accessed 5 January 2016.
Landesman, P. (2004, January 25). The girls next door. *New York Times Magazine*, http://www.nytimes.com/1998/01/11/world/contraband-women-a-special-report-traffickers-new-cargo-naive-slavic-women.html?pagewanted=all, 21 February 2016.
Los Angeles Times. (2001, November 18). Laura Bush Addresses State of Afghan Women. *Los Angeles Times*. http://articles.latimes.com/2001/nov/18/news/mn-5602, date accessed 21 February 2016.
Marsden, L. (2012). Bush, Obama and a Faith-based US Foreign Policy. *International Affairs, 88*(5), 953–974.
Mastanduno, M. (1997). Preserving the Unipolar Moment: Realist theories and U.S. grand strategy after the cold war. *International Security, 21*(4), 49–88.

Mertus, J. (2004). *Bait and switch: Human rights and US Foreign Policy*. New York: Routledge.

Nayak, M. (2006). Orientalism and 'Saving' US State Identity after 9/11. *International Feminist Journal of Politics, 8*(1), 42–61.

O'Brien, E., Hayes, S., & Carpenter, B. (2013). *The politics of sex trafficking: A moral geography*. Basingstoke: Palgrave.

Peters, A. (2013). "Things that involve sex are just different": US anti-trafficking law and policy on the books, in their minds, and in action. *Anthropological Quarterly, 86*(1), 221–256.

Piehl, M. (2014). Perspectives on religion in Twentieth Century American History. In B. Schulman (Ed.), *Making the American Century: Essays on the political culture of twentieth century America* (pp. 141–15). Oxford: Oxford University Press.

Reich, S. (2010). *Global norms, American Sponsorship and the emerging patterns of world politics*. Basingstoke: Palgrave.

Risley, A. (2015). "America will not tolerate slave traders": Counter-trafficking policies and US Power. *Journal of Women Politics and Policy, 36*(2), 213–238.

Russo, A. (2006). The Feminist Majority Foundation's Campaign to Stop Gender Apartheid: The Intersections of Feminism and Imperialism in the United States. *International Feminist Journal of Politics, 8*(4), 557–77.

Schulman, B. (2014). *Making the American Century: Essays on the political culture of twentieth century America*. Oxford: Oxford University Press.

Slaughter, A.-M. (2007). *The idea that is America: Keeping faith with our values in a dangerous world*. New York: Basic Books.

slaveryfootprint.org. (2016). How many slaves work for you? slaveryfootprint.org: http://slaveryfootprint.org/, date accessed 21 February 2016.

Soderlund, G. (2005). Running from the rescuers: New US crusades against trafficking and the rhetoric of abolition. *NWSA Journal, 17*(3), 64–87.

Specter, M. (1998, January 11). Contraband Women—A Special Report. Traffickers New Cargo Naive Slavic Women. New York Times. http://www.nytimes.com/1998/01/11/world/contraband-women-a-special-report-traffickers-new-cargo-naive-slavic-women.html?pagewanted=all, date accessed 21 February 2016.

Stolz, B.-A. (2007). Interpreting the U.S. Human Trafficking Debate Through the Lens of Symbolic Politics. *Law and Policy, 29*(3), 311–338.

TiP Report. (2001–2015). *Trafficking in Persons Reports 2001–2015*. Office to Monitor and Combat Trafficking in Persons, US State Department. http://www.state.gov/j/tip/rls/tiprpt/ date accessed 23 March 2016.

TVPA. (2000). Trafficking Victims Protection Act. 28 October 2000, US Department of State, http://www.state.gov/j/tip/laws/, date accessed 21 February 2016.

TVPA 2003. (2003). Trafficking Victims Protection Reauthorization Act of 2003. 7 January 2003, US State Department: http://www.state.gov/j/tip/laws/61130.htm, date accessed 21 February 2016.

UN Treaty Collection. (1990). International convention on the protection of the rights of all migrant workers and members of their families. 18 December 1990, United Nations Treaty Collection. https://treaties.un.org/Pages/ShowMTDSGDetails.aspx?src=UNTSONLINE&tabid=2&mtdsg_no=IV-13&chapter=4&lang=en, date accessed 20 February 2016.

UN Treaty Collection. (2000). Protocol to prevent, suppress and punish trafficking in persons, especially women and children, supplementing the United Nations Convention against Transnational Organized Crime New York, 15 November 2000, United Nations Treaty Collection. https://treaties.un.org/Pages/ViewDetails.aspx?src=TREATY&mtdsg_no=XVIII-12-a&chapter=18&lang=en, date accessed 20 February 2016.

UN webcast. (2003). Statement by His Excellency Mr. George W. Bush, President of the United States of America Address to the United Nations General Assembly 23 September 2003. http://www.un.org/webcast/ga/58/statements/usaeng030923.htm, date accessed 20 February 2016.

Vance, C. (2011). States of contradiction: Twelve ways to do nothing about trafficking while pretending to. *Social Research, 78*(3), 933–948.

VAWA. (2000). Victims of Trafficking and Violence Protection Act of 2000, 28 October 2000, Division B - Violence Against Women Act 2000. http://www.state.gov/j/tip/laws/61124.htm, date accessed 21 February 2016.

Wall, W. (2014). Symbol of unity, symbol of pluralism: The "Interfaith Idea" in Wartime and Cold War America. In B. Schulman (Ed.), *Making the American Century: Essays on the political culture of Twentieth Century America* (pp. 171–187). Oxford: Oxford University Press.

Weitzer, R. (2010). The movement to criminalize sex work in the United States. *Journal of Law and Society, 37*(1), 61–84.

Wofford, T. (2014, July 21). Governor Rick Perry to Deploy National Guard to U.S.-Mexico Border. *Newsweek.* http://europe.newsweek.com/gov-rick-perry-deploy-national-guard-usmexico-border-260089?rm=eu, date accessed 21 February 2016.

Wooditch, A. (2011). The Efficacy of the Trafficking in Persons Report: A review of the evidence. *Criminal Justice Policy Review, 22*, 471–493.

Zimmerman, Y. (2010). Religion and politics from Bush to Obama: Rethinking sex and religion in the United States' initiative to combat human trafficking. *Journal of Feminist Studies in Religion, 26*(1), 79–99.

Zimmerman, Y. (2011). Christianity and human trafficking. *Religion Compass, 5*(10), 567–578.

Zimmerman, Y. (2013). *Other dreams of freedom: Religion, sex and human trafficking.* Oxford: Oxford University Press.

CHAPTER 5

Norm Socialisation: Localising the Global, Regionalising the Local

Introduction

Why do states begin to comply with international norms—or to put it more precisely certain versions of certain norms? The norm lifecycle model suggests this happens through processes of socialisation (Finnemore and Sikkink 1998). This implies that states adopt norms as they learn over time what is necessary in order to conform and perform as acceptable actors in the international society of states. As mentioned in Chap. 2, predominant accounts of such socialisation processes tend to work from the 'top down' or the 'outside in'. For example, norm socialisation is depicted as occurring when elite nation state bureaucrats working in international or regional bodies become aware of new expectations and transfer them downward to their domestic contexts or when transnational moral proselytisers work assiduously to carry norms conscientiously across borders from the global to the local. Elements of such 'outside-in' dynamics are undoubtedly an important part of the norm socialisation process and indeed the last chapter clearly demonstrated the role of a hegemonic power in impressing normative expectations through its foreign policies on the domestic politics of others in the international system. Chapter 4 contained several examples of nation-states enacting anti-trafficking measures in response to US pressure and the fear of a TiP report shaming. Yet, that chapter also argued that the zeal of the US to 'push' a particular version of the anti-trafficking norm can only be understood after recognising the foreign policy-shaping impact of conjoined domestic forces in the form of American radical

G. Wylie, *The International Politics of Human Trafficking*,
DOI 10.1057/978-1-137-37775-3_5

feminism and conservative Christianity. As Chap. 2 proposed, therefore, it is necessary to inflect our understanding of socialisation within the norm lifecycle with recognition of both the complex intersections of domestic and international actors in the process and with an understanding of the exercise of power politics, which make certain norm socialisation processes more effective than others.

This chapter explores these socialisation dynamics further through a case study of the adoption of anti-trafficking norms in the Republic of Ireland and Northern Ireland. Both of these jurisdictions are currently within the European Union and, as many authors note, the EU does play a vital role in conditioning and socialising its members. It is therefore not surprising that the Republic and Northern Ireland have found it necessary to respond to the anti-trafficking architecture and directives that the EU has elaborated in the years since Palermo. These EU initiatives will be outlined later in this chapter and their impact reveals the manner in which norm socialisation processes do flow from the 'outside in'. Yet, I think that here again it is possible to see socialisation dynamics running in both directions. As this chapter will detail, both the Republic and Northern Ireland have been sites of intense civil society activism around human (although again, more precisely, sex) trafficking and in the pan-European context these civil actors are in the vanguard of forwarding neo-abolitionist legal proposals regarding prostitution, pitched as anti-trafficking measures. In forwarding such proposals civil society actors in Ireland, North and South, depend upon channelling external influences, most notably through reference to the beacon provided for their campaigning by the neo-abolitionist framework already existing in some of the Nordic states, particularly Sweden. So, as I will show below, the politics of norm persuasion and contestation do not just travel from the regional institution to the member states, but also vice versa. Through this chapter I will therefore be analysing the lifecycle of norm socialisation by identifying not only the localisation of global and regional norms, but also the regionalisation of the local, showing how prevailing normative politics in domestic contexts can impact on the agenda of a regional international institution.

As already stated in the paragraph above, anti-trafficking norms in the Irish Republic and Northern Ireland once again boil down to a predominating concern with sex trafficking. Moreover, the familiar correlations among prostitution, sex trafficking and violence against women re-emerge as central to the processes of norm shaping and adoption in these jurisdictions. In Chap. 3 I suggested, with reference to Janet Halley, that the success of such 'governance feminist' policy proposals often carries unintended consequences (Halley 2006). At the close of this chapter, I will argue that one of the unintended consequences of this particular localisation of anti-trafficking norms is the reinforcement by feminists of securitised border politics on the island of Ireland.

Theories of Norm Socialisation

In general sociological terms, socialisation theory tries to make sense of how people learn to behave or think in certain ways. As such the idea of socialisation is associated with social constructivist worldviews. As one example, this approach was particularly influential in gender studies, where it formed a key intellectual plank in moves from the 1970s onwards to break away from the historically commonplace understanding that for humans 'anatomy was indeed destiny' (Bradley 2007, 11). In basic outline, the argument runs that while we may be born with a biological sex, we are constructed as gendered people through processes of social learning. From infancy onwards we are socialised by numerous influences including family, education and culture in how to 'properly' embody and enact our gender. It is notable that socialisation theory in this bald formulation runs from the external to the internal; we learn to conform to what the outside world expects of us. At the same time though there is epistemological hope in socialisation theory because, from this perspective, gender is something we learn and this implies malleability and the possibility of change, thus freeing people up from the determinism of biological essentialism.

Socialisation theory incorporated to International Relations and the 'first wave' of norm studies transposes this understanding of learning and its trajectory from outside world to interior realm. In this rendering of the theory, international organisations, international non-governmental organisations and nation-states are understood to be active agents of socialisation, in relation to each other and in relation to domestic polities. In international contexts, political and civil elites learn what is expected of them through engagement in international society and act accordingly. For example, those states that are integrated into international bodies and become subject to the prevailing mores of the collective learn what is expected of them and transpose this to the local arena of domestic politics. Socialisation happens therefore as states perceive an interest or an appropriateness in 'copying the behaviour of others' (Greenhill 2010, 129).

A prime example of this kind of dynamics at work is found in the working of regional organisations, of which the EU is probably the most obvious and well-covered case in point (see for example articles by Braun 2014; Piedrafita 2012; Silander and Nilssen 2013; van Schaik and Schunz 2012; van Kersbergen and Verbeek 2007). For instance, a central element of the whole process of EU enlargement into Central and Eastern Europe is premised on applicant states learning to conform to the terms and conditions of what is considered appropriate behaviour for states seeking EU membership. Some of these conditions are material (for instance having a functioning and stable economy) but many are normative. Expectations around evincing 'Western European' values of civil liberties, human and minority rights, democratic consolidation and free market principles are just some headline examples of norms to be learned and demonstrated by applicant states (Tatham 2009).

Besides international and regional organisations, the other key 'teachers' of norms often identified in 'first wave' IR norm writing are transnational moral entrepreneurs, advocacy networks or social movements that mobilise support for normative change across borders and into nation-states (Acharya 2004, 242). The existence of these external moral entrepreneurs as those who frame, name and shame states into norm adoption is discussed throughout the work of Margaret Keck and Kathryn Sikkink (1998). Their seminal work on transnational advocacy networks discusses numerous examples of these agents at work in regard to spreading environmental values, human rights norms and opposition to violence against women. From this perspective, it is through such transnational moral activism that states get connected to 'a global culture of human rights norms' (Greenhill 2010, 130) and learn to change their behaviour and identities accordingly.

While social constructivist accounts of norm adoption do stress the kinds of dynamics mentioned just now (elite learning, moral shaming, changing identities, amending behaviour), it is important not to lose sight of the coercive dynamics that are also part of the story of norm socialisation. This enforced aspect of socialisation was demonstrated in the last chapter within the discussion of the extent to which the US is capable of flexing its hegemonic power to ensure compliance with its definition of anti-trafficking standards, through the threat of economic sanctions or public outing via the TiP report. Recognising the reality of such power play, Jeffrey Checkel advocates for a more rounded, synthesised account of norm socialisation processes. He points to the need to build a bridge between those constructivist accounts of norm diffusion that emphasise learning and those rationalist accounts that reveal the elements of coercion and calculations of costs and benefits that accompany state decisions to adopt new normative standards (Checkel 2001, 553). In effect, the adoption of new norms always emerges from what Ethan Nadelmann refers to as complex processes involving 'economic and security interests as well as moral ones' (Nadelmann 1990, 480).

In further support of this analysis, it is appropriate to revert again to the EU example and note that normative conditionality in its enlargement process always entails a mixing of 'carrots and sticks' (Greenhill 2010, 132). Learning EU values was and is not simply a voluntarily imbibed process evolving from elite interactions. Rather the material power to withhold EU membership from those deemed not to be learning, endorsing or enacting EU norms rests with those already inside the Union and so makes norm compliance a mix of voluntary and coerced policy adoption. As ever, it is not wise to 'neglect the role of power' in the international system when accounting for norm diffusion (Epstein 2012, 135).

Another key criticism of the 'first wave' accounts of norm socialisation is that they tend to imagine the process as a one-way street, giving 'one-sided account(s) of 'teaching and persuasion' (Adler-Nissen 2014, 151). As with classic socialisation theory in gender studies, teaching in IR accounts usually comes from the socialiser (in this context states, international organisations or transnational NGOs, which could all be read as analogous to the adult world in gender theory) and is directed at 'the socialisee' (other states and domestic societies, in this case analogous to the child). It is for these reasons that Charlotte Epstein sees a problematic 'infantilization' of the socialisee at work in many accounts of international norm socialisation that consequently fail to see the possibilities for localised resistance to new normative expectations. Epstein's focus on the possibility of local resistance echoes the case discussed by Kravtsov (2009), mentioned in Chap. 2, concerning objection to the promotion of anti-retroviral drugs (ARVs) in South Africa due to contending norms surrounding questions of HIV's cause and treatment. Similarly Rebecca Adler-Nissen (2014, 144) argues that some states may almost relish their stigmatisation as a 'badge of honour' if they fail to adapt to new norm expectations. While Adler-Nissen, Epstein and Kravtsov all focus on the issue of localised resistance to learning global norms, other writers note more broadly that local reception—which might be positive or negative—needs to be part of the story of norm socialisation. As Maria Krasnodębska notes the predominance of one-sided normative accounts of EU enlargement downplay the agency of Eastern European states and the extent to which they shape Western institutions (Krasnodębska 2014, 8). Whether a norm will be 'localised', 'displaced' or 'resisted' depends on pre-existing normative and cultural contexts (Acharya 2004). In order to illustrate this insight Amitav Acharya provides his readers with a helpful diagram to capture the complex multi-directional interactions between the local and the global in norm socialisation (Acharya 2004, 254). His case is made by reference to the degree to which new Western security norms have received a mixed reception in Association of South East Asian (ASEAN) states. While notions related to collective security are successfully localised, objections to humanitarian interventions as a threat to the respect for sovereignty at the heart of ASEAN make that norm non-transferable to local Asian contexts. Acharya's overarching point is that 'local actors do not remain passive targets and learners as transnational agents acting out of a universal script produce and direct norm diffusion in world politics' (Acharya 2004, 269). Whether norms will float or sink in any localised context depends in his analysis on pre-existing local norms and values, the actions of local norm entrepreneurs and whether local 'norm takers' believe that new norms will enhance their authority (2004, 248).

I take from all the works cited in this section that in order to tell the story of why certain norms get socialised in certain ways in particular contexts (or not) there is a need to account for a potent mixing of local, regional and global power dynamics, alongside the sway of pre-existing domestic and external norms and the activities of 'norm taking' states and civil societies. Some evidence of these intersections was already clear in Chap. 4, but in the next sections I turn to the case study of Ireland and Northern Ireland in the context of global and regional politics to explore how local mores, activist civil society entrepreneurs and domestic and regional politics combine to produce locally specific socialisations of the global anti-trafficking norm. One skein in the interweaving influences that play a vital part in formulating the tenor of the localisation of global norms in Ireland is the European context, so it is to this that I turn first.

From the Global to the Regional

A knock-on effect of the UN Palermo Protocol and its increasing number of signatories and ratifications after 2000 (not to mention the bolstering given by US activism in the field) was the transposition of anti-trafficking concerns to the regional levels of world politics. As noted in the introduction to this book, these include the ASEAN Declaration against Human Trafficking Particularly Women and Children of 2004, the African Union's Ouagadougou Plan of Action on Trafficking in Human Beings Especially Women and Children (the Ouagadougou Action Plan of 2006) and the establishment of an Anti-Trafficking in Persons Unit within the secretariat of the Organization of American States (OAS).

In this same period human trafficking also made a substantial mark in a number of pan-European bodies (Stoyanova 2013, 66). For example, the Council of Europe (a human rights body in Europe with 47 member states) created its own Convention on Action against Trafficking in Human Beings (Council of Europe Convention 2005). The Convention's wording specifically records that it takes its cue from the Palermo Protocol but many commentators note that this Convention is more promising as a human rights instrument than Palermo because of its focus on rights to be afforded to those identified as victims of trafficking (Gallagher 2015a). The Convention also established a monitoring mechanism, the Group of Experts on Action Against Trafficking in Human Beings (GRETA), tasked with reporting on member states implementation of the Convention. GRETA commissioners make monitoring visits to member states to quiz and report back on relevant stakeholders' anti-trafficking laws and practices (GRETA 2015). Similarly, the 57 member states of the Organisation for Security and Cooperation in Europe (OSCE) took up the human trafficking issue in 2003 with the establishment of an anti-trafficking office and a post of Special Representative and Coordinator for Combating Trafficking in Human Beings. The role of this Representative includes building anti-trafficking alliances across the OSCE through hosting an annual international high-level conference for representatives of political and civil societies and helping participating states develop and implement effective policies. The Special Representative also visits member states to monitor progress and issue recommendations (OSCE 2015). Looking at these two examples, it is possible to identify elite-level, top-down socialisation processes in action as these bodies charge their secretariats and monitors to oversee, check up on and encourage member states to adopt what they consider to be good anti-trafficking practices.

Of course in the European context, the regional body with the greatest clout is the European Union. Its status differs from organisations like the Council of Europe and the OSCE because of its impact on the sovereignty of its members by virtue, for example, of the legally binding nature of its directives on member-states. In the years since Palermo, the EU too has created anti-trafficking architecture through a number of European Council framework decisions and directives. Key elements of these are the original Framework Decision of 2002 on Combatting Trafficking in Human Beings (2002/629/JHA); the 2004 Council Directive on Short-term Residency Permits for Victims of Trafficking who Cooperate with the Authorities (2004/81/EC); the 2011 Directive on Preventing and Combating Trafficking in Human Beings and Protecting its Victims (replacing the 2002 Framework Decision) (2011/36/EU); and the 2012 Directive on Support to Victims of Crime (2012/29/EU). EU concerns with human trafficking are also reflected in funding for social initiatives and academic research related to the issue, the convening of expert working groups, statistics gathered through Eurostat, discussions in European parliamentary committees and resolutions before the European Parliament, to name but a few intra-EU contexts where the issue is dealt with.

There are some important points to draw out from reflection on this complex EU architecture. First, while frequent reference is made in EU contexts to trafficking as a human rights issue, frameworks and directives to date largely view human trafficking through the lenses of crime and security, to the extent that the humanitarian intentions of EU Directives tend to be trumped by border control concerns (Krieg 2009, 776). For example, the 2002 and 2011 Directives translate the three-element Palermo definition of trafficking into EU frameworks with the same consequent narrowing of the possibility of identifying victims, who must tick all three boxes of coercion/deception, movement and exploitation in order to be deemed victims of trafficking. The Palermo emphasis on transnational crime, prosecution and punishment also flavours the Directives. The 2004 Directive, for example, offers temporary residence to people identified as victims but on the pre-condition that they collaborate with the policing authorities to further prosecutions of traffickers. The Prevention Directive of 2011 also focuses on the issues of encouraging pan-European policing and prosecution through EUROPOL and EUROJUST and upping criminal sanctions for traffickers, with space given to victims' rights only in brief Article 11 (2011/36/EU). Interestingly, the 2011 Directive also makes reference to the necessity of member-states taking preventative action intended to 'discourage and reduce the demand that fosters all forms of exploitation related to trafficking in human beings' (Article 18). This 'demand' focus, which was missing from the original 2002 Framework

Decision, is indicative of an increasingly influential lobby and framing of the issue in the EU, as will be explored further below.

Over the years some other wings of the EU machinery have advocated a broadening of the understanding of trafficking to lessen the crime and border control concerns evident in the Directives and make 'exploitation' the key concern in anti-trafficking initiatives. This was proposed by the EU's Expert Group in 2004, which reasoned that regardless of how people find themselves in difficulties, EU responses to trafficking should be driven less by the concern to establish whether people are moved across borders under conditions of deception and coercion but more with what happens to them at the end of the journey. Recognising the complexity of people's migration stories and seeking to get to the ethical core of the issue, the EU Experts Group asserted (2004, 7) that,

> From a human rights perspective, the primary concern is to combat the exploitation of human beings under forced labour or slavery like conditions, no matter whether such exploitation involves a victim of trafficking, a smuggled person, an illegal immigrant or a lawful resident.

However, the continuing key concern of the Directives with addressing organised crime and preventing illicit border movement suggests that this 2004 recommendation did not impact on the general crime/security/ border control tenor of EU anti-trafficking efforts. The EU's 'migrant crisis' of summer 2015 onwards reveals this pervasive tendency to view trafficking through a crime control lens. Prominent discourses about the crisis place blame on 'people traffickers' in Turkey and North Africa and the EU increasingly seeks consensus for a securitised response to the crisis, such as the destruction of trafficking rings and traffickers' boats (Lynch 2015). This representation of the problem will be returned to in Chap. 7 where the unintended consequences of this approach to the crisis will be discussed.

A second key theme to draw out of EU Directives to date is that, like Palermo, they echo the definition of exploitative outcomes that acknowledge human trafficking can be for multiple ends, opening the definition to include forced labour, begging and marriage (2011/36/EU). However, like so many other international formulations, there is still a special listing and privileging of trafficking for the sexual exploitation of women and children (Krieg 2009, 780). This tendency and a consequent move to support the politics of neo-abolitionism are particularly obvious in European parliamentary committees and resolutions concerning the issue, most recently the 2014 'Honeyball Resolution' to the European Parliament (2013/2103/INI) and the report on 'Sexual Exploitation and Prostitution and its Impact on Gender Equality' (Schulze 2014) based on research requested by the European Parliament's committee on Women's Rights and Gender Equality.

The Resolution presented to the European Parliament by Mary Honeyball MEP opens by bringing the full weight of anti-trafficking legal architecture to bear on the European Parliament. The preamble cites 43 relevant pieces of international legislation and frameworks. It then goes on to state bluntly that prostitution is a gendered phenomenon, a form of slavery, a form of violence against women, incompatible with dignity and rights, linked to human trafficking and maintained through demand. The Resolution then goes on to advocate 'the Nordic model' (2013/2103/INI, points 31 and 32) arguing that such legislation should be introduced as a key means of combatting trafficking and as a means of 'establishing what acceptable norms are in society' (point 36). Despite a little wobble in tone where there is an admission that research is needed into which policies work, this Resolution ends with trenchant neo-abolitionist statements to the effect that any alternative policy (e.g. regulation or legalisation of prostitution) would lead to 'sexual slavery and gender inequality' (2013/2103/INI). The European Parliament adopted the non-binding resolution in February 2014 by 343 votes to 139, with 105 abstentions (European Parliament News 2014).

Such a resolution can only make its way into the Parliament on the basis of a pre-history of research, lobbying and framing of the issue by the MEP and parliamentary committee concerned but also by actors engaged in European civil and political societies. Key agents in this respect are the committee on gender equality and women's rights inside the parliament and the European Women's Lobby outside.

The Honeyball Resolution emerged on the basis of an 'own initiative' report on 'Sexual Exploitation and Prostitution and its Impact on Gender Equality' undertaken by the Women's Rights and Gender Equality Committee. The committee's work was underpinned by research it requested from the Policy Department on Citizens' Rights and Constitutional Affairs into the international literature on sexual exploitation and prostitution and its impact on gender equality (Schulze 2014). This research used Palermo and the EU Directives for its definitional basis and statistics provided by the abolitionist French NGO Foundacion

Scelles. Its findings supported the view that 'the concept is gaining ground that prostitution cannot be supported as a legitimate business because it is fundamentally contradictory to the Charter of Fundamental Rights' (Schulze 2014, 9) and also that consensus exists in 'international law and literature...that prostitution is hardly separated from sexual exploitation and trafficking in human beings' (2014, 6). Demand for sexual exploitation is also named as a key cause of these interlinked forms of exploitation and once again 'the Swedish model' is favourably reviewed (Schulze 2014, 53).

The 'Swedish' or 'Nordic' model refers to the 'sex purchase ban' initiated by the Swedish government in 1999. Initially a law that sought to abolish prostitution because it was seen as incompatible with Swedish norms around gender equality, the law was increasingly presented and legitimated as an instrument to prevent sex trafficking in women (Swanström 2016). Norway followed suit in adopting a similar law, so the term 'Nordic model' also often comes into play to describe the system but as May-Len Skilbrei and Charlottta Holmström (2013) point out this is a misnomer as other Nordic states, notably Finland and Denmark, have rejected the model on the grounds of their assessments that it does not work to prevent either prostitution or trafficking. There is plenty of heated debate across European political and civil societies about the normative underpinnings and actual effects of this law (for opposing views see for example Ekberg 2004 and Jordan 2012) but it has undoubtedly become the aspired to model for many European neo-abolitionist feminists.

Debates about the ideas behind the Swedish law and assessments of its impact run along the same highly charged 'sex war' lines that marked the intra-feminist debates around Palermo, as discussed in Chap. 2. What is of interest here in terms of the theme of this chapter is that advocacy of the Swedish law has become 'regionalised' because it is admired by so many lobbyists across the EU. For example it became a touchstone for Irish neo-abolitionist lobbyists, as the case to be detailed below will show. In terms of actual uptake the Swedish model is still under debate in many places and other EU states take very different views, with regulation and legalisation of prostitution also practiced across the member-states. At the same time the question does arise as to whether the transposition of a norm from 'the Nordic' region to the rest of Europe is feasible. The Swedish model reflects very particular and long-lived characteristics of that country's domestic politics. These include the tradition of social democracy, gender equality and strong alliances between feminists and the welfare state

(Swanström 2016). Others would point to the intersection of these traditions with what Arthur Gould refers to as Sweden's 'fear of the foreign', emerging in reaction to threats to the sanctity of Sweden's strong welfarist traditions coming from neo-liberalism, globalisation and migration, epitomised by more women in prostitution coming from abroad (Gould 2001, 452–453). These are key factors creating a context conducive to the normative legitimacy of the 'sex purchase ban' in Sweden. Given this idiosyncratic context, are Swedish policies transferable to other European societies that do not share this very particular socio-political background? This is a question I will return to in discussing Ireland but what is clear is that one particularly vociferous lobby in European civil society does think that the "Nordic" local is regionalisable—and that is the European Women's Lobby (EWL).

An important aspect of the functioning of EU institutions is being seen to be lobbied. EU bodies are aware of their perceived democratic deficit, given that turnout in European elections is small and the most influential European institutions are not connected to any electorates (especially the European Commission). Given this situation the EU tries to encourage the impression that it is open to all comers among civil society lobbyists but at the same time seeks to manage its relationships with civil society through encouraging the formation of umbrella lobbies it can relate to. Obvious examples of such 'partnership arrangements' include that between DG Development and CONCORD (European NGO confederation for Relief and Development) as the designated umbrella body for development NGOs (Greenwood 2010, 202–207). The parallel in relation to women's issues and gender equality is surely the European Women's Lobby (EWL).

The EWL is an umbrella lobby encompassing 2000 women's groups from throughout 31 European states. Its policy positions stand in the tradition of radical feminism with key policy planks built around encouraging women's political participation and economic empowerment while opposing violence against women (womenlobby.org 2015). Violence against women is analysed by the EWL as rooted in pervasive 'male violence against women (embedded in) a structural system of patriarchal values by which violence against women and girls is tolerated, legitimized and even trivialized'. From this structural analysis it follows that manifestations of violence against women are understood very broadly and include prostitution. Prostitution is understood as a form of male violence because, '(it) is a question of patriarchy: it is the ultimate way in which men control women's bodies and sexuality, through an exchange of money' (European

Women's Lobby 2010, 2 and 8). On the basis of this position, EWL launched its 'Brussels Call' in 2012 declaring that 'abolition of prostitution is a shared value across Europe' and also claimed the connection that 'the system of prostitution fuels and perpetuates trafficking in human beings for sexual exploitation' (European Women's Lobby 2012). The EWL website showcases the 200 organisations and 50 plus MEPs who have joined the cause.

The bold statement that abolitionism is a common value across Europe is hyperbolic. As mentioned above not all states are enamoured of the 'Swedish model', nor are all women's groups (most notably networks of sex work projects). The EU does steer away from prescribing prostitution policies for its members, yet there is undoubtedly a strong tendency in the European context to combine concern with the framing of trafficking as a problem of serious organised crime and corruption coupled with issues of gender inequality and violence against women (Meriläinen and Vos 2015, 18), leading to an ever increasing abolitionist tone to most of the positions emerging from Brussels on this issue.

These regional developments circulate to the local, as will be shown in the next section where the localisation of the anti-trafficking norms of the UN and EU in the Irish context will be explored. Looking back, the Brussels Call offers a curious clue as to the salience of the prostitution/sex trafficking issue for Irish civil society. For such a small country in terms of population there is an over-representation of signatories to the Brussels Call by NGOs from the Republic of Ireland. There are 64 Irish organisations' logos appended to the Call, compared to countries with enormous populations like Germany with only four NGO logos represented (European Women's Lobby 2012). The roots of this wild over-representation of Irish NGOs in the Brussels Call is indicative of the highly effective uptake of neo-abolitionism in Irish civil society over the last ten years, leading to a very context-specific localisation of a global and regional norm.

Anti-trafficking Politics in the Republic of Ireland

In European terms the Republic of Ireland came late to ratification of the Palermo Protocol and the uptake of European Directives. Final ratification of Palermo only occurred in 2010, following a flurry of developments from 2008 onwards, which saw the Criminal Law (Human Trafficking) Act passed, as well as the creation of a dedicated Anti-Trafficking Unit in the Department of Justice, a National Action Plan and the creation of consultative mechanisms among state, policing and civil society actors. An important element in this final push to ratify Palermo came from the embarrassment of a poor showing in the State Department TiP reports as Ireland slid from Tier 1 to Tier 2 status over a couple of years (see the TiP Reports of 2006 and 2008). Ireland has also opted into the 2011 EU Directive and amended the Human Trafficking Act (in 2013) to take into account that Directive's broad definition of trafficking to include forced begging and a definition of forced labour (European Commission 2015). A recent court case in Ireland did however criticise the extent to which the Irish state is fully compliant in its transposition of the 2011 EU Directive into law, particularly as it affects the treatment of suspected victims of trafficking (O'Faolain 2015). This is indicative of the on-going process of norm socialisation, occurring as domestic political and judicial actors work to interpret the meaning of new normative requirements coming from 'outside' to the local context. As a member of the OSCE and the Council of Europe, Ireland is also subject to monitoring visits by the OSCE and GRETA, which both evaluated Ireland's anti-trafficking record in 2013 (OSCE 2013 and GRETA 2013).

It is clear therefore that external prodding by powerful agents of norm socialisation, like the US, EU, OSCE and Council of Europe, undoubtedly formed part of the impetus behind the evolution of Ireland's anti-trafficking framework and architecture. Yet, Ireland is also a classic illustration of Acharya's argument that the trajectory of norm socialisation and adoption is significantly shaped by local agency. Ireland's eventual, if tardy, formal endorsement of international expectations was provoked not only by external pressure but also by a vociferous civil society campaign for action against human trafficking, with strong local roots and good transnational connections. That campaign, under the umbrella title 'Turn Off the Red Light' (TORL), was and is solely concerned with trafficking in women and children for sexual exploitation.

Eilís Ward's (2016) genealogy of this campaign traces its roots to Irish feminist activists associated with the local and global anti-violence against women campaigns of the 1990s onwards. TORL's own timeline (TORL 2015a) dates its official starting point to the publication of a handbook on the links between prostitution and trafficking by Grainne Healy and Monica O'Connor, two radical feminist women's rights advocates (Healy and O'Connor 2006). The provenance of their study is clear in that it was the result of a project among CATW (Coalition Against Trafficking in Women), EWL and the Swedish and US governments. Following this publication, the campaign evolved under the TORL umbrella, led by the Immigrant Council of Ireland. The campaign, as it name suggests, is primarily concerned to abolish prostitution, and by extension sex trafficking, through lobbying for the adaptation of the 'Nordic' style criminalisation of sex buyers policy to the Irish context.

In terms of developing a range of forms of collective action, the TORL campaign is an extremely impressive and strategically astute organisation. Through a range of tactics such as commissioned research, public propagation of statistics, cultural events, supporting women who can speak of personal horrific experiences in prostitution, European networking and ultimately through very effective political and civil society alliance building, TORL has come to dominate the public space in the formation of Irish anti-trafficking norms (Ward 2016), even to the extent of excluding all other voices by claiming to speak for 'all Irish women' (FitzGerald and McGarry 2015, 15). Through careful building of associations with political parties, trades unions, local government councils, church-based anti-trafficking networks and NGOs across a spectrum of activities related to prostitution, migration, women's rights, children's rights and so on, TORL created an apparent civil and political society consensus in favour of neo-abolitionism as an anti-sex trafficking and anti-prostitution policy for contemporary Ireland. Their alliance of 70 plus NGOs, political parties and local councils (TORL 2015b), which translated into a claim to enjoy the combined support of 1.6 million members (TORL 2015a), explains the heavy Irish presence on the EWL's Brussels Call.

Politicians sympathetic to the campaign shepherded Swedish style proposals through the Irish houses of parliament and provoked uptake of the issue by the Joint Oireachtas (parliamentary) Committee on Justice. In 2012 this committee opened a public hearing on the question of the future of prostitution policy, and as well as inviting submissions and holding public hearings on the issue, the committee made a fact- finding visit to Sweden. As a consequence the Justice Committee published a report fully endorsing the neo-abolitionist position (Oireachtas Joint Committee on Justice, Equality and Defence 2013) and in late 2014 the Irish government accepted the arguments for Swedish style laws, introduced into the Criminal Law (Sexual Offences) Bill of 2015.

As a result of this campaigning, the TORL's success is pretty secure and any opposition is muted. There is a Sex Worker's Rights Alliance in the Republic (SWAI 2015) bringing together sex workers, social and health professionals and researchers but it is comparatively small and those who oppose the law are outnumbered. It is important for me to acknowledge that as an academic researcher and a participant in public discourses in Ireland, I am not a supporter of the TORL campaign (nor am I a member of SWAI, though my biases are towards them). With my colleague Eilís Ward, I made a submission to the Oireachtas committee critical of the Nordic model. We have written elsewhere about our experiences of occupying a contrary stance to that endorsed by an overwhelming majority of Irish feminists and civil and political actors. As participants in the public debates, we became very aware of the difficulties of opposing a discourse that became hegemonic, as we were often cast as being either clueless academics or prostitution's legitimisers for taking an oppositional stance. As I indicated in this book's introduction the politics of trafficking tends to become highly personal for all who get involved, even those who enter the issue as self-deludingly neutral academics. Yet, acknowledging our own uneasiness and drawing inspiration from Wanda Pillow's idea of the 'reflexivity of discomfort' (Pillow 2003), we did gain analytical and methodological insights from our experiences about researching in the context of the power play surrounding the issue (Ward and Wylie 2014, see also Ryan 2016).

As detailed above the TORL campaign is comprehensive in reach and very astute. As well as local alliance building, it leveraged strong support in the EU, EWL and Sweden. Yet its salience is not just due to its clever and multiple tactics. As Acherya suggests, norm socialisation rests in the mores of the norm takers, as much as the external pressure from the norm socialisers (Acherya 2004). There are strong locally specific reasons as to why the anti-prostitution/anti sex-trafficking/neo-abolitionism nexus finds strong root in Ireland. The alliance is built between those who touch very different chords in the social mores of Ireland. The role of radical feminists very much engaged with issues of violence against women was highlighted above and their success in this campaign is all the more surprising given that feminism has faced a tough context in Ireland in the past, when Church and State together created an inhospitable setting. However, 'governance feminism' has made inroads in Ireland over the last 30 years and women's voices are strongly organised in the National Women's Council, and so on. Ironically, the hangovers of 'old fashioned morality' related to church and state are probably equally a key part of the social acceptability of anti-prostitution measures, particularly those aimed at men who buy sex. The churches are at one in their support of neo-abolitionism with Catholic religious congregations in Ireland behind 'Action to Prevent Trafficking', which is again supportive of TORL and linked to pan-European religious networks such as RENATE—Religious in Europe Networking Against Trafficking and Exploitation (APT 2015). While formal church structures certainly play a less influential role in contemporary Irish society, as secularism bites and religious attendance falls off, the mark of church influence is still strong. For example, sex education in schools is still provided within the ethos of primary and secondary schools, the vast majority of which are under Catholic or other Christian patronage. Therefore the tendency in the Relationships and Sexuality curriculum is to emphasise relationships rather than sexuality, value heteronormativity and (though this is changing post the 2015 Marriage Equality Referendum) reinforce expectations for conventional marriage (Sherlock 2012).

Representatives from TORL also played a part in promoting neo-abolitionist discourses north of the border in Ireland. The devolved Northern Ireland Assembly was the first layer of government within the UK to adopt neo-abolition policies with the passing of a private member's Bill sponsored by Lord Morrow of the Democratic Unionist Party, which became the Human Trafficking and Exploitation [Criminal Justice and Support for Victims) Act (Northern Ireland) 2015] (royal assent was given in January 2015). Clause 6 of this Act criminalises the purchase of sex with the implied intent that this will reduce the demand for sex trafficking. In the consultation process leading to the acceptance of 'Lord Morrow's Bill', TORL representatives made submissions and were invited to give evidence to the Stormont committee (TORL 2015a). As will be recounted below, the embedding of this version of the anti-trafficking norm in Northern Ireland owes much to the socio-political and cultural particularities of that jurisdiction but the cross-border lobbying involved is again illustrative of the complex weaving from the local to the regional to the global, which goes into the process of norm socialisation relating to human trafficking.

Northern Ireland

Northern Ireland is still politically part of the UK. As such British anti-trafficking laws and architecture influence the Northern Irish context (for example, Northern Ireland was included in UK-wide anti-trafficking policing operations, as will be explained below). Although the UK's scepticism about belonging to the EU is well known and it opts out of many Directives impinging on issues of migration control or justice, it did opt in to the 2011 Directive (European Commission 2011) and is party to the Council of Europe Convention on Action against Trafficking in Human Beings. Therefore, as in the case of the Republic of Ireland, there is a degree to which external socialisation processes impinge on the adoption of anti-trafficking norms in Northern Ireland. However, Northern Ireland is also subject to another layer of governance; the devolved power-sharing Stormont Assembly set up as part of the Belfast Agreement (1998) intended to end the on-going violence between nationalists and unionists with their contending aspirations for Northern Ireland's future political belonging. In 2014 the Stormont Assembly became the first of the UK's devolved assemblies to adopt a neo-abolitionist law criminalising the purchase of sex, framed as an anti-prostitution and anti-trafficking measure. Although guided through the political system by Lord Morrow of the Democratic Unionist Party, the proposal accrued near unanimous political support. Given that unanimity is such a rarity in divided Northern Ireland, it is important to decipher why consensus was achieved on this issue. In order to do so, Acharya and Epstein's advice to pay attention to the mores and agency of local norm takers is useful once again.

As elsewhere, knowledge production about the 'problem' of human trafficking, particularly sex trafficking, in Northern Ireland surfaced in the early years of the 2000s. An initial report by Rebecca Dudley for Women's Aid (2006) acknowledged that fast figures could not be put on the extent of the problem but concluded, on the basis of expert interviews and newspaper surveys, that all forms of trafficking, but most particularly sex trafficking of women and unaccompanied minors, was a growing problem in the region. The ability to say this with any certainty was complicated by the fact that interviewees from the Police Service of Northern Ireland (PSNI) did not think the problem affected Northern Ireland but other interviewees from victim support services were sure that trafficking existed in the jurisdiction. In this report human trafficking for sexual exploitation was named clearly as 'an evil', 'a form of violence against women' and the necessity of trained policing, prosecutorial severity for traffickers, greater protections for victims and the tackling of demand for sexual services were all broached in its recommendations (Dudley 2006). A second piece of research on the nature and extent of trafficking in the region was undertaken in 2009 under the auspices of the Northern Ireland Human Rights Commission (Martynowicz et al. 2011). Again this report's authors acknowledge the unreliability of statistics and admit that they occasionally had to change interview tack as some interviewees largely lacked ‘experience of practical engagement with victims of trafficking’ (2011, 3). However, this report did refer to five trafficking-related arrests in Northern Ireland that occurred after a UK level anti-trafficking policing operation, Pentameter Two, in 2009 [although it is worth noting that the apparent success of the Pentameter operations faded away as most of the arrests failed to result in any prosecutions, still less convictions (Davies 2009)]. Nonetheless Martynowicz and her co-authors did conclude that on ‘bitty’ evidence it was possible to make a ‘reasonable assumption’ that human trafficking—for labour and sexual exploitation—was occurring in Northern Ireland. Interestingly and unusually, this report did give strong attention to labour trafficking and noted the problems for undocumented migrants stemming from work permit abuses and unscrupulous businesses as underpinning causes of the exploitation of migrant workers. Women’s Aid was identified as the body best placed to offer support services to women and children trafficked for sexual exploitation, while Migrant Helpline was recommended as support to male victims of sexual exploitation and those trafficked for forced labour.

As ever, as I laid out in the introduction to this book, no amount of acknowledgement that knowledge is slight and partial, or admission that sources might be sensationalist or biased, or awareness of the complex scenarios that exploited migrants experience, prevents trafficking statistics gaining life or the enthusiastic elaboration of new anti-trafficking laws and convoluted anti-trafficking architecture. The claim, even on admittedly ‘bitty’ evidence, that there is definitely a problem and that it is associated with ‘demand’ for sexual exploitation has taken political wing and flown in several contexts. In this case Northern Ireland has forged ahead of other constituent parts of the UK to adopt neo-abolitionist policies as anti-sex-trafficking measures and why it has done so needs contextually sensitive explanation.

The lobby for neo-abolitionist approaches to combatting trafficking in Northern Ireland is once again the product of intriguing civil and political society alliances. In this case, Lord Morrow—the promoter of the 2015 Act—comes from the Democratic Unionist Party, a socially and politically conservative party that believes that Northern Ireland is and must remain an integral part of the UK. The party has strong associations with conservative and evangelical Protestantism in Northern Ireland. Lord Morrow told the Northern Assembly that his Bill was ‘very much motivated by my Christian faith' (Emerson 2015) and attributed his intense concern about human trafficking to reading the biography of William Wilberforce, a key nineteenth-century Christian activist in the abolition of the slave trade (Clarke 2012). This personal interest was augmented by advice from CARE (Christian Action Research and Education), a conservative Christian NGO focusing on issues to do with family values as well as opposition to prostitution and sex trafficking (CARE 2015). Representatives of CARE accompanied Lord Morrow at the formulation, readings and committee stages of his Private Member's Bill in the Stormont Justice Committee. Alongside Lord Morrow and CARE at a key stage of the Stormont process was Gunilla Ekberg, Swedish feminist, researcher and advocate of the Swedish sex purchase ban. Their appearance together at the parliamentary committee in September 2013 to explain and defend 'clause 6'of Lord Morrow' Bill—the proposed sex purchase ban—epitomises the coming together of strange bedfellows in relation to this policy position (Hansard 2013).

As in the Republic very few opponents of the Bill testified to the Justice committee. Some witnesses who did present critical perspectives on neo-abolitionism were subject to an unprecedented personal barrage. One academic from Queens University Belfast had his personal e-mails to Ms Ekberg, in which he questioned her alliance with the DUP, read publically by a committee member leading to highly charged and personalised discussions (Hansard 2014b). A sex workers' representative was also quizzed intently with intrusive questions raised about her motives and conduct (Hansard 2014a).

In 2014 the Assembly's Department of Justice did commission research into the nature and extent of prostitution in Northern Ireland, which the Justice Minister intended as an evidence base to underpin the on-going debates about Lord Morrow's Bill and Clause 6 in particular. The successful tender for this research went to Queens University Belfast and National University of Ireland, Galway—and I must confess again to a small part in the process as I was a member of the international advisory board.

The research design was intended to be comprehensive, trying to connect with as many sources of information as possible by sending out a questionnaire and doing interviews with women and men who sell sex in Northern Ireland, 'scraping' websites to build a picture of sex for sale, interviewing clients and interviewing area experts (police, service providers and so on). There were definite limitations to the report such as the acknowledged problems of contacting 'hidden populations' and dealing with 'selection bias', that is people willing to come forward for interview over-representing a particular view. That said, in its report the research offered a complex account of sex workers and clients in Northern Ireland but also clearly concluded that the sex purchase ban was not supported by the majority of those identifying as sex workers in the Northern Irish context (Huschke et al. 2014).

This research too became caught up in the politics surrounding sex trafficking. When it was commissioned Lord Morrow dismissed the research as a 'typical civil service trick to send clause 6 into the long grass' (Hansard 2014c). After its publication one NGO originally associated with the research, Women's Aid, condemned its findings and rejected its recommendations as failing to recognise prostitution as violence against women (Women's Aid 2014). In the end however, political momentum upstaged the research, which was made public just one day before the crucial vote on the Bill was taken in the Stormont Assembly. Eventually an unusual degree of cross-party support for the Bill was evidenced. The republican, nationalist party Sinn Fein, which rarely finds itself in accord with Unionist proposals, overcame its original scepticism of the Bill, shifting position because of unprecedented lobbying and feminist framing of the issue as one of women's rights.

Out of the processes detailed above, the two jurisdictions on the island of Ireland have reached the same normative understanding of human trafficking as primarily an issue of the sexual exploitation of women that requires a 'demand' reductionist policy to address it adequately. There are common factors leading to this, including the international context of European and UN norm socialisation 'from above'. Yet, far from being 'infantilised norm takers', it is the vociferous and well-organised lobbying by local coalitions of convinced parties who have effectively inculcated this norm in their civil and political contexts, while relying on the regional example set by the Nordic model to provide an exemplar for their policy prescriptions. Importantly, this story of the common adoption of neo-abolitionism also has to account for the differences in social mores between the two places. For example, in Northern Ireland the impact of Protestant conservative religious belief is a strong factor in terms of casting the moral landscape, and this differs from the secularising context in the contemporary Irish Republic, where evangelical Protestants are a tiny minority and feminist-led coalition building has been key. As the new legal frameworks take shape it will be fascinating (or worrying) to see what implementation brings, yet as with all victories for 'governance feminists' and their allies (Halley 2006) there may already be some unintended consequences to be discerned.

Neo-abolitionism and Its Consequences

In both parts of Ireland, local civil society moral entrepreneurs connected to regional European networks succeeded in creating legislative changes in line with their reading of human trafficking as being primarily about sexual exploitation and prostitution, understood as forms of violence against women. Writing about France, where neo-abolitionist currents are also highly persuasive, Barbara Ticktin suggests that feminist lobbying for policies to curb sexual violence has easily been co-opted into government discourses of border control (Ticktin 2008, 864). In the French case, Ticktin argues that abolitionism, by seeking to 'save' a few select women from the evils of the violence in prostitution, serves to differentiate those women from other people who do not have the right to belong to the French state, that is criminal migrant men accused of trafficking and pimping or women who do not conform to the state's 'rescuing' of them. She draws a parallel between this consequence of abolitionist rhetoric and the contemporaneous framing of Islamic veiling as a coercive form of violence against women. Again this discourse of violence enables the drawing of borderlines, with only un-veiled women seen as belonging to the idealised, secularised French Republic, while religious men who are accused of forcing veiling on women become rank outsiders.

I would suggest that there are similar ways in which discourses around trafficking and prostitution as sexual violence have become part of the politics of border control in Ireland and the UK but also between the two jurisdictions (that is, the Republic and Northern Ireland). Elsewhere I have written with Deirdre Coghlan about how the Irish government uses discourses of human trafficking to securitise migration, labelling 'organised criminal' traffickers as a security threat and categorising victims of trafficking as a minority of abused migrants, deserving of state protections but set apart from the vast majority of all other categories of 'undeserving' irregular migrants (Coghlan and Wylie 2011). Similar discourses that position trafficking as a threat to security and a reason for tightening border controls against all but the few who are deemed innocent and deserving of protection, particularly women who have experiences of sexual exploitation, are to be found in the UK (Anderson 2013). Intriguingly, these are discourses that NGOs end up replicating in their determination to secure protections for their client groups or to ensure they are included in state consultative or funding mechanisms (Coghlan and Wylie 2011, 1516).

At another level though, that of the two jurisdictions on the island of Ireland, there are ways in which discourses of sex trafficking and prostitution understood as violence against women have become part of the politics of bordering in a manner unique to the politics of a divided island. As is well known, since the 1990s Northern Ireland is the context for a long-drawn out peace process, which attempts to resolve the political divisions and violence caused by colonial history, material inequalities and divided identities. As well as being a process aimed at establishing peaceable politics within Northern Ireland, it is a process with both North-South (Northern Ireland and the Republic) and East-West dimensions (relating to Irish and British relations). Part of the peace process is the lessening of the everyday significance of the physical border between Northern Ireland and the Republic—a space that used to be militarised and visible to cross—while equally accepting the border's continuing presence through the political formulation that accepts that it will exist as long as a majority of people in Northern Ireland wish to remain in the UK. In effect, the peace process accomplishes an ambiguous trick of both diminishing and reinforcing the North-South border.

Advocates of neo-abolitionism have used this border ambiguity to press home their arguments. They express the fear that if one side criminalises the buying of sex but the other does not then criminality and exploitation related to prostitution in the borderlands and beyond will increase exponentially on the side without a sex purchase ban. For example, after the passage of Lord Morrow's Bill the TORL released a statement that, 'sex buyer laws which will come into force in Northern Ireland this weekend (June 1st 2015) will make southern border counties and Dublin far more attractive for pimps, traffickers and thugs' (TORL 2015c). The porousness of the border requires that both jurisdictions should act to criminalise, or traffickers and those who sell sex will just move North or South. By contrast if both sides adopt neo-abolitionism then the border will be secured, sealing off the space for the traffickers and trafficked by the adoption of mutually compatible legislation. If they do not, the possibility of on-going easy movement 'across the land border' (Dudley 2006) will negate the anti-trafficking bite of neo-abolitionist measures. As Rebecca Dudley argued when she presented her research to the UK Parliament,

> Police sources noted the ease with which the land border can be crossed within Ireland and also increased use of Northern Ireland as a route through the UK from the Republic of Ireland and going in the other direction. We know the border is used every day for all sorts of activities from going to work to going to the dentist, so it is very, very easy to cross. (UK Parliament Joint Committee on Human Rights 2006)

As the citations above indicate, fear of the consequences of slippage through the border cracks made for key arguments legitimising the call for joined up neo-abolitionist policies on both sides of it. As well as arguing for border control, the advocates of neo-abolitionism are also keen on enhancing prosecution, custodial sentences and state punishment of organisers and buyers of sex (Dudley 2006). In these ways Irish neo-abolitionists, North and South, epitomise the carceral feminism defined by Elizabeth Bernstein (2010). By arguing for policies of border control they find themselves closely aligned with the securitisation agendas of states in ways that might seem odd for feminist advocates.

Conclusion

The norm lifecycle model suggests that the uptake of new norms in the political systems happens as a result of socialisation processes from the international level to the local. International civil servants and politicians are tasked to learn of new normative expectations in global or regional organisations and transmit the learning back home. Undoubtedly elements of this process are discernible when looking at the localisation of international trafficking norms. The increasingly elaborate anti-trafficking architecture of the UN, EU and other regional organisations does impact on member states. Yet the process of socialisation is not all one way. While domestic polities are usually imagined as 'norm takers' in this scenario, understanding how, why and in what form norms are elaborated in domestic contexts also requires paying attention to local activism and mores. In the case of the adoption of anti-trafficking norms in the two polities on the island of Ireland, the activism of civil society entrepreneurs whose inclinations accord with the wider societal mores explains why European ideals translate in particular ways to the local context. A further layer to this complex story comes from 'sideways' moves where Irish norm entrepreneurs look to regional exemplars—in this case Sweden and Norway—to legitimise particular formulations of the problem and its solutions. Anti-trafficking politics do not take the same shape everywhere—for example, neo-abolitionism has not gained purchase in all other European contexts (Ward and Wylie 2016)—so there is a need to look at discourses and power play inside local civil and political societies to see what will find approbation in local contexts. The case study in this chapter of the interweaving of anti-trafficking politics among Ireland, Europe and Sweden shows all these socialisation dynamics in action.

What they also show once again, reiterating the other chapters of this book so far, is that anti-trafficking politics tends to boil down in international and local contexts to an omnipresent obsession with trafficking as sexual exploitation. Issues of trafficking for labour exploitation receive cursory mention but rarely become the impassioned focus of civil society efforts, policies or interventions. In the Republic of Ireland, for instance, one of the very few cases to result in successful prosecution for human trafficking so far led to convictions in a Romanian court of men who exploited people for agricultural labour in the southeast of the country. Yet, only one NGO doggedly presses the case that attention needs to be paid to trafficking for forced labour. This is a common occurrence. Although Palermo and the laws and architecture it spawned always make reference to trafficking for ends beyond sexual exploitation, reference to other forms of exploitation rarely go beyond paying lip service. This returns us to the puzzle, which was raised in Chap. 2, about norms that do not follow the lifecycle at all. The question of why this occurs will be explored in Chap. 6 in relation to the case of trafficking for labour exploitation.

Bibliography

Acharya, A. (2004). How ideas spread: Whose norms matter? Norm localization and institutional change in Asian regionalism. *International Organization, 58*(2), 239–275.

Adler-Nissen, R. (2014). Stigma management in international relations: Transgressive identities, norms, and order in International Society. *International Organization, 68*(4), 143–176.

Anderson, B. (2013). *Us and them: The dangerous politics of immigration control.* Oxford: Oxford University Press.

APT. (2015). Act to prevent trafficking. http://www.aptireland.org/, date accessed 21 September 21 2015.

Bernstein, E. (2010). Militarized humanitarianism meets Carceral Feminism: The politics of sex, rights, and freedom in contemporary anti-trafficking campaigns. *Signs, 36*(1), 45–72.

Bradley, H. (2007). *Gender* (Volume 38 of Polity Key Concepts in the Social Sciences series) (1st editon). Cambridge: Polity.

Braun, M. (2014). EU Climate Norms in East-Central Europe. *Journal of Common Market Studies, 52*(3), 445–460.

CARE. (2015). CARE—Our causes: Human exploitation—Human trafficking—prostitution. http://www.care.org.uk/our-causes/human-exploitation/prostitution, date accessed 28 September 2015.

Checkel, J. (2001). Why Comply? Social learning and European Identity Change. *International Organization, 55*(3), 553–588.

Clarke, L. (2012). Morrow right to keep driving trafficking bill. *Belfast Telegraph*, 26 October 2012.

Coghlan, D., & Wylie, G. (2011). Defining trafficking/Denying justice? Forced labour in Ireland and the consequences of trafficking discourse. *Journal of Ethnic and Migration Studies, 37*(9), 1513–1526.

Council of Europe Convention. (2005). CoE convention on action against trafficking in human beings. 16 May 2005, https://www.coe.int/t/dghl/monitoring/trafficking/Docs/Convntn/CETS197_en.asp, date accessed 26 February 2016.

Davies, N. (2009, October 20). Inquiry fails to find single trafficker who forced anybody into prostitution. *The Guardian*.

Dudley, R. (2006). *Crossing borders: Preliminary research on human trafficking in Northern Ireland*. Belfast: Women's Aid Federation of Northern Ireland.

Ekberg, G. (2004). The Swedish Law that prohibits the purchase of sexual services best practices for prevention of prostitution and trafficking in human beings. *Violence Against Women, 10*(10), 1187–1218.

Emerson, N. (2015, June 7). DUP finds a more seductive look for Christian Fundamentalism. *The Sunday Times*.

Epstein, C. (2012). Stop telling us how to behave: Socialization or infantilization? *International Studies Perspectives, 13*, 135–145.

EU Experts Group. (2004). *EU Experts Group Report on Trafficking in Human Beings*. Brussels: Directorate-General on Justice, Freedom and Security European Commission.

European Commission. (2011). Directive 2011/36/EU Applied to United Kingdom, European Commission—Together against Trafficking in Human Beings. https://ec.europa.eu/anti-trafficking/legislation-and-case-law-eu-legislation-criminal-law/directive-201136eu-applied-united-kingdom_en, date accessed 28 September 2015.

European Commission. (2015). Ireland—Europe against trafficking in human beings, Together against trafficking in human beings. https://ec.europa.eu/anti-trafficking/content/nip/ireland_en, date accessed 9 July 2015.

European Parliament. (2013). Motion for a European Parliament Resolution on Sexual Exploitation and Prostitution and its Impact on Gender Equality.

http://www.europarl.europa.eu/sides/getDoc.do?pubRef=-//EP//TEXT+REPORT+A7-2014-0071+0+DOC+XML+V0//EN#title1, date accessed 9 July 2015.

European Parliament News. (2014). Punish the client, not the prostitute. http://www.europarl.europa.eu/news/en/news-room/content/20140221IPR36644/html/Punish-the-client-not-the-prostitute, date accessed 31 August 2015.

European Women's Lobby. (2010). *Towards a Europe Free from all forms of male violence against women*. Report prepared by the EWL Centre on Violence against Women. Brussels: EWL.

European Women's Lobby. (2012). Brussels' call 'together for a Europe free from prostitution. http://www.womenlobby.org/spip.php?article4374, date accessed 31 August 2015.

Finnemore, M., & Sikkink, K. (1998). International norm dynamics and political change. *International Organization, 52*(4), 887–917.

FitzGerald, S., & McGarry, K. (2015). Problematizing prostitution in law and policy in the Republic of Ireland: A case for reframing. *Social and Legal Studies*. doi:10.1177/09646639156148861-21.

Gallagher, A. T. (2015a). Two cheers for the trafficking protocol. *Anti-Trafficking Review, 4*, 14–32.

Gould, A. (2001). The criminalization of buying sex: The politics of prostitution in Sweden. *Journal of Social Policy, 30*(3), 437–456.

Greenhill, B. (2010). The Company you keep: International socialization and the diffusion of human rights norms. *International Studies Quarterly, 54*, 127–145.

Greenwood, J. (2010). Regulating NGO participation in the EU: A de-facto accreditation system built on representativeness. In J. Steffek & K. Hahn (Eds.), *Evaluating Transnational NGOs: Legitimacy, accountability, representation* (pp. 200–219). Basingstoke: Palgrave Macmillan.

GRETA. (2013). Report concerning the implementation of the Council of Europe Convention on Action against Trafficking in Human Beings by Ireland, http://www.coe.int/t/dghl/monitoring/trafficking/docs/Reports/GRETA_2013_15_FGR_IRL_public_en.pdf, 7 September 2015.

GRETA. (2015). Council of Europe Group of Experts on Actions Against Trafficking in Human Beings. http://www.coe.int/t/dghl/monitoring/trafficking/Docs/Monitoring/GRETA_en.asp, date accessed 31 August 2015.

Halley, J., Kotiswaran, P., Shamir, H., & Thomas, C. (2006). From the International to the local in feminist legal responses to rape, prostitution, sex work and sex trafficking: Four studies in contemporary governance feminism. *Harvard Journal of Law and Gender, 29*, 335–423.

Hansard. (2013). Human trafficking and exploitation (Further provisions and support for victims) Bill: Briefing from Lord Morrow MLA/CARE/Former Swedish Government Special Adviser, 12 September 2013 (Belfast: Hansard—Official Parliamentary Record).

Hansard. (2014a). Human trafficking and exploitation (Further Provisions and Support for Victims) Bill: International Union of Sex Workers. Belfast: Hansard—Official Parliamentary Record.

Hansard. (2014b). Human trafficking and exploitation (Further Provisions and Support for Victims) Bill: Dr Graham Ellison and Dr Susann Huschke, Queen's University Belfast, 30 January 2014, Northern Ireland Assembly—Committee for Justice. Belfast: Hansard—Official Parliamentary Record.

Hansard. (2014c). Committee for Justice Official Report, Human Trafficking and Exploitation (Further Provisions and Support for Victims) Bill: Lord Morrow and Dr Dan Boucher. Belfast: Hansard—Official Parliamentary Record.

Healy, G., & O'Connor, M. (2006). *The links between prostitution and sex trafficking: A briefing handbook.* Report prepared for the Joint Project Coordinated by the Coalition Against Trafficking in Women (CATW) and the European Women's Lobby (EWL) on Promoting Preventative Measures to Combat Trafficking in Human Beings for Sexual Exploitation: A Swedish and United States Governmental and Non-Governmental Organisation Partnership.

Huschke, S., Shirlow, P., Schibotz, D., Ward, E., Probst, U., & Ni Dhonaill, C. (2014). *Research into Prostitution in Northern Ireland* report commissioned from Queen's University Belfast by Department of Justice, Northern Ireland.

Keck, M., & Sikkink, K. (1998). *Activists beyond borders: Advocacy Networks in International Politics.* Ithaca, New York: Cornell University Press.

Krasnodębska, M. (2014). Socialization as a power discourse: Conceptualizing the Eastern Enlargement of Western International Institutions. *Poznan University of Economics Review, 14*(3), 7–22.

Kravtsov, V. (2009). ARV treatment and AIDS Entrepreneurs in South Africa: Domestic opposition to an International Norm (1999–2004). *Global Society, 23*(3), 295–316.

Krieg, S. (2009). Trafficking in human beings: The EU approach between Border Control, Law Enforcement and Human Rights. *European Law Journal, 15*(6), 775–790.

Lynch, S. (2015, May 19). New EU Military Mission will target and destroy boats used by migrant traffickers. *Irish Times.*

Martynowicz, A., Toucas, S., & Caughey, A. (2011). The nature and extent of human trafficking in Northern Ireland: A scoping study. *Trends in Organized Crime, 14,* 198–223.

Meriläinen, N., & Vos, M. (2015). Public Discourse on Human Trafficking in International Issue Arenas. *Societies, 5,* 14–42. doi:10.3390/soc5010014.

Nadelmann, E. (1990). Global prohibition regimes: The emergence of norms in international society. *International Organization, 44*(4), 479–525.

O'Faolain, A. (2015). Law fails to comply with EU trafficking directive, rules High Court. http://www.irishtimes.com/news/crime-and-law/courts/high-court/law-fails-to-comply-with-eu-trafficking-directive-rules-high-court-1.2177347, date accessed 7 September 2015.

Oireachtas Joint Committee on Justice, Equality and Defence. (2013). Report on hearings and submissions on the Review of Legislation on Prostitution June 2013. http://www.oireachtas.ie/parliament/media/committees/justice/1. Part-1-final.pdf, date accessed 7 September 2015.

OSCE. (2013). Report by Maria Grazia Giammarinaro, OSCE Special representative and co-ordinator for combating trafficking in human beings, following her visit to Ireland from 30 January to 2 February 2012, http://www.osce.org/cthb/99775, date accessed 7 September 2015.

Piedrafita, S. (2012). Instrumental Action and Norm Compliance in EU Enlargement Negotiations. *Journal of European Integration, 34*(3), 277–295.

Pillow, W. (2003). Confession, catharsis, or cure? Rethinking the uses of reflexivity as methodological power in qualitative research. *International Journal of Qualitative Studies in Education, 16*(2), 175–196.

Ryan, P. (2016). Conducting sex work research in a politically contentious climate: Lessons from Ireland. In I. A. Crowhurst (Ed.), *Sexualities research: Critical interjections, diverse methodologies and practical applications.* London: Routledge.

Schulze, S. E. (2014). *Sexual exploitation and prostitution and its effect on gender equality.* Brussels: European Parliament, Policy Department on Citizens' Rights and Constitutional Affairs.

Sherlock, L. (2012). Sociopolitical influences on sexuality education in Sweden and Ireland. *Sex Education, 12*(4), 383–396.

Silander, D., & Nilssen, M. (2013). Democratization without enlargement? the European Neighbourhood Policy on Post-communist Transitions. *Contemporary Politics, 19*(4), 441–458.

Skilbrei, M.-L., & Holmström, C. (2013). *Prostitution Policy in the Nordic Region: Ambiguous sympathies.* Farnham: Ashgate.

Stoyanova, V. (2013). The crisis of a definition: Human trafficking in Bulgarian Law. *Amsterdam Law Forum, 5*(1), 64–79.

SWAI. (2015). *Sex Worker's Alliance Ireland.* http://sexworkersallianceireland.org/, 21 September 2015.

Swanström, Y. (2016). From contested to consensus: Swedish politics on prostitution and trafficking. In E. Ward & G. Wylie (Eds.), *The politics of neo-abolitionism: Feminism, neo-liberalism and the State.* London: Routledge.

Tatham, A. (2009). *Enlargement of the European Union.* Kluwer Law International: Alpen aan den Rejn.

Ticktin, B. (2008). Sexual violence as the language of border control: Where French Feminist and Anti- immigrant Rhetoric Meet. *Signs, 33*(4), 863–889.

TORL—Turn Off the Red Light. (2015a). TORL—The campaign so far. Accessed from http://www.turnofftheredlight.ie/about/the-campaign-so-far/, on 21 September 2015.

TORL—Turn Off the Red Light. (2015b). "Who are we?" http://www.turnofftheredlight.ie/about/whos-involved/, date accessed 21 September 2015.

TORL—Turn Off the Red Light. (2015c). Campaigners Call for Immediate Publication of New Sex Offences Bill as NI laws take Effect. 10 August 2015, http://www.turnofftheredlight.ie/2015/08/campaigners-call-for-immediate-publication-of-new-sex-offences-bill-as-ni-laws-take-effect/, date accessed 24 March 2016.

van Kersbergen, K., & Verbeek, B. (2007). The politics of international norms: EU subsidiarity and the imperfect competence regime of the European Union. *European Journal of International Relations, 13*(2), 217–238.

van Schaik, L., & Schunz, S. (2012). Explaining EU activism and impact in global climate politics: Is the union a norm- or interest-driven actor? *Journal of Common Market Studies, 50*(1), 169–186.

Ward, E. (2016). Ireland: A neo-abolitionist shoe-in? In E. Ward & G. Wylie (Eds.), *The politics of neo-abolitionism: Feminism, prostitution and the State.* Abingdon Oxon: Routledge.

Ward, E., & Wylie, G. (2014). Reflexivities of discomfort': Researching the sex trade and sex trafficking in Ireland. *European Journal of Women's Studies, 21*(3), 251–263.

Women's Aid. (2014). Women's Aid Statement on Queen's University Belfast/ Department of Justice Research on Prostitution. http://www.womensaidni.org/womens-aid-statement-queens-university-belfast-department-justice-research-prostitution/, date accessed 28 September 2015.

CHAPTER 6

The Neglected Norm: Trafficking for Forced Labour

Introduction

In 2009 two men were convicted in a Romanian court of human trafficking into Ireland. They were sentenced to prison terms of between five and seven years. In their trial evidence was served that the men forced a group of Romanian migrant workers into agricultural labour in the southeast of Ireland, using threats of physical violence to ensure the workers' compliance and extorting most of their earnings to service alleged debts (O'Brien 2009). This is one of the very few cases involving human trafficking into Ireland that has resulted in a legal conviction. Yet, as shown in Chap. 5, civil and political interest within Ireland on the trafficking issue obsesses around trafficking for sexual exploitation and the links drawn between trafficking and prostitution. Indeed whenever allegations of trafficking in 'other' industries surface in Ireland—as they do sporadically in relation to e.g. fishing, domestic labour and cannabis farming (Carr 2015; Duncan 2014; Irish Times 2015)—those involved in anti-trafficking activism often use them as a springboard to rehearse their views on the necessity of neo-abolitionism as the essential anti-trafficking architecture. For example, the revelation of a potential case of trafficking in men for exploitation in car washing in Donegal allowed the Immigrant Council of Ireland to condemn all trafficking while ingeniously using this case to stress the urgent necessity of implementing Ireland's new laws that 'targeting demand for sex trafficking' and demonstrating that Ireland is not soft on 'trafficking, pimping and organized crime' (The Journal 2015).

G. Wylie, *The International Politics of Human Trafficking*,
DOI 10.1057/978-1-137-37775-3_6

This is just a small illustration of what is a relative blanking out of international engagement in relation to trafficking for labour exploitation when compared to the issue of sex. Chapter 3 did detail the discussions within the Palermo Protocol's formation process that eventually teased out an expansion of the definition of human trafficking beyond its historical roots of being solely about the sexual exploitation of women and children. Yet, although these discussions ended in seeming acknowledgment that trafficking can be for other exploitative ends—specifically labour, forced servitude and the removal of organs—this definitional shift was, even from the outset, becoming occluded by the Protocol's title as being 'especially' about the sexual exploitation of women and children. In effect, before but even since Palermo, sex trafficking remains 'front and center in the larger anti-trafficking movement' (Zhang 2012, 470). Statistics gathering exercises, international and local legal developments, civil and political entrepreneurship and even academic research mirror and perpetuate this tendency. The silence about issues beyond sexual exploitation in Chaps. 4 and 5 of this book is also evidence that concern about trafficking for labour exploitation has not provoked a notable norm lifecycle in its own right.

The agenda for this chapter is to understand why this is the case. As I mentioned in Chap. 2 when discussing the second wave of more critical studies about norms in international politics, there are several scholars who draw attention to the question of norms that do not 'catch on', failing either to inspire vociferous entrepreneurship or to reshape states' identities and interests. This literature provides clues as to why politics 'within' the community of moral entrepreneurs or 'without' in the wider political world might militate against a norm lifecycle flourishing on certain issues. With regard to the particularities of trafficking for labour exploitation, I will suggest that labour issues provoke less concern because they do not fit easily with many of the key concerns and discourses that fuel interest in sex trafficking among moral entrepreneurs. Writing about trafficking discourses, Neil Howard suggests that within them lie binary views of the world, that it is possible to draw clear distinctions between coercion and consent or between situations that are exploitative or legitimate in terms of employment (Howard 2014, 125). I would suggest that these intrinsic binaries within trafficking discourses could be multiplied to include the possibilities of clear dichotomies between victimhood and agency, innocence and complicity, femininity and masculinity, sex and work. In relation to all of these binaries labour trafficking arguably falls on the 'wrong' side of each, so failing to inspire anti-trafficking moral entrepreneurs' engagement. Moreover, in relation to politics 'without', I will argue that the issue of trafficking for labour exploitation fails to reshape states' identities and interests or to provoke state activism given the context of international neo-liberalism and the necessity of exploitable labour to the globalising world economy.

Trafficking for Labour Exploitation as a Neglected Norm

It is safe to say that trafficking for labour exploitation is the 'poor cousin' of the anti-trafficking cause. If resistance to expanding the trafficking definition to include labour issues at the Palermo-producing talks was evident, a little but not much has changed since then. Hila Shamir suggests that the expansion of the global anti-trafficking framework has come at the expense of 'tending to ignore labor trafficking' (Shamir 2012, 79) or at the very least there is a 'passing interest' in labour exploitation issues (van Schendel et al. 2012).

Evidence for this neglect can be demonstrated in several ways. As the introductory chapter to this book demonstrated, trafficking statistics tend to focus on the issue of sexual exploitation. The US State Department's TiP Report, for example, regularly returns the figure that 70–80 % of global trafficking cases relate to the sexual exploitation of women and children. As my introduction intended to make clear, how statistics are gathered in this field depends on many things, including pre-suppositions about what constitutes the problem. Therefore the notion that trafficking is primarily about sexual exploitation pre-determines the terms of reference and so the outcomes of many statistical reports. In Elzbieta Godziak and Micah Bump's overview of published English language empirical studies on human trafficking, they found that 30 out of 39 publications focused on sex trafficking and seven on child trafficking but only three of the sampled studies concerned labour exploitation and only two considered men as trafficking victims (Godziak and Bump 2008). Similarly in Amy Farrell's review of 110 sources on trafficking only 17 were concerned with labour trafficking (Farrell et al. 2009 cited in Zhang 2012, 470). Statistical exercises therefore compound the sense that trafficking is primarily an issue of the sexual exploitation of women and children.

'Common knowledge' about human trafficking is not just constituted through statistical exercises and reports. According to Finnemore and Sikkink's discussion of the norm lifecycle the last stage of the cycle occurs when a new norm acquires the status of common knowledge and this idea will be dwelt on in greater detail in the next and final chapter. However, it suffices to say here that common knowledge is constituted in many ways including popular media accounts, as well as fictional and cultural representations of human trafficking. In the main, media and cultural representations of human trafficking reiterate the notion that trafficking is primarily about sexual exploitation. Popular journalistic accounts of the issue, such as Victor Malarek's *The Natashas* (2004) and Nicholas Kristof and Sheryl WuDunn's *Half the Sky* (2010), are exclusively concerned with sex trafficking. Cultural representations in film and television productions reprise the same fixation with sex trafficking including *Lilya 4 Ever*, *Eastern Promises* and the *Taken* series.

In terms of moral entrepreneurs, while the influential international coalition CATW describes its mission as 'to end human trafficking in our lifetime' (CATW 2016), the coalition's work is singularly focused on sexual exploitation, prostitution and trafficking. Other organisations campaigning against sex trafficking do show the 'passing interest' in labour issues remarked on by van Schendel et al. (2012). So, for example, a key moral entrepreneur in the field like the International Justice Mission presents its work as dealing with the general violence of exploitation in many developing world contexts. However, their key activities—to rescue and restore victims—do centre on people they deem to be victims of sex trafficking and prostitution. In Kemala Kempadoo's critical analysis of trends in contemporary anti-trafficking activism she notes the prevalence of 'anti-slavery activists' who are predominantly 'white, male, middle class "rescuers" of "uncivilized people"', and while they are not exclusively focused on the sex trade, these groups give much attention to 'women and girls in what is identified as forced prostitution'. The other two obvious trends she identifies in anti-trafficking activism—feminist abolitionism and celebrity endorsements—are also chiefly concerned with sex trafficking (Kempadoo 2015).

On the issue of state socialisation into norms, the adoption of new frameworks and laws surrounding labour trafficking has often been slower than those concerning sexual exploitation. In some of the case study countries referred to in the earlier chapters this is very marked. Sweden, so often seen as the leading light in anti-trafficking activism by many, only added a legal prohibition on labour trafficking belatedly in 2004, several years after the anti-sex trafficking justification was given as a reason for supporting the adoption of the sex purchase ban. The issue still receives comparatively little attention or law enforcement activity in Sweden (Hulting 2012). During the Bush administration years, as we saw in Chap. 3, sex trafficking, prostitution politics and the anti-prostitution pledge predominated in the US understanding of the problem. In the UK, early anti-trafficking legislation in 2002 dealt with sex trafficking and trafficking for forced labour was only addressed in 2007 (Anderson 2013, 141). In Ireland, although lifting Palermo language into law meant labour trafficking joined the statute books along with sex trafficking in 2008, a lack of clarity about the meaning of forced labour in the law was only rectified in 2013 when new legislation was passed that adopted the International Labour Organization's definition of forced labour, as well as including other provisions such as extending trafficking to include forced begging (Darcy 2013). Writing of criminal investigations into cases of trafficking, Anne Gallagher finds another instance of this in-built bias towards sex trafficking in relation to victim identification. Of 44,758 potential victims identified globally in 2013, only 20 % were victims of labour exploitation, showing in her words that 'the old tired idea of trafficking—as being solely about sexual exploitation—is alive and well' (Gallagher 2015b, 65).

The evidence above is not intended to occlude the existence of work on the issue of trafficking for labour exploitation, which has emerged more recently in the contexts of politics, moral entrepreneurship, the production of common knowledge and academic research. As one example, political shifts can swing attention somewhat towards broader labour abuses. During the lifetime of the Obama Administration the State Department's Office to Monitor and Combat Trafficking in Persons' focus in relation to trafficking expanded to include concerns about exploitation in global supply chains, with reports and activism on the issue heightened (see for example the Verite 2015 report to the OMCTP). Cultural representations of labour trafficking do exist in films such as Crash (2004), which begins with a scene involving imprisoned male Asian workers in a van in Los Angeles who are bought and sold between protagonists in the film. This is a portrayal intended to create 'a strong impression of trafficking for forced labour' in the minds of viewers (Quayson and Arlim 2012, 2). The International Labour Organization is one example of an international body that now incorporates the issue into its work. A survey of ILO reports over the last 15 years shows an exponential increase in references to labour trafficking in its research output, from a small base of less than ten publications per year through the 1990s to 11 publications in 2000 and then a steady and ever increasing rise to 256 in 2015 (International

Labour Organization 2016). Also over recent years, some of the moral entrepreneurs referred to in earlier chapters, like the Global Alliance Against Traffic in Women (GAATW) and La Strada International, have ever more consciously framed their concerns as being with all forms of trafficking and insist on analyses that relate trafficking to broader labour and migration issues (La Strada International 2016a; GAATW 2016a), although for GAATW the emphasis of their project work remains on women's migration and the particular problems they encounter in the sex industry and domestic service (GAATW 2016b). Moreover, both emphasise the need for a human rights framework to counter trafficking, yet as a means of tackling labour exploitation this has some drawbacks. As Hila Shamir points out the emphasis on human rights individualises the issues (such as La Strada's campaign for compensation for individual victims of trafficking, see La Strada 2016b) and while this 'certainly extends some assistance to trafficked persons, it fails to deal with the economic, social, and legal conditions that create workers' vulnerability to exploitation' (Shamir 2012, 80). This is an important point to be revisited later in this chapter.

There is also academic work consciously trying to break the grip of obsession with trafficking for sexual exploitation. As one example, I was part of a European Science Foundation-funded research project aiming to discover and analyse evidence of trafficking in industries other than the sex industry in several European countries funded under the European Science Foundation's EUROCORES research programme in 2005. This project explicitly intended to 'address the fact that so far the identification, assistance and protection strategies for victims of trafficking are designed almost exclusively to address the needs of persons trafficked into the sex industry. Project outcomes...should improve the understanding of the issue of trafficking for labour exploitation and ensure that it is mainstreamed in the EU' (European Science Foundation 2005). A key publication following that project is Human Rights and Migration: Trafficking for Forced Labour edited by the ESF project's principal investigator, Christien van den Anker and Ilse van Liempt (2012). Across the contributors' chapters details emerge of exploitative practices endured particularly by migrant workers in sectors such as domestic work, catering, agriculture and informal markets in many European countries. Despite the project's determination to broaden the discourse about trafficking beyond the sex industry it is notable that several chapters in the book recognise that it is an uphill struggle to extend the discourse because government projects and international funding (see for example, Cezaru Nanu on Moldova) or the institutional environment and media portrayals (Madeleine Hulting on Sweden) all focus on sex trafficking. Importantly too—and this will be discussed in more detail below—a key issue for the researchers in all the countries involved was making sense of the concept of labour trafficking and the related issue of defining exploitation (van den Anker and van Liempt 2012, 8). Given the three-pronged legal definition of trafficking, vagueness on exploitation, the complexity of many migrant workers' experiences and their own subjectivity concerning their journeys and working conditions, it was difficult to determine where on 'a continuum of exploitation' (Coghlan and Wylie 2012, 131) many people found themselves and whether trafficking for forced labour was ever simple to discern or a useful concept in terms of challenging exploitative situations.

In more recent years, there is an increasing body of academic studies discussing and critically analysing the presence of labour trafficking in industries such as quarrying in west Africa (Howard 2014), football migration from Africa to Europe (Essen 2015a and 2015b), domestic work in Asia, the Middle East and Europe (Huling 2012; Vlieger 2012; Vivar 2012) and agriculture (Palumbo and Sciurba 2015), to name just a few. They too tend to raise complex questions about the utility of framing all labour exploitation as trafficking given the complicated situations many migrant workers find themselves in. As Neil Howard argues, trafficking discourses rely on clear binaries, i.e. that we can demarcate between consent and coercion, normal work and abusive conditions, legitimate work and exploitation. Yet, people's realities are full of ambiguity and contingency and always framed by the structural context in which they exist, as Howard found out in his interviews with adolescent boys working in the tough conditions of African quarries. While NGOs labelled these kids as trafficked, the boys rejected this designation and avoided engagement with anti-trafficking interventions. They explained that they opted for this labour over farm work and the chance quarrying brings for gaining cash earnings, resources for families and social status associated with manhood (Howard 2014, 125–131).

In this section the strong predominance of the issue of sex trafficking throughout trafficking studies, knowledge, activism, politics, legal architecture and law enforcement has been illustrated. Yet the section also shows that, when attention does turn to labour issues, the re-emergence occurs of some of the familiar difficulties we already encountered about the meaning and stability of the anti-trafficking norm. The complexity around issues of conceptualisation and definition, questions of human agency versus structural constraints and debates over policy responses that mark all trafficking discussions surface once again. All of these points will necessarily be returned to as this chapter develops explanations for the general neglect of labour trafficking in comparison to sex in the anti-trafficking norm lifecycle. To develop these explanations, I will first return to the literature about norms in international politics and theories developed to explain norm neglect.

The Causes of Norm Neglect

There is a tendency in writing about norms to focus on norms that work. Attention is focused on ideals and values that inspire moral entrepreneurs, who then frame their ideas so compellingly and lobby so energetically that intersecting global and local socialisation processes kick in and state identities and interests eventually change. Yet, as Krook and True remind us, 'not all norms will gain salience' (2012, 112). By way of example Chap. 2 referred to Charli Carpenter's discussion of the lack of norm emergence regarding responsibility towards babies born of war rape (2007) despite huge international civil and political interest in the issue of sexual violence in warfare over the last decades. Carpenter's point continues to ring true. The issue of sexual violence in warfare has become increasingly salient, as epitomised by the global summit in London in 2014 on the issue spearheaded by William Hague for the British government and Angelina Jolie (UK Government 2014). Yet the fate of babies born of rape in war is still not an issue attracting much attention. Carpenter explained this neglect with reference to the internal politics of NGOs and the turf wars and resource allocation decisions that preclude involvement in all issues that might be of relevance to campaigners. Other authors were cited in Chap. 1 as pointing towards more conventional statist interests in keeping normative concerns from growing salient. One example was Jeffrey Legro's discussion of how the utility of certain weaponry for states silenced moral concerns around their usage (1997).

Further analyses of failures to promote or change norms offer additional and alternative explanations as to why some norms do not gain traction. Material power does not always lead to norm change or neglect as Vincent Keating shows in his work on the Bush administration's attempts to change international prohibitions against torture in favour of accepting the legitimacy of 'enhanced interrogation techniques' to pursue the 'war on terror'. His research demonstrates that existing normative commitments held by the liberal state allies the Bush administration was trying to persuade were not so easily swayed despite the material power of the US. Prevailing human rights frameworks and a strong evidence base contradicting the utility of torture led to resistance to normative change by US allies such as France and Germany (Keating 2014). Similarly the push for a universal international reproductive rights norm or a globally agreed definition of what constitutes reproductive health has also proven problematic. Although pressed from feminist standpoints at UN conferences such as Beijing and Cairo, 'the language and the idea of reproductive health never enjoyed consensus' because contested notions about the meaning of life and the admissibility of abortion prevent normative consensus between states, religious communities and civil society organisations (Yoshihara 2012–2013).

Each of these cases relates to failures of norm salience, yet they do all point to different reasons why certain ideals flounder. Sometimes the reasons relate to politics within the community of moral entrepreneurs where certain ideas may not inspire intense activism or where no consensus can be reached. Other times norm failure relates to the unshakeable resonance of pre-existing normative commitments and at others it stems from the material power of states to determine whether norm change is in their interests or not. The answer to the question of norm neglect therefore probably lies in the complex intersection of some or all of the above and it certainly needs to be discussed with reference to the particularities of each case where norms fail to fly. The sections below will relate these broad brush strokes, which bring up a range of factors relating to politics 'within' and 'without', to the particular case study of trafficking for labour exploitation, which in terms of norm salience, as was shown above, pales into insignificance compared to the normative entrepreneurship and successful socialisation of states surrounding trafficking for sexual exploitation.

Labour Exploitation: Challenging the Sexing and Gendering of Trafficking

One of the theories about why some norms do not find salience, as suggested by Keating above, relates to the difficulty of challenging a well-established framing of an issue and the normative values associated with it. In relation to human trafficking, despite the move to broaden the definition in the Palermo Protocol, trafficking was and remains primarily associated with the sexual exploitation of women and children. This is an understanding of the issue that is hard to budge because it bears the gravitas of long usage, beginning with the late nineteenth-century white slavery panic and extending from there. As Gretchen Soderlund suggests the association of trafficking with sexual exploitation may have been 'first popularized in 1880s England, but by the twentieth century's first decade (it) became deeply embedded in the Western imaginary such that even today the term "trafficking" (and, increasingly, "prostitution") connotes sexual enslavement, captive innocents, and mercenary villains' (Soderlund 2011, 194). The 1949 UN Convention consolidated these associations and anti-sex trafficking activists from CEDAW to Beijing to Palermo have capitalised on this predominant take on the issue. In these few lines we read again that historically and enduringly trafficking is essentially understood to be something that affects women, who are primarily pictured as innocent victims of sexual exploitation in the form of prostitution. By referring back to Howard's insights about the dualities intrinsic to trafficking discourses, it is possible to deduce what trafficking is generally not understood to be from the silences around the other sides of this essential definition. So, it can be surmised that in common understanding trafficking is not something affecting men or anyone who cannot be imagined to be 'innocent', nor does it readily encompass other forms of exploitation. In one bald example of the difficulty of expanding definitions of trafficking beyond 'innocent' women, coercion and sex, Pardis Mahdavi writes that in her public presentations on trafficking to audiences of NGOs and policy makers she is often met with incredulous responses to her assertion that men are trafficked and subject to forced labour (Mahdavi 2014).

Such incredulity about men and other forms of forced labour as trafficking does stem from historical usage but also from prevailing gendered notions of agency, victimhood and innocence. In the socially constructed world of dichotomous gender relations, men and masculinity are stereotypically associated with possessing power over others, exercising agency and acting rationally, whereas women and femininity form the other halves of these dyads, associated with seeking empowerment, being enmeshed in relationships and subject to emotions (Hutchings 2008). In the field of international politics, for example, the core subject matter concerns war, weaponry, geo-politics and strategy. Feminist IR scholars' interventions over the last few decades reveal that in focusing on this core, mainstream IR scholars are in effect describing a world ruled by men and so 'presume a male and masculine subject position' as the agents of international political life. In this situation of male power hierarchy, the international political world lauds the exercise of the 'man-shaped' qualities of rational calculation and self-interest in the pursuit of state interests (Carver 2014, 116). This analysis of a masculine power hierarchy and the valourisation of male values in international politics is an important revelation made by feminist scholars in the field. Equally too this allows for a recognition of women's subordinate positioning in the power-driven world of international politics and the ways gendered institutions and expectations perpetuate this relative powerlessness. The work of scholars such as Cynthia Enloe have been key in identifying the spaces inhabited by women in international politics and writing in their neglected importance in the functioning of global economy, military practices and diplomatic life (Enloe 2014).

These are helpful analyses in many ways, undertaking long overdue work about the ways in which gendered power relations and attributes shape the international world. Yet there is a danger that in some renderings such analyses also contain and perpetuate a lack of awareness of differences amongst men and amongst women by offering a rigidly binary reading of the gendered power order in global politics. For example, a radical feminist analysis of global politics stresses the omnipresence of male power and the global subordination of women. As Janet Halley summarised this viewpoint, 'everything about the relationship of males to females manifests domination and subordination' (Halley 2006, 33–57 and 27). Contemporary gender studies however show more awareness of the fluidity of gendered lives across different times and places and challenge the necessary coupling of 'sexed bodies' with particular performances of gender. Third World or post-colonial feminism offers one retort to the assumed unity of experience amongst women, pointing out the power differentials and diverse interests between women across the globe on the basis of intersecting identities of nation, race, poverty and colonial legacies (Parpart and Zalewski 2008). With regard to men, the assumption that masculinity confers power and agency on all persons possessing male bodies is rife in many feminist analyses, but equally problematic. Writing of prevailing academic discourses about development, Adam Jones finds a dynamic at play whereby gender and development theories (usually referred to in the literature by the acronym 'GAD') generally reiterate women's oppression and assume male power, failing to pay attention to the complex lives of 'ordinary (and extraordinary) men in the global South' and relaying stereotypes that depict men's relationships with women as universally 'exploitative and aggressive' (Jones 2006, xviii).

As with the post-colonial feminist analysis of women, more nuanced thinking would acknowledge 'differences among men and different kinds of masculinities', including the existence of hegemonic and subordinated masculinities across time, place and context without losing sight of on-going gender inequalities' (Gutmann 1997, 398).

Although post-colonial feminisms and contemporary masculinity studies suggest that the gendered realities of peoples' lives are complex, the legacy of those earlier and more straightforward gender and feminist analyses that depict dichotomous divisions of power, characteristics and attributes between two distinct genders is still very salient in everyday discourses and expectations about gender around the world. They have certainly left their mark in relation to trafficking discourse and politics.

In most depictions of human trafficking men are assumed to be the traffickers, not the trafficked. Victor Malarek (2004) and Siddharth Kara (2009) among others who have produced investigative journalism or popular academic research into human trafficking, almost unfailingly depict men as perpetrators. In Malarek's *The Natashas*, for example, the victims of post-Soviet trafficking rings are all innocent and duped women sold into prostitution, whereas the perpetrators are manly 'sweaty goons' of post-Soviet mafia style outfits (Malarek 2004). Such depictions perpetuate Western stereotypes of Eastern Europe as the slightly less civilised 'demi-orient' to West European normality (Wolff 1994), while also reflecting gendered notions in relation to trafficking. In such notions men cannot be victims. Adam Jones detects the existence of a similar trope in his work on men in the global South, where he notes that academic discourses about gender and development are incapable of imagining male vulnerability. By way of exemplification, Jones undertook a search engine survey of GAD literature that produced 28,500 references to 'women's vulnerability', compared to only 291 for the phrase 'men's vulnerability' (Jones 2006, xiv).

Written in to these striking figures is the dichotomous expectation that while men are ascribed agency, women are universally expected to be vulnerable by virtue of their place in the gendered power hierarchy. With vulnerability comes the possibility of victimhood and because trafficking definitions require that the victim be utterly deceived, coerced and then innocently subject to their exploitative experiences, prevailing gendered assumptions about power and agency play against the identification of men as victims. Given these normative gendered assumptions about female vulnerability and male agency, it is little surprise that the label 'victim of trafficking' is rarely ascribed to men (Allais 2013, 45).

Undoubtedly many migrant men do find themselves in labour situations that could be described as exploitative, in agriculture, construction, catering, fishing or sex industries to name but a few. Yet, their cases are not often investigated as ones of human trafficking as evidenced by the poor representation of male victims and labour exploitation cases in overall trafficking investigations, as noted with reference to Anne Gallagher's article earlier. Rather, because men are ascribed agency in popular gendered imaginings, they are more often presumed by state agencies to be 'illegal' migrants or smuggled people who are culpable in their own irregular migration and responsible for their own fate, rather than 'innocent' and 'vulnerable' trafficking victims. In effect 'gender biases result in men not being identified as victims of trafficking' (Allais 2013, 45). Interestingly too, as Van den Anker and van Liempt (2012) point out, it is not just state agents or anti-trafficking NGOs that operate out of these gendered assumptions but men who find themselves in exploitative labour situations rarely associate themselves with the label 'victim of trafficking' as they too are imbued with gendered norms which socialise 'men to endure' and not consider themselves victims.

The paragraphs above have explored the workings of some of the binaries underpinning trafficking discourses and how they create obstacles to expanding the anti-trafficking norm to recognise that men (or indeed people who do not fit into rigid gender categories) could be considered vulnerable to trafficking. Gendered expectations about masculinity and femininity and imaginings related to them of agency, innocence and victimhood militate against recognising men as trafficked. A further binary militating against the generation of moral entrepreneurship around labour exploitation is the impact of dichotomous thinking about sex and work.

For exciting moral fervour, debates about sex and norms are perhaps hard to equal. In her inspired article title, Alexis Peters suggests that 'Things that involve sex are just different' (Peters 2013). Writing of the passage of the US Trafficking Victims Protection Act she reveals that law to be 'a rich cultural text, reflecting social and political anxieties over prostitution, victimisation and women's sexuality'. Although the TVPA does deal with all kinds of trafficking, it makes a distinction between 'sex trafficking' and 'non-sex trafficking' and so ends up privileging the former and diverting attention away from 'other labour sectors' and 'men all together'. What this also reveals is that in the culture of the alliance between the Bush administration, radical feminists and Christian evangelicals, sexual exploitation is understood as 'uniquely horrid' (Peters 2013, 222–235).

For radical feminists, as we saw in Chap. 3, prostitution is at heart a form of violence against women. It involves an attack on the integrity of women's bodies that cannot genuinely be consented to when considered in the light of women's wholesale subordination in gendered power relations. From this perspective sexual exploitation is not comparable to exploitative conditions in other forms of work. Agriculture, construction, catering, fishing and so on, are forms of work in which exploitation, even incidences of violence, might happen—but they are not expressions of violence in themselves. It is for these reasons that neo-abolitionists resist the very terms 'sex work' and 'sex workers' due to the apparent legitimacy they confer by giving the dignity of 'work' to what they understand to be violence (Shamir 2012). Frankly put, 'prostitution is not and never can be work' for neo-abolitionists (Anderson 2013, 147). Resistance to broadening understandings of 'exploitative ends' to encompass other forms of work has therefore been marked or only grudgingly accepted from neo-abolitionist quarters. Chapter 3 also recounted the debates around this point between the two feminist coalitions at Palermo. Although the Palermo definition was broad enough in the end to include various kinds of exploitation, the practice of anti-trafficking architecture and activism continues to privilege sex over labour rather than treating sex as labour.

This discussion of resistance from some quarters to norm expansion suggests that Charli Carpenter's point is valid. Turf wars and gatekeeping by forceful lobbyists can result in norm neglect and so are of relevance in explaining the failure to develop a strong normative framework concerning trafficking for labour exploitation. Yet, another reason is also to be found in the very difficulty of deciding when labour conditions are so exploitative that they might be defined as constituting 'trafficking'. This brings us to another of the dichotomies in trafficking discourses, the possibility—or impossibility—of dividing forced from free work (Anderson 2013, 147).

Exploitation and Work

As has been argued in earlier chapters, the threefold definition of human trafficking is always hard to operationalise. Proving that movement under conditions of deception and coercion for exploitative ends has occurred to someone is complex. In relation to labour trafficking defining exploitation is particularly challenging.

The idea that work under capitalist conditions involves a degree of exploitation has a long provenance. Most famously it was central to Karl

Marx's discussion of unequal class relations. Exploitation was both a descriptive and normative term for Marx. It was descriptive in capturing the reality of capitalism—people's labour being bought and used to create profit for others—and normative in criticising the potential injustices of this system (Warren 2015, 287). This double meaning, which suggests labour relations are by definition exploitative while such exploitation can be bad, implies that it is hard to determine where unacceptable exploitation begins. From a liberal perspective the same dilemma exists but from a different analysis. A liberal market should enable all to choose employment freely but the reality is that all kinds of personal and structural constraints limit freedom of choice. Liberalism aims to draw a clear line between forced and free labour (Anderson 2013, 147), yet such delineation is hard to pin down in reality. Whatever philosophical angle we begin from, it can be said that most of us who work exist somewhere on a 'continuum of exploitation' (Skrivankova 2010) between the relative freedom of a chosen career and good working conditions—but still beholden to expectations of bosses and varying terms and conditions of employment—through degrees of exploitation to outright slavery. The question is how to identify where in this spectrum conditions become so poor that the degree of exploitation is unacceptable and 'labour trafficking' might even be said to exist. The International Labour Organization, for example, grapples with this problem by using the concept of a 'forced labour continuum' to try to classify the experiences of workers (van Schendel et al. 2012, 10).

This was certainly a conundrum we encountered in the ESF EUROCORES research project on trafficking in industries other than the sex industry, which was mentioned above. In the Irish context we found that for some of our interviewees (who included service providers, trade unionists, labour inspectors and law enforcement officials), labour conditions in some industries, such as fruit picking, circus work and catering, were by definition extremely arduous and therefore whether the exploitation experienced by migrant workers was unacceptable or even possibly definable as trafficking for forced labour was indeterminable (Coghlan and Wylie 2011, 1522). Interestingly for the Polish research team, interviews with migrant workers themselves showed that although conditions were appalling the workers did not consider themselves exploited. This surfaced in discussions with irregular migrant workers from Vietnam who accepted that their first years working in informal street trading in Poland would be extremely harsh until they became established in the hierarchy of the shadow economy (Szulecka 2012). As these workers own opinions so poignantly reveal 'framing all forms of exploitation...as "trafficking" ignores the agency of migrant workers' (van Schendel et al. 2012, 11).

Child labour may seem the simpler case to take in relation to recognising exploitation. Yet even among child workers a complex intersection of the structural constraints they live within and the children's own agency emerges in ethnographic research. This was already referred to in relation to Neil Howard's studies concerning adolescent miners in African quarries. Similarly, ethnographic research by Roy Huijsmans and Simon Baker concerning adolescent girls moving across the Lao-Thai border in the Greater Mekong Sub-region of Asia to work as nannies, shop assistants and karaoke bar hostesses shows the 'complex subject positions' of young people in relation to exploitative working conditions (Huijsmans and Baker 2012, 935–937). In all these cases the young people involved existed in local cultural contexts where maturity comes before 18 and where changing economic possibilities and expectations around provision for households and migration led them to make certain choices in relation to work. They did not self-define as victims or trafficked children.

While it is very hard to define a clear line between free and forced labour and between consent and coercion, it is not the case that ethically this should allow us to abandon the cause of trying to define when exploitation is unacceptable and what norms of 'decent work' need to be established and defended locally or globally. Establishing such norms should not be beyond the bounds of possibility and certainly there are plenty of ILO conventions, international rights based conventions (such as the UN Convention on the Rights of Migrant Workers and their Families) and local laws on working conditions, which should make 'decent work' realisable. The problem is that many of these frameworks are honoured in the breach. As is well known, for example, the UN Convention on the Rights of Migrant Workers is poorly signed and not ratified. The 37 signatories are all migrant-sending states of the global South not the migrant-receiving states of the global North (UN Treaty Collection 1990). And here lies another reason for the failure of a norm lifecycle to emerge in relation to trafficking for labour exploitation. As Legro put forward, norm neglect can also be the result of a failure by states to see their interests being met in a new norm (1997). With regard to preventing trafficking for labour exploitation, it is not in many states' interests to promote such a norm or allow themselves to be socialised into it. The workings of global neo-liberal capitalism and its accompanying migration regime militate against this, as will be discussed in the section below.

Trafficking for Forced Labour in the Context of Global Economics and Security

One of the downsides of human trafficking discourses, according to Hila Shamir, is that emphasis on the fate of trafficked persons and the associated impetus to rescue victims has individualised responses to issues of migration and exploitation and so turned attention away from a necessary analysis of root causes. For Shamir the existing anti-trafficking framework 'fails to deal with the economic, social and legal conditions that create workers' vulnerability to exploitation' (Shamir 2012, 80). These conditions emerge largely as a consequence of neo-liberal globalisation and its economic and political manifestations. It can be argued that because many states benefit from the workings of globalisation, anti-labour trafficking architecture and activism get neglected.

Globalisation is a term coined to capture and analyse the sense that we are now living in a 'runaway world' (Giddens 2003). While global interactions are nothing new, post-Cold War international politics, marked by the end of ideological blocs and the augury of probable world dominance by Western ideals and capitalism, seemed to require a new conceptualisation. The phrase 'globalisation' was invented to describe, analyse and also often criticise the near universal spread of free market ideals and neo-liberal economics and associated expectations around the growing reach of democratisation and political liberalism. The concept of globalisation also tries to capture the novel speed and intensity of connections across time and space, the cultural effects of world-shrinking technology and media and the impact all this has on people's senses of identity and security as they are affected by living in a world where traditional ways of life and physical borders appear to be eroding.

Contemporary globalisation is very much premised upon economic neo-liberalism. This is an economic theory and its ensuing policy prescriptions that originated in the academic work, such as that of the Chicago School from the 1940s onwards, but gained political bite because of its adoption by governments in the 1980s. Neo-liberalism postulates the necessity of freeing markets and rolling back state interventions in economy and social welfare because such policies are seen as the means to secure economic growth and create enterprising societies. The 'Washington Consensus' in favour of neo-liberalism, as adopted by the International Monetary Fund and the World Bank from the 1980s onwards, ensured that this model became a key underpinning of globalisation processes (Holton 2005).

In order to realise the twin ideals of market liberalisation and state diminution, neo-liberal globalisation requires the dismantling of barriers to economic freedom and mobility. Thus the globalising world is imagined as increasingly 'borderless' (Diener and Hagen 2009). Financial transactions happen round the clock because markets are always open somewhere, economically protectionist measures are increasingly taboo, transnational corporations manifest their presence in many places simultaneously and new technologies enable constant communication globally.

Yet globalisation contains a great contradiction (Munck 2008). While goods, services, currencies, information and companies all move freely in the globalising world, people do not. Simply put, the world is not borderless for everyone. The apparent freedoms of globalisation are regulated by exclusionary migration regimes put in place by governments of the global North. These migration regimes sometimes take obvious forms, such as the external regulation of EU borders through FRONTEX operations around 'fortress Europe' or even physical barriers like fences in the borderlands between Mexico and the US, but they are also manifest in complex legal categorisation of migrants (as skilled or unskilled workers, regular or irregular migrants, trafficked or smuggled people and so on), which operate to create 'desirable' and 'undesirable' entrants to states.

In such ways migration regimes 'discipline the transnational mobility of people' (Geiger and Pécoud 2013). Economically, migration restrictions such as travel visas and work permit rules effectively structure labour mobility in the globalising context. This manifests in several ways. For instance there is the categorisation of 'skilled' and 'unskilled' workers, which operates to determine which workers' movements will be legally facilitated. Those from the global South deemed to be 'skilled' might be 'cherry-picked' for regularised access to the global North but those considered to be 'unskilled' are prevented from moving legally. So, for example, in Ireland the economic boom years of the late 1990s to early 2000s were enabled by an unprecedented openness to economic in-migration by the Irish state (Fanning 2010) but this was emphatically geared to seeking out fellow EU citizens first and only then allowing workers with requisite education and skill levels to migrate from beyond Europe. When workers were of necessity recruited to 'low-skilled work' in, for example, agricultural labour, visas and work permits were so restrictive that movement between employers or the possibility of long-term stay was highly circumscribed.

The disciplining of global labour mobility works to the benefit of companies and consumers too. Many corporations operate global supply chains that end in the labour-intensive extractive or manufacturing sectors of the global South. Poor social protections (as required by the neo-liberal economic model) and restricted migratory possibilities ensure a supply of workers who provide cheap goods, services and low wage bills for powerful economic actors and consumers (Bang 2013). Feminist international political economy has effectively demonstrated the gendered nature of some of these supply chains, such as the reliance on women's 'unskilled' labour in the tax-free maquiladoras of the Mexican side of the US border (Bachour 2015). Recent assessment of the maquiladoras suggests that after a massive expansion in the 1990s, the sector has impacted negatively on welfare and the development of skilled workers in Mexico (Heid et al. 2013).

On the other side of these global labour dynamics, those who desire or are compelled to migrate but are unable to secure legal entry to developed economies tend to end up working in shadow economies. In effect workers with the status of 'irregular' or 'undocumented' migrants constitute a 'reserve army of labour' made docile in the face of their fear of deportation should they come to the attention of the authorities (Khosravi 2012, 51). For example, although 'irregular migrants' are entitled to their very fundamental rights—such as basic health care—those in undocumented situations are wary of accessing these rights. Sharam Khosravi tells of one undocumented friend who died from a heart condition rather than draw attention to his family's irregular status (Khosravi 2011). What is more, these people generally work in the 3D industries, those that are considered dirty, dangerous or demeaning. Often they are care workers, domestic workers or kitchen workers dealing with the waste products of developed societies. It is both because they are dealing with waste and are consigned by their irregular status to living on the margins of society that Zygmunt Baumann refers to such people as the 'human waste' of globalisation (Baumann 2004).

It is their positioning in the contradictions of globalisation that makes many migrant workers (or 'low skilled' workers in general) vulnerable to exploitation, forced labour and practices that might be defined as trafficking. In the case study of Ireland we undertook for the EUROCORES project, for example, it was clear that people's vulnerability to exploitative labour conditions often related to their undocumented migration status and their lack of work permits and visas. Even those who held permits were exploitable, as movement away from deplorable working conditions was made impossible by the fact that employers held the work permits (Coghlan and Wylie 2011). Such status meant that undocumented migrants were often (though not always) silent in the face of unacceptable conditions. More recent cases in Ireland concerning alleged abuses against domestic staff in diplomatic households again show the vulnerability created by other migration regulations. Because of diplomatic immunity such households are exempt from local legal provisions, making the workers involved virtually unreachable (Migrant Rights Centre Ireland 2011). Likewise studies of domestic workers in a range of countries such as Germany, Saudi Arabia and Malaysia show that positioning in the 'black economy' and the privacy of homes, accompanied by a lack of legal protections, creates scenarios where exploitation is almost 'the standard labour condition' (Vlieger 2012, 180).

As each of these examples shows, by simultaneously encouraging economic liberalisation while disciplining labour mobility, the complex workings of globalisation create conditions for many people that could be labelled as trafficking or exploitation. Because many people for economic or political reasons are driven to migrate and look for work, they strategise irregular means of migration creating 'complex (unruly and new) patterns of international movement' (Conway and Heynen 2006, 13), which so often end up in the shadow worlds of 'illegal' status, black economies and precarious labour. However what the examples also show is that such migration regimes work to the benefit of many states, companies and consumers by providing cheap and quiet workers. As Karen Bravo writes, 'states outsource to the human smuggler-trafficker their own labor recruitment function. That is, while the state enacts and enforces anti-immigrant and anti-mobility laws, human smuggler-traffickers "informally" supply the demands of domestic labor markets for low-cost and compliant labor' (Bravo 2015, 28). And this is not necessarily only the case for Northern states and consumers in receipt of migrant workers but also states that send them. The Philippines, for example, has long encouraged migration as a source of remittances and national development (the policy of 'bagong bayani'). Though domestic concerns about the exploitation of such workers has grown in recent years, replacing discourses about the 'heroism' of migrant workers with concerns over their potential 'martyrdom' (Tigus 2012, 28), the reliance on these workers' economic returns prevents strong political action on their behalves. The benefits that sending and receiving countries accrue from this situation are tantamount, in Alice Huling's opinion, to enabling 'state conditioned expressions of human trafficking' (Huling 2012, 640).

It is not, however, just for economic reasons that states are interested in the attempt to discipline the transnational mobility of people. Physical traversing of borders may be one last thing states can try to control in the 'runaway world'. Therefore, regulating movement across borders allows states to present to their populations the idea that they are securing them against the unruliness of the outside world. Migration restrictions are therefore strongly related to the political aims and rhetoric surrounding national identity preservation, crime control and state security. In this context, human trafficking discourses are used by states to this end. As Claudia Aradau summarises, politicians make use of trafficking discourses for two purposes. The first is to stir up a 'politics of pity' and suggest the need to respond to or rescue individual trafficking victims. As Shamir (2012) underlines, this individualisation detracts attention from the kind of political and economic structures that cause exploitation and have been under discussion here. The second purpose is to prompt a 'politics of fear' and so legitimise the need to close borders and manage migration (Aradau 2004). The association of human trafficking with the supposed connections drawn between irregular migration, organised crime and security threat is now a frequent part of states' discourses in the contemporary world. In this light, tackling trafficking becomes a crucial element of states' rationales for tightening border controls. The development of 'common knowledge' that trafficking and migration are security threats is now well embedded, with many unforeseen consequences for those migrating. Chapter 7 will develop this final discussion about human trafficking, common knowledge and negative consequences.

Conclusion

In a book concerned with tracing the lifecycle of the human trafficking norm, the issue of trafficking for labour exploitation presents an anomaly. While human trafficking has excited so much concern, activism and architecture building, the real impetus for the lifecycle comes from activism and politics around the issue of trafficking for sexual exploitation. As this chapter shows, this is evident in respect to the weight of moral entrepreneurship, the statistics collected, the focus of research agendas and state socialisation as reflected in legal frameworks, policy implementation and policing efforts.

To understand why the labour exploitation aspect of the human trafficking issue is the subject of norm neglect, this chapter first explored some theories derived from other case studies in which particular normative issues have not provoked lifecycles and then related them to the labour issue. Those studies implied that norms might not gain traction if settled normative understandings are too well embedded, if moral entrepreneurs are uninspired or conflicted, or if the material interests of states militate against the lifecycle developing. The relative neglect of the issue of labour exploitation can be explained with reference to each of these elements. The historic association of trafficking with the sexual exploitation of women and girls, the impact of broader gendered preconceptions of victimhood, the unwillingness of key entrepreneurs to countenance broader definitions and the contradiction between neo-liberal economic interests and taking measures to end labour exploitation are all elements of an explanation as to why the labour norm does not fly. Exploring the neglect of this norm has also ultimately brought the argument back to the intersection of human trafficking norms and contemporary migration regimes. It is this key conjunction and its consequences that will require further exploration as this book reaches the last stage of the norm lifecycle—the point at which norms become 'taken for granted'.

Bibliography

Allais, C. (2013). The profile less considered: The trafficking of men in South Africa. *South African Review of Sociology, 44*(1), 40–54.

Anderson, B. (2013). *Us and them: The dangerous politics of immigration control.* Oxford: Oxford University Press.

Aradau, C. (2004). The perverse politics of four-letter words: Risk and pity in the securitisation of human trafficking. *Millennium Journal of International Studies, 33*(2), 251–277.

Bachour, M.-K. (2015). Disrupting the myth of Maquila Disposability: Sites of reproduction and resistance in Juárez. *Women's Studies International Forum, 48*, 174–184.

Bang, N. (2013). Unmasking the Charade of the Global Supply Contract: A novel theory of corporate liability in human trafficking and forced labor cases. *Houston Journal of International Law, 35*(2), 255–322.

Baumann, Z. (2004). *Wasted lives: Modernity and its outcasts.* Cambridge: Polity.

Bravo, K. (2015). Interrogating the State's role in human trafficking. *Indiana International and Comparative Law Review, 25*(1), 9–31.

Carpenter, C. (2007). Setting the Advocacy Agenda: Theorizing issue emergence and non-emergence in Transnational Advocacy Networks. *International Studies Quarterly, 51*, 99–120.

Carr, A. (2015, November 3) 'Use of illegal migrants on Irish Trawlers a 'National Disgrace'. *Irish Times.*

Carver, T. (2014). Men and masculinities in International Relations Research. *The Brown Journal of World Affairs, xxi*(1), 113–126.

CATW. (2016). Coalition against trafficking in women: Who we are: Mission. http://www.catwinternational.org/WhoWeAre/Mission, date accessed 5 January 2016.

Coghlan, D., & Wylie, G. (2011). Defining trafficking/Denying justice? Forced labour in Ireland and the consequences of trafficking discourse. *Journal of Ethnic and Migration Studies, 37*(9), 1513–1526.

Coghlan, D., & Wylie, G. (2012). Speaking with a forked tongue: Contrary political discourses and the Irish State's construction of human trafficking. In C. van den Anker & I. van Liempt (Eds.), *Human rights and migration: Trafficking for forced labour.* Palgrave MacMillan: Basingstoke.

Conway, D., & Heynen, N. (2006). *Globalization's contradictions: Geographies of discipline, destruction and transformation.* Abingdon Oxon: Routledge.

Darcy, S. (2013). Irish Companies can now be prosecuted for forced labour. https://businesshumanrightsireland.wordpress.com/2013/07/03/irish-companies-can-now-be-prosecuted-for-forced-labour/, date accessed 5 January 2016.

Diener, A., & Hagen, J. (2009). Theorizing borders in a 'Borderless World': Globalization, territory and identity. *Geography Compass, 3*(3), 1196–1216.

Duncan, P. (2014, September 12). Guidelines issued to protect domestic staff in embassies. *Irish Times.*

Enloe, C. (2014). *Bananas, beaches and bases: Making Feminist Sense of International Politics.* Completely Revised and Updated. Berkley: University of California Press.

Essen, J. (2015a). Escape to victory: Development, youth entrepreneurship and the migration of Ghanaian Footballers. *Geoforum, 64*, 47–55.

Essen, J. (2015b). Better off at home? Rethinking responses to trafficked West African Footballers in Europe. *Journal of Ethnic and Migration Studies, 41*(3), 512–530.

European Science Foundation. (2005). Awarded Projects ECRP 1. http://www.esf.org/coordinating-research/eurocores/completed-programmes/ecrp-i-2005.html, date accessed 5 January 2016.

Fanning, B. (2010). From Developmental Ireland to Migration Nation: Immigration and shifting rules of belonging in the Republic of Ireland. *The Economic and Social Review, 41*(3), 395–412.

Farrell, A., McDevitt, J., Perry, N., Fahy, S., Chamberlain, K., & Adams, W. (2009). *Review of existing estimates of victims of human trafficking in the United States and recommendations for improving research and measurement of human trafficking.* Washington, DC: Humanity United.

GAATW. (2016a). Strategic thematic directions, GAATW. http://www.gaatw.org/what-we-do/2011-2013-strategic-direction, date accessed 5 January 2016.

GAATW. (2016b). Power in Migration and Work Projects 2015. http://www.gaatw.org/190-what-we-do/812-power-in-migration-and-work-projects-in-2015, date accessed 5 January 2016.

Gallagher, A. T. (2015b). Exploitation in migration: Unacceptable but inevitable. *Journal of International Affairs, 68*(2), 55–74.

Geiger, M., & Pécoud, A. (2013). *Disciplining the transnational mobility of people*. Basingstoke: Palgrave MacMillan.

Giddens, A. (2003). *Runaway World: How Globalization is shaping our Lives.* New York: Routledge.

Godziak, E., & Bump, M. (2008). *Data and research on human trafficking: Bibliography of research-based literature*. Georgetown, Washington, DC: Institute for the Study of International Migration, Walsh School of Foreign Service.

Gutmann, M. (1997). Trafficking in MEN: The anthropology of masculinity. *Annual Review of Anthropology, 26*, 385–409.

Halley, J., Kotiswaran, P., Shamir, H., & Thomas, C. (2006). From the International to the local in feminist legal responses to rape, prostitution, sex work and sex trafficking: Four studies in contemporary governance feminism. *Harvard Journal of Law and Gender, 29*, 335–423.

Heid, B., Larch, M., & Riaño, A. (2013). The rise of the Maquiladoras: A mixed blessing. *Review of Development Economics, 17*(2), 252–267.

Holton, R. (2005). *Making globalization*. Basingstoke: Palgrave, MacMillan.

Howard, N. (2014). Teenage Labor Migration and Anti-trafficking Policy in West Africa. *The Annals of the American Academy of Political and Social Science, 653*, 124–140.

Huijsmans, R., & Baker, S. (2012). Child trafficking: 'Worst Form' of child labour, or worst approach to young migrants? *Development and Change, 43*(4), 919–946.

Huling, A. (2012). Domestic workers in Malaysia: Hidden victims of forced labour. *International Law and Politics, 44*, 629–680.

Hulting, M. (2012). Hidden labour: Knowledge production of trafficking illustrated by a Swedish Case Study. In C. van den Anker & I. van Liempt (Eds.), *Human rights and migration: Trafficking for forced labour.* Basingstoke: Palgrave MacMillan.

Hutchings, K. (2008). Cognitive short cuts. In J. Parpart & M. Zalewski (Eds.), *Rethinking the man question: Sex, gender and violence in international relations.* London: Zed Books.

International Labour Organization. (2016). ILO Publications. http://www.ilo.org/Search4/search.do?sitelang=en&locale=en_EN&consumercode=ILOHQ_STELLENT_PUBLIC&searchWhat=ILO+reports+on+human+trafficking&searchLanguage=en, date accessed 4 January 2016.

Irish Times. (2015, April 16). Vietnamese Woman in Trafficking Claim Brings Court Case. *Irish Times.*

Jones, A. (2006). Worlding men. In A. Jones (Ed.), *Men of the Global South.* London: Zed Books.

Kara, S. (2009). *Sex trafficking: Inside the Business of Modern Slavery.* New York: Colombia University Press.

Keating, V. (2014). Contesting the International Illegitimacy of Torture: The Bush Administration's Failure to Legitimate its Preferences within International Society. *British Journal of Politics and International Relations, 16*(1), 1–27.

Kempadoo, K. (2015). The Modern-Day White (Wo)Man's Burden: Trends in anti-trafficking and anti-slavery campaigns. *Journal of Human Trafficking, 1*(1), 8–20.

Khosravi, S. (2011). *'Illegal' Traveller: An auto-ethnography of borders.* Basingstoke: Palgrave MacMillan.

Khosravi, S. (2012). An ethnography of Migrant 'Illegality' in Sweden: Included yet excepted. In C. van den Anker & I. van Liempt (Eds.), *Human rights and migration: Trafficking for forced labour* (pp. 46–68). Basingstoke: Palgrave MacMillan.

Kristof, N., & WuDunn, S. (2010). *Half the sky: How to change the World.* London: Virago.

Krook, M., & True, J. (2012). Rethinking the Lifecycles of International Norms: The United Nations and the Global Promotion of Gender Equality. *European Journal of International Relations, 18*(1), 103–127.

La Strada International (2016a) Home Page, La Strada International, http://lastradainternational.org/, date accessed 5 January 2016.

La Strada. (2016b). COMP.ACT—European Action for Compensation for Trafficked Persons. http://lastradainternational.org/about-lsi/projects/compensation-for-trafficked-persons, date accessed 5 January 2016.

Legro, J. (1997). Which norms matters? Revisiting the failure of internationalism. *International Organization, 51*(1), 31–63.

Mahdavi, P. (2014). *From trafficking to terror: Constructing a global social problem.* New York: Routledge.

Malarek, V. (2004). *The Natashas: The new global sex trade.* Toronto: Viking Books.

Migrant Rights Centre Ireland. (2011). Protecting domestic workers employed by diplomats in Ireland. http://mrci.ie/wp-content/uploads/2012/10/Policy-Paper-Diplomatic-Immunity-2011.pdf, date accessed 24 March 2016.

Munck, R. (2008). Globalisation, governance and migration: An introduction. *Third World Quarterly, 29*(7), 1227–1246.

O'Brien, C. (2009, December 3). Three men jailed for trafficking into Ireland. *Irish Times.*

Palumbo, L., & Sciurba, A. (2015). Vulnerability to forced labour and trafficking: The case of Romanian Women in the Agricultural Sector in Sicily. *Anti-Trafficking Review*, *5*, 1–9. DOI: 10.14197/atr.20121556.

Parpart, J. L., & Zalewski, M. (2008). *Rethinking the man question: Sex, gender and violence in international relations*. London: Zed Books.

Peters, A. (2013). "Things that involve sex are just different": US anti-trafficking law and policy on the books, in their minds, and in action. *Anthropological Quarterly*, *86*(1), 221–256.

Quayson, A., & Arlim, A. (Eds.). (2012). *Labour migration, human trafficking and multinational companies: The commodification of illicit flows*. Abingdon, Oxon: Routledge.

Shamir, H. (2012). A labor paradigm for human trafficking. *UCLA Law Review*, *76*, 78–136.

Skrivankova, K. (2010). *Between decent work and forced labour: Examining the continuum of exploitation*. York: Joseph Rowntree Foundation.

Soderlund, G. (2011). The rhetoric of revelation: Sex trafficking and journalistic expose. *Humanity: An International Journal of Human Rights, Humanitarianism and Development*, *2*(2), 193–211.

Szulecka, M. (2012). The Right to be Exploited: Vietnamese workers in Poland. In C. van den Anker & I. van Liempt (Eds.), *Human rights and migration: Trafficking for forced labour* (pp. 161–192). Basingstoke: Palgrave MacMillan.

The Journal.ie. (2015). Arrest in Donegal 'Highlights need for action on trafficking'. http://www.thejournal.ie/letterkenny-donegal-human-trafficking-investigation-2358973-Sep2015/, date accessed 4 January 2016.

Tigus, J. (2012). Agency by Proxy: Women and human trafficking discourse in the Philippines. In W. L. van Schendel, L. Lyons, & M. Ford (Eds.), *Labour migration and human trafficking in Southeast Asia: Critical Perspectives*. Abingdon Oxon: Routledge.

UK Government. (2014). Global summit to end sexual violence in conflict, 9–13 June. https://www.gov.uk/government/topical-events/sexual-violence-in-conflict, date accessed 9 January 2016.

UN. (1949). Convention for the suppression of the traffic in persons and of the exploitation of the prostitution of others. http://www.ohchr.org/Documents/ProfessionalInterest/trafficpersons.pdf, date accessed 27 February 2015.

UN Treaty Collection. (1990). International convention on the protection of the rights of all migrant workers and members of their families. 18 December 1990, United Nations Treaty Collection. https://treaties.un.org/Pages/ShowMTDSGDetails.aspx?src=UNTSONLINE&tabid=2&mtdsg_no=IV-13&chapter=4&lang=en, date accessed 20 February 2016.

van den Anker, C., & van Liempt, I. (Eds.). (2012). *Human rights and migration: Trafficking for forced labour*. Basingstoke: Palgrave.

van Schendel, W., Lyons, L., & Ford, M. (2012). *Labour migration and human trafficking in Southeast Asia: Critical perspectives*. London: Routledge.

Vivar, M.-T. (2012). The right to always wear a smile: Migration policies and the exploitation of domestic workers 'Labour in Germany'. In C. van den Anker & I. van Liempt (Eds.), *Human rights and migration: Trafficking for forced labour*. Palgrave MacMillan: Basingstoke.

Vlieger, A. (2012). Domestic workers in Saudi Arabia and the Emirates: Trafficking Victims?. *International Migration*, doi. 10.1111/j.1468-2435.2012.00785.x

Warren, P. (2015). In defense of the Marxian Theory of Exploitation: Thoughts on Roemer, Cohen, and Others. *Social Theory and Practice, 41*(2), 286–308.

Wolff, L. (1994). *Inventing Eastern Europe: the Map of Civilization on the Mind of the Enlightenment*. Stanford: Stanford University Press.

Yoshihara, S. (2012–13). Lost in translation: The Failure of the International Reproductive Rights Norm. *Ave Maria Law Review, 11*, 2, 367–409.

Zhang, S. (2012). Measuring labor trafficking: A research note. *Crime Law and Social Change, 58*, 469–482. doi:10.1007/s10611-012-9393-y.

CHAPTER 7

The Far End of the Norm Lifecycle: Common Knowledge and Its Consequences

Introduction

The 'far end' of Finnemore and Sikkink's lifecycle is reached when a norm becomes 'common knowledge'. This is the stage beyond moral entrepreneurship, beyond cascade from the international to the domestic, beyond legal and bureaucratic socialisation within state elites, to the point where the norm has become 'taken for granted' or internalised in societies more broadly (Finnemore and Sikkink 1998, 895). In this closing chapter, I intend to show that in many ways the idea that human trafficking is a pervasive problem and a 'bad thing' needing governance (Walters 2008) is now common knowledge. If 20 years ago very little was said about human trafficking, it is a well-known issue now. For example, in the last weeks of writing this book, I caught a strange item on the radio news. Human feet in sports shoes are being found washing up regularly on the shores of British Colombia. In an interview a local journalist remarked that speculation was rife that this might well be the result of human trafficking. However when DNA analysis identified the feet, it emerged that they all belonged to people whose deaths were sorrowful but unsuspicious, probably the results of suicide. Bizarrely it emerged that modern sports shoe technology possesses remarkable, if gruesome, preservative effects. Among the many striking aspects of this story for me was the automatic assumption that such a case would relate to human trafficking. The concept is so familiar to the listeners

G. Wylie, *The International Politics of Human Trafficking*,
DOI 10.1057/978-1-137-37775-3_7

that it needs no explanation. There is common knowledge that human trafficking is an insidious reality, the trafficked are helpless victims and traffickers are 'the folk devils' (Dagistanli and Milivojevic 2013, 237) of our times.

In this chapter I will suggest that common knowledge about human trafficking is constructed in many ways. As this radio vignette exemplifies, widespread public knowledge about trafficking is implanted in ways beyond the reportage of statistics or the public processes of law making and anti-trafficking architecture building. Common knowledge about the problem and the need for response are constituted through the work of awareness-raising campaigns and training schemes, 'celebritisation' of the cause, cinematic representations, investigative journalism and the association of trafficking with major sporting events, to focus on just a few ways in which wide social knowledge is created. Later in the chapter each of these examples will be expanded upon in relation to their effect on public space, particularly in Europe and the US.

Yet, as has been my emphasis throughout this book, this is not uncontested or stable knowledge. Although the need to oppose human trafficking might now have a 'taken for granted quality' (Finnemore and Sikkink 1998, 904), neat ends to norm lifecycles are unlikely. Debates about the nature and extent of the problem and the best policy responses to it are vociferous, as earlier chapters of this book recount, and norm contestation continues and will persist. However, as this chapter will show some widespread understandings of the problem do become more hegemonic in public imagination than others. Unsurprisingly probably, these relate again to trafficking as a horror that befalls vulnerable women and children, that is perpetrated by masculine organised crime networks and that requires the shoring up of state borders. And crucially, such common knowledge is not neutral but produces and legitimates political consequences. The idea that discourses, policy prescriptions and political actions concerning trafficking have consequences (intended and unintended), particularly for migrants in the globalising world, is a frequent motif throughout this book. I will close this chapter by reiterating this theme and copper-fastening it by analysing how common knowledge about human trafficking is being played out in contemporary international politics by examining how it is used to legitimise securitised responses by European states to the crisis for migrants seeking refuge in Europe in 2015 and 2016.

The Politics of Common Knowledge at the Lifecycle's 'Far End'

Finnemore and Sikkink's discussion of the 'far end' of the norm lifecycle is fairly brief. They suggest that 'norm internalization' occurs when 'norms acquire a taken-for-granted quality and are no longer a matter of broad public debate' and they give a few examples to illustrate the kind of moral consensus they are talking about. 'Few people today discuss whether women should be allowed to vote, whether slavery is useful, or whether medical personnel should be granted immunity during war' (Finnemore and Sikkink 1998, 895). Explaining why such social consensus exists on these particular norms, they suggest that it is because these kinds of issues stir empathetic responses from fellow humans, particularly because they relate to the wounding of vulnerable bodies. And they suggest that such consensus is built not just by elaborating new normative frameworks, but also by their wide habituation through professional training and bureaucratic practices (Finnemore and Sikkink 1998, 905).

Just as with the examples given above, few people today would question whether human trafficking is an abuse of people that requires response. To express any doubts about this would be like questioning the goodness of 'motherhood and apple pie' in Bridget Anderson's words (Anderson 2007, 3). Or as Walters puts it, 'who could possibly be in favour of human trafficking' (Walters 2008, 281)? Echoing Finnemore and Sikkink, it seems as though trafficking constitutes a paradigmatic case of our apparently natural empathetic response to other humans who have been wounded. Because trafficking victims are understood to be innocent people, who are deceived, coerced, moved and exploited (most often sexually), they constitute a classic case of the way in which human responses can be motivated by 'the politics of pity' for others in distress (Aradau 2004). Moreover, as Finnemore and Sikkink suggest, this is also a case where bureaucratic habituation of responses to the problem has evolved. The professionalisation of responses to human trafficking is legion. In the Irish context (as across Europe) police and border guards are trained regularly in how to identify victims of trafficking. Indeed the spread of knowledge includes and goes beyond these front-line professionals. As Bravo (2015, 11) writes,

> Human trafficking is very "*au courant.*" School groups learn about and are appalled by its existence. Police officers, hotel workers, social workers,

> and taxi drivers are trained to recognize it on street corners, in restaurants, nail salons, and hospitals, and to report it to law enforcement officials. Committed and dedicated activists and non-governmental organizations rescue and rehabilitate its victims, and lobby their legislators for the adoption and implementation of anti-human trafficking campaigns.

As this quotation suggests, common knowledge about human trafficking is often generated by means that are to be expected, particularly NGO campaigns, but also in ways that are less overt such as inclusion in school curricula and in workplace training beyond the obvious profession of policing. Additional means by which knowledge becomes widespread, as will be exemplified in the next section, include fictional and 'non-fictional' presentations of the problem and support from celebrities for the cause.

Yet, before proceeding to the examples, it is important to remember that common knowledge is neither completely settled nor neutral. Finnemore and Sikkink's account of common knowledge does seem to imply that with it comes a death of controversy, its replacement with technocracy and virtual automatic norm conformance. Such a dynamic can be seen around human trafficking to some extent, given for instance the high ratification rates for Palermo and its regional counterparts and the complex anti-trafficking architecture that emerged consequently. Yet, as this book touches on repeatedly, controversy surrounding the nature and extent of trafficking and the best responses to it persists, as evidenced for example by the debates within feminism that have not diminished over the years.

However what the examples below will reiterate is that common knowledge about human trafficking still privileges a particular version of the issue. Cinematic and journalistic accounts, celebrity foundations and discourses around global sporting events still focus especially on certain narratives. These primarily relate to sex trafficking, female vulnerability, male criminality and security threats rather than spreading knowledge about the complex experiences and multiple ends of exploitable migrant journeys and the international economic and political structural constraints that underpin their troubles. The fact that certain versions of knowledge about trafficking are more socially engrained than others is a reminder that 'knowledge is not neutral or objective' but rather 'embedded in power relations' (Hochmüller and Müller 2014, 707) and can be used to legitimate certain interventions that further the agendas of the globally privileged.

Olivier Nay offers an analysis of one example of the playing out of the politics of knowledge in the contemporary world in his discussion of the concept of 'failed states'. Borrowing a phrase from Appadurai, he traces the 'social life' of this idea (Nay 2014, 211) from its genesis in the World Bank and the Organization for Economic Cooperation and Development (OECD) outwards, demonstrating how momentum grew around this framing of the problems of certain states. After gaining traction, the idea of 'failed states' became a legitimating discourse, enabling the West to spread what it considers 'good practice' government to the global South in the form of 'benchmarking', new public management practices and setting policy standards. Although resistance to the 'failed state' concept does arise, the powers that be tend to assimilate such criticisms, adjusting the dominant framing somewhat to take the sting from criticisms, ensuring the preservation of a dominant paradigm (Nay 2014, 224). In a similar vein, as will be shown below, a dominant paradigm concerning trafficking persists although some morphing does occur to assimilate critique. Yet in the end a powerful common understanding of human trafficking persists and as a form of hegemonic knowledge is used by states to justify certain responses to the problem, entangling the issue with state-centric accounts of security preservation in the globalising world.

Common Knowledge About Human Trafficking

Every time I walk through the arrival channels at Dublin airport, I am struck by the ageing A4 poster on the walls before passengers reach the Garda National Immigration Bureau's passport control booths. The poster features the pensive face of a young woman against a black background and the question in various languages, 'sex slave'? A hotline to access help appears at the bottom of the poster. I am not sure if any young, migrant woman arriving in Ireland for whatever reason would identify herself as a potential 'sex slave' but the poster is surely also intended to speak to the general travelling public. It foments a notion of the possible danger of sexual exploitation for single women audacious enough to travel alone. In some other instances poster campaigns are not so subconsciously targeted at the general public. In the UK and Ireland the Blue Blindfold campaign, with its scary skull-like logo in Ireland, uses posters, a website and YouTube to warn the public that human trafficking is all around, urging us to 'open our eyes' to the signs of trafficking and recruiting our help to report any suspicious behaviour that might indicate trafficking, including children 'who travel in groups with persons who are not relatives' or women 'whose mobile phones ring all the time when they are out' (Blue Blindfold 2016). Such campaigns create a sense of human trafficking as a menace in so-called countries of destination and parallel campaigns are prominent in countries assumed to be places of origin for victims of trafficking.

Writing of anti-trafficking poster campaigns, it is interesting the Rutvica Andrijasevic and Bridget Anderson are equally struck by the posters they see in arrivals at UK airports (Andrijasevic and Anderson 2009, 22) but another focus of their critical engagement with such campaigns is how they are presented in places deemed to be 'countries of origin' in Central and Eastern Europe (Andrijasevic 2007). Andrijasevic analyses some striking examples of campaigns sponsored by the International Organization for Migration (IOM) in Eastern Europe. The imagery used includes women with puppet strings hooked into their flesh, women held in massive tight masculine fists, voyeuristic images of women in prostitution and shady male background characters exchanging money. In Andrijasevic's reading of these posters they dualistically fetishise women and reduce them to inanimate objects, while 'foster(ing) the assumption of wide criminalization of Eastern European societies' (Andrijasevic 2007, 27), with men the assumed perpetrators. Similar critiques of anti-trafficking campaigns exist in the work of other authors. Roy Huijsmans notes that the students he meets undertaking Development Studies in The Netherlands all come with an existent knowledge of the problem of human trafficking. Asking where such awareness comes from he points to the work of some development NGOs that take part in the process of 'globalizing knowledge' about trafficking. In particular he analyses a billboard and social media campaign generated by the NGO 'oneMen', which targets young people. Huijsmans discusses this NGO's anti-trafficking posters containing images of Indian women with bar-coded foreheads, which are designed to attract support for efforts to rescue women from Indian brothels. As he suggests, these posters are problematic in their gifting of agency to the Dutch donor, while denying it to the Indian woman, who cannot see the barcode on her forehead. As such this campaign, as many in the development sector do, replicates unequal global power relations in its production of knowledge about human trafficking (Huijsmans 2011). A further point Huijsmans makes is that nowhere in the oneMan campaign, with its emphasis on rescue efforts, are the underlying dynamics of migration regimes or other structural factors behind trafficking discussed. Indeed it might be said that one aims of all these posters is to create angst about women's migration, link migration to criminality and suggest that the safest place for women is to stay at home (Andrijasevic 2007).

Andrijasevic does write of how she took the opportunity to criticise the International Organization for Migration for the nature of its campaigns during a public debate and the surprised and chastened reaction she received from the IOM representative (Andrijasevic and Anderson 2009, 150–151). Perhaps partially due to such interventions, some contemporary IOM campaigns are not as erotic in relation to women or as shady in their depiction of men as erstwhile. For example, IOM's more recent animated anti-trafficking infomercials on YouTube feature generic characters and trafficking for various forms of labour (see for example IOM Tunisia 2013 and IOM South Africa 2009). Perhaps this is a good example however of how critical perspectives can get assimilated into hegemonic knowledge as proposed by Nay (2014, 224). Despite the changes in representation, the subliminal message of all these campaigns remains the frightening individual criminal perpetrator, the dangers of migration and the wisdom of staying at home, rather than any questioning of, for instance, the impact of migration barriers in the globalising world.

Going beyond NGO or government-fostered information campaigns, today's public perceptions of trafficking are also generated by other forms of media and artistic representation. For instance, cinematic portrayals of human trafficking are plentiful and a number of films were already mentioned in earlier chapters. Sallie Yea presents a compilation list of 23 recent film portrayals of human trafficking (a combination of feature length documentaries and works of fiction), remarking on the fact that they are virtually exclusively concerned with sex trafficking of women and children. She also discusses the use of cinema in the cause of activism, as generated by the use of post-film discussions in many places. Writing of Singapore, Yea notes that 'the filmic production and cinematic performance of the girl trafficking victim...is the principal mobilizing device of anti-trafficking solidarity and intervention'. The emotional impact of a dramatic film followed by a question-and-answer session with experts creates an 'intimate audience' who wish to do something about the problem (Yea 2015). In discussing the well-known film concerning sex trafficking from Russia to Sweden, *Lilya 4-Ever*, Emily Schuckman Matthews equally proposes that such films are intended to inspire 'post-diegetic activism' (Schuckman Matthews 2015).

Popular journalistic accounts and investigative exposés are also key generators of knowledge about human trafficking, just as they were in the earlier era of the foundation of sensationalist journalism. Gretchen

Soderlund's work (2011 and 2013), in which she demonstrated the centrality of nineteenth-century 'white slavery' trafficking stories to the historical development of newspapers, was discussed in Chap. 3. In her work she establishes how the 'rhetoric of revelation' in old and new press accounts of trafficking establish the authority of the journalist and legitimise the truth-value and generalisability of their narrative (Soderlund 2011, 208). In a similar vein, Roxana Galusca argues that American male investigative journalists covering sex trafficking today are also engaged in establishing a 'popular regime of truth'. Through their 'rescue sprees' in Asian brothels and their depictions of all the women they encounter as victims of gender violence and trauma, journalistic accounts have fed into US public perceptions and abolitionist foreign policy under Bush (Galusca 2012, 1 and 4). Chapter 4 carried a number of examples of such contemporary US newspaper stories, with reference to several major features in the *New York Times* over the last 20 years by Michael Specter, Tod Landesman and Nicholas Kristof. Kristof's work on the topic in particular is prolific, mushrooming into activism through his involvement in the 'Half the Sky Movement' (2016). Indeed his book of the same name, which features a strong focus on stories of sex trafficking and advocates for rescue from prostitution and the implementation of abolitionism, is a national bestseller (Kristof and DuWunn 2009). The Half the Sky Movement is also proud to draw attention on its website to the support it enjoys from a number of 'A-list actor celebrities'. This points to the tendency towards the 'celebritization of human trafficking' as discussed by Dina Francesca Haynes. Haynes is intrigued by the emergence of celebrities as experts on human trafficking, noting how prominent actors were called to give testimony to Congressional hearings in the run up to the TVPA reauthorisations, each offering 'confident, reductionist narratives which sway public opinion' (2014, 30). Carol Vance also remarks on the role of celebrities in advancing public knowledge of trafficking. She puzzles over the manner in which an actress who portrayed a trafficking victim (Mira Sorvino) becomes an acknowledged expert on the issue, while others devote their Foundations to tackling the problem (for example, Demi Moore and Ashton Kutcher's DNA Foundation) (Vance 2011, 941). For Haynes the allure of the trafficking issue for celebrities lies in a focus on sexual exploitation and the opportunity to pose as the 'celebrity-as-rescuer' of fetishised victims. She points out that when the issue is framed as one of migrant labour and weak protections in the context of globalisation, celebrities do not rise to the bait (Haynes 2014, 25–26).

Returning to the European space, media coverage with its wide reach into public consciousness is an important part of the cultural creation of knowledge about trafficking in this context too (Dittmer 2003). In Chap. 5 I referred to Victor Malarek's book *The Natashas* (2004) as one investigative journalistic account of trafficking of women for sexual exploitation from Russia and the Soviet successor states to Western Europe and the Middle East. Despite Malarek's investigative skills, the book is steeped in the cultural tropes common in the West that map out Eastern Europe as a barbaric and yet sexually alluring place (think *Dracula*!—Dittmer 2003). Every Russian 'trafficker' Malarek encounters is 'a goon' or a 'sweaty thug', while nightclubs are run by 'sleazy eastern European émigrés with misbegotten fortunes and visions of untapped criminal proceeds'. The 'countries of origin' for trafficked women are lands of 'discarded children' and 'brutal orphanages'. He uses terms such as 'the Wild East' to describe Russian cities or a 'pathetic corner of the world' for the Balkans. Meanwhile every Western character involved in anti-trafficking rescue work is cast in heroic light. A Western police officer is 'strapping', 'blunt', 'straight', determined to 'restore law and order to the tiny, war-ravaged Balkans', while a Catholic mission in Southern Italy literally 'saves' women from the traffickers (for further discussion of these points see Wylie 2009). Overall *The Natashas* relies on and reinforces public perception of trafficking as being about the sexual exploitation of vulnerable and naive women caught up in the dangers to the West emanating from a tawdry Eastern Europe and its criminalised masculinity.

Shorter newspaper reports about sex trafficking in daily and weekly newspapers are prolific (with one of the most enticing headlines of recent days coming from the UK *Sun* newspaper, 'Jhadis, Voodoo Murders, Sex Trafficking...We can stop them all if we leave the EU' (The Sun 2016)). To focus on one particular area more systematically, however, the conjoining of newspaper coverage with anti-trafficking campaigning has been heightened in the last decade by the implied association of sex trafficking with major sporting events. This putative connection first emerged in 2006 when Germany hosted the FIFA World Cup, prompting civil society petitions to the German government and the EU. CATW, for instance, organised an on-line petition ('Buying Sex is Not a Sport') in five languages. It was signed by more than 150,000 individuals and organisations from 125 countries and delivered to German Embassies in all the major world regions at the onset of the Games (CATW 2006).

The supposed link has re-emerged regularly ever since in relation to other World Cups and Olympics. Indeed coverage of the issue produces another of the 'vampire numbers' of trafficking statistics (Vance 2011, 936). In 2006 the expected number of 40,000 women likely to be trafficked for sexual exploitation at the World Cup surfaced through NGO activism and media accounts. This figure bobs up repeatedly whenever the connection between major sporting events and trafficking is alleged (Cooper and Branford 2013, 18). The fact that nothing like that number of cases is ever detected does nothing to puncture the estimate. Rather, the probable politics behind the number is worth exploring. Noting that the first time these allegations emerged was with respect to an event hosted by Germany, Selda Dagistanli and Sanji Milivojevic conclude that associating the World Cup with sex trafficking was a deliberate ploy. A nexus of neo-abolitionist campaigners, faith-based organisations, the Bush administration and EU officials raised the potential increase in sex trafficking in order to target Germany's liberal prostitution laws. The predicted numbers of sex trafficking victims did not transpire but the added police attention to the possibility led to arrests and deportations of sex workers (Daglistanli and Milivojevic 2013, 238).

The London Olympics of 2012 offered another occasion at which these allegations were rehearsed in public. Newspapers reported, often with tabloid-style relish, on the expected influx of prostitutes and sex trafficking victims to the UK (see for example Daily Telegraph, 2011, Morning Star, 2011, The Times, 2011, Mail Online, 2012). British politicians took up the cause and subsequently an extra £60,000 pounds was found to support anti-trafficking policing around the games. Art installations, visited by 11,725 people, were created around the venues of the games to create public awareness about the experiences of trafficking victims (Cooper and Branford 2013). Kate Cooper and Sue Branford discuss the implications of all this attention in their report commissioned by the Central American Women's Network (CAWN). Mirroring the findings of Dagistanli and Milivojevic (2013), they suggest that the press, parliament and NGOs generated a 'moral panic' about the purported problem but the outcome was not a rise in detected cases or 'rescued victims' but increased police raids on sex workers and deportations. They also note the 'inherently racist' coverage of the issue in the UK press, which homed in on allegations about Roma gangs arriving in London to beg, rob or engage in prostitution (Cooper and Branford 2013, 21).

The section above shows the myriad ways in which common knowledge about human trafficking is generated and embedded in public consciousness. Examples from newspapers, radio, film, books and campaign materials have been presented to demonstrate the pervasive presence of the problem of human trafficking in American, European and also Singaporean public discourses. Sometimes these different media even become entangled with each other in their reproduction of representations of trafficking, as for example when Landesman's *New York Times* editorial "The Girls Next Door" from 2004 was turned into the movie *Trade* (Galusca 2012, 5). Furthermore, this is only a snapshot of the range of possible materials I could refer to in order to build a picture of the spread of common knowledge about human trafficking. Others would include the wide reach of the youth-focused MTV-Exit campaign (MTV 2016) or the designation of high-profile anti-trafficking days by global or regional international organisations, such as the 'World Day against Trafficking in Persons' overseen by the UN Office on Drugs and Crime (UNODC 2016). I cannot of course substantiate a claim here that all these forms of knowledge promotion demonstrably impact the people who are exposed to them. However, an interesting interjection from a film studies scholar on this question is worth noting. Dina Iordanova recalls the scepticism her paper on the role of films in creating awareness of human trafficking provoked when presented to an audience of political scientists, one of whom asked whether films did anything more than entertain. She retorts,

> It never occurred to me that one could question the importance of popular cultural representations, especially from an 'impact' point of view—after all, a popular TV sitcom or a 'Hollywood blockbuster' has got a much broader public reach (and influence over minds) than a government white paper. (Iordanova 2010, 110)

Accepting this suggestion, my intent here is first and simply to show the omnipresence of representations of human trafficking across multiple media, and so suggest common knowledge is being created. It becomes 'taken for granted', in Finnemore and Sikkink's words, that a problem exists that is a source of worry for societies and requires responses. However, second, there are certain aspects of the framings discussed that are important to stress because they relate to the earlier point that knowledge is neither neutral nor inconsequential. In the material presented above an overwhelming (though not exclusive) focus is on sex trafficking. The vulnerability of women and children to exploitation is a perpetual feature of the various representations. Labour or broader migration issues are largely missing, as are men as anything other than criminal perpetrators or sex buyers. Importantly too orientalist, even racist framings are prevalent through references to the vulnerability of exotic female 'others' to exploitation by dodgy male characters. So, for example, analyses of cinematic portrayals of sex trafficking victims reveal the ways in which 'third world girl children' or 'post-Soviet women' are seen voyeuristically and denied any agency of over their lives through such depictions (Yea 2015; Arthurs 2012). More broadly, in his study of African women's migration to Europe, Tyron Woods proposes that discourses of human trafficking as modern day slavery (emphasising the role of parents in selling children or local agents in facilitating irregular migration) recreate colonial notions of Africa as being associated with criminality and barbarism (Woods 2013, 123). Overall, common knowledge around human trafficking can reinforce global inequalities (Huijsmans 2011), legitimate asymmetrical power relations in the world system (Nay 2014, 211) and also reinforce problematically gendered accounts of international politics.

Moreover, despite the likely intentions of the purveyors of knowledge to raise sympathy for victims of trafficking, common knowledge can backfire by encouraging and legitimating 'carceral' responses by states to the issue. Carceral approaches, as defined by Elizabeth Bernstein, involve promoting essentially 'law and order' type responses to social issues. Tracing the development of this approach as part of neo-liberal political agendas, she charts alongside this general trend the rise of 'carceral feminism' that brings activists into surprising allegiance with states. In her view feminist abolitionists in particular have fastened themselves to this carceral approach through their alliances with law enforcers to prosecute traffickers and their advocacy of laws that punish the clients of sex workers (Bernstein 2010, 47). Jennifer Musto applies this critique of 'carceral feminism' to the work of anti-trafficking NGOs in The Netherlands, who tie themselves into close cooperation with the police because gaining protections for victims depends upon those victims agreeing to be involved in prosecutions (Musto 2010, 384). The case already mentioned above of the rise in raids on brothels and deportations of migrant sex workers during heightened concerns about sex trafficking at the Olympics is another such outcome of carceral approaches to human trafficking. Similarly, Woods' study of Nigerian women in Italy shows that even when they are categorised as potential victims, 'Nigerian women in Western Europe are often incarcerated for crimes associated with drugs and commercial sex while being labeled Victims of Trafficking' (Woods 2013, 121).

Carceral approaches to human trafficking find their legitimation in the prevalent forms of common knowledge about the problem. Because the dominant ways of knowing the issue rest on notions of female vulnerability to sexual violence, male criminality and migratory threats to state security [the elements Milivojevic and Pickering (2013, 586) refer to as the 'three pillars of the global trafficking complex'], certain ways of dealing with the issue get prioritised. Thus the general tenor of many of the public campaigns described above aim to dissuade women from migrating, so reinstating paternal control over female border crossers (Milivojevic and Pickering 2013, 588). Western governments too instrumentalise 'the idiom of the vulnerable female, trafficked migrant to extend…border and immigration control capacity overseas' (Fitzgerald 2012, 228). Meanwhile, the neglect of the potential of male victimhood persists, for the reasons concerning masculinity and agency discussed in Chap. 6, and men are associated with criminal activities of either trafficking or exploiting women as sex purchasers. Both of these depictions are useful to justify carceral responses. Overall, the 'moral panic' abroad in many societies about human trafficking leads to the promotion of 'conservative interests that revolve around punitive criminal justice and exclusionary migration policies' (Dagistanli and Milivojevic 2013, 231). Drawing on this last point, it is becoming ever more clear how reliance on common knowledge about human trafficking is being used by governments to shore up nation-state borders. This has been exceptionally evident in the EU response to the migration crisis of 2015–2016.

Knowledge About Trafficking and the Legitimation of Securitised Responses to the Crisis for Migrants in Europe

When I began writing this book in 2013, I did not foresee that it would end in this way. Yet, events in Europe over the last year brought forcefully into focus the way in which being able to draw on common knowledge about human trafficking has become a key reference for European governments in pursuing a securitised response to the current migration crisis. The frequent use of language advocating militant action and border closures against 'traffickers and smugglers' has been very noticeable in regional and national governmental discourses around this crisis.

Over the year 2015–2016 there was an enormous movement of people towards Europe. Regular and irregular migration to Europe is nothing new. People move to Europe because of all kinds of war-related horrors, economic pressures or migratory desires. However, the main impetus for the heightened numbers in the 2015–2016 period was refugee flows from the civil war in Syria, alongside people fleeing conflicts in Afghanistan, Iraq and Eritrea. There are several routes, across sea and land, into Europe from the global South and East. Records from the EU's Frontex border agency reveal that in the year 2013–2014, 50,834 people moved through the 'Western Balkan route' but by 2016 these annual figures had become monthly ones, with 65,345 people on that route in the month of January 2016 alone (deSisto 2016; FRONTEX 2016).

Throughout 2015 (and since) European governments were divided and confused in their response to this human crisis. Some governments were initially willing to accept large numbers of those seeking asylum, but many others balked at allowing entry, passage, refuge or quotas. The Schengen Agreement allowing open borders within the EU for European citizens is fraying badly as several members reimpose border controls to stem migratory movements. Since September 2015, 8 of the 26 Schengen countries have reimposed border controls (The Guardian 2016a). As a result of this crisis the political and practical capabilities of the EU have been thrown into question, as have the self-professed values of the Union. The foundational values of the EU as written into its treaties include respect for human rights, equality and dignity, as well as pluralism, tolerance, justice, solidarity, non-discrimination, well-being and peace (europa.eu 2016). All appear in disarray, as so many governments and peoples attempt to shut down refugee movement and refuse to accept quotas of those on the move, leaving some Southern European countries to become 'warehouses of souls' in the haunting phrase of Greek prime minister Alexis Tsipras (The Guardian 2016b).

There is much that needs to be said about the ethics and politics of this situation. For the purposes of this book, however, the focus is necessarily more narrowly on how the international politics of human trafficking are playing out in this scenario. What is notable to me is the frequent recourse European governments make to the language of preventing human trafficking as reason to pursue securitised, even militarised, responses to this movement of people.

The securitisation of migration in the European space does pre-date the current crisis. Prior to the 1990s migration was treated as an issue of either economics or humanitarian response but this changed with the defrosting of Cold War politics. Jeff Huysmans' article on '*The European Union and the Securitization of Migration*' (2000) was among the first to analyse this trend. Huysmans argued that the completion of the internal European market and the formation of the Schengen Agreement were integral to each other. The abolition of internal borders led to the necessity of external border control and so the socio-economic project of the single European market and internal mobility spilled over into a security one. Solidifying internal cohesion came at the cost of 'reifying dangers from outside' and presenting migration as 'a danger to public order, cultural identity and labour market stability' with Schengen explicitly connecting immigration to 'terrorism, transnational crime and border control' (Huysmans 2000, 756). Sometimes it seems we are caught in a time warp as the politicians of 2015/16 continue to connect migration to these very phenomena, although the internal European cohesion this security discourse was meant to generate seems to be in far greater doubt now than before.

There are numerous examples that can be drawn from the statements of pan-European organisations and individual governments that can illustrate the connections between policing and/or military deployments against migration and the use of anti-trafficking language as justification. In one instance from Spring 2015, the European Council committed itself to 'strengthen the EU's 'presence at sea, to fight the traffickers, to prevent illegal migration flows and to reinforce internal solidarity and responsibility'. The Council also considered whether to seek consent from the UN Security Council and Libya to undertake intelligence gathering to be followed by military manoeuvres intended to 'destroy suspect boats' of traffickers and smugglers near the Libyan coast' (European Parliament at a Glance 2015).

By early 2016, EU states allied in NATO agreed to send three naval vessels to Turkish Mediterranean waters with the dual intent of returning migrants rescued from boats to Turkey and monitoring the movement of vessels in order 'to feed information to the national authorities in Greece and Turkey, to help them crack down on human trafficking and criminal networks fuelling the migration crisis' (Deutsche Presse-Agentur 2016). The International Organization for Migration mirrored these associations between trafficking and the plight of migrants. An IOM spokesman reported that, 'migrants arriving in Italy are often in "very bad conditions, having been subjected to violence by smugglers in Libya", he said, adding that women were subjected to human trafficking' (Mailonline 2016). This, perhaps unwittingly, reveals once again gendered assumptions about migration. While women might be trafficking victims, men are consciously intent on being smuggled. EUROPOL too noted 'a disturbing cross-over between organized gangs helping to smuggle refugees into the EU and human-trafficking gangs exploiting them for sex and slavery' (The Observer 2016).

Among individual European governments, the Hungarian government under Victor Orban has been particularly vociferous in using the issue of human trafficking as a means to legitimate a militarised response to migration. This is a government that makes frequent public use of a putative connection among migration, terrorism and threats to national security (Nagy 2015). Unsurprisingly, therefore, the Hungarian government was the first among EU states to decide to block its borders against migrants in a dauntingly physical manner. The Hungarian border fence, four metres of steel topped with razor wire, stretches for over 300 km at Hungary's borders with Croatia and Serbia (and in all probability Romania next). Whenever Victor Orban or members of his government speak of it they usually focus on two functions they argue it fulfils; it is both a means to secure Hungary and Europe from the criminality associated with migration and a means to keep Hungarian 'Christian' culture free of alien influences. In justifying the razor wire fence, Prime Minister Orban frequently and specifically invokes its utility as an anti-human trafficking device. For example, he referred to the fence as a means to stop or catch human traffickers, promising that Hungary will mete out 'punishment for human trafficking that will be so severe that it will be really deserved by those who do business with the life and fate of others' (NBC News 2015). At the time of writing, Orban announced an intention to extend the fence along Hungary's border with Romania on the grounds that this would 'teach Brussels, the human traffickers and the migrants that Hungary is sovereign country' (Associated Press 2016).

Prime Minister Orban might be the most flagrant user of the spectre of human trafficking as bogeyman to justify his intent to stop migrants from entering Hungary and Europe. Yet, as the paragraphs before also demonstrated, it is a language frequently resorted to by the EU, NATO, Europol and the IOM as well. In coverage of the issue and in official statements there is also a notable tendency to conflate trafficking and smuggling (despite the immense efforts back in the Palermo process to distinguish the two) and associate both with criminality, painting traffickers and smugglers as the 'folk devils' of the transnational organised criminal world (Dagistanli and Milivojevic 2013, 237) and as threats to European security. Such framing is easily achieved, despite the complex reality of the stories behind some of these people labelled as traffickers and smugglers and their activities. Sharam Koshravi who was himself an 'illegal traveller' (in his own words) reminds that not all those who profit from arranging irregular migration are easily pigeon-holed as criminals. Some are family members and some understand their actions as providing a necessary service (Khosravi 2011). However we judge the morality or otherwise of their actions, there seems little doubt that the recourse by migrants to the help of those who can facilitate entry to or passage within Europe is only exacerbated by the lack of regular and safe migration channels. Victor Orban and his ilk seem immune to the harmful consequences of their actions.

Erecting fences and denying people the opportunity to exercise their rights to claim asylum in the name of preventing human trafficking may seem a rather bizarre outcome of the anti-trafficking politics of the last two decades. Although, remembering the genesis of the Palermo Protocol inside the UN Transnational Organized Crime Convention, this should not be utterly surprising. Transnational organised crime is now identified by governments as one of several new security threats emerging in the contemporary world. By extension, the association of human trafficking with this form of crime enables states to ensure that those deemed either 'traffickers' or 'smugglers' are labelled in the public mind as organised, criminal threats to European states and security responses to them can therefore be legitimised. These discourses rely on accumulated common knowledge about human trafficking, particularly the two pillars of the 'global trafficking complex', which focus on migration and criminality (Milivojevic and Pickering 2013). And it is the accumulated common knowledge of these aspects of human trafficking, reinforced by repeated references in the context of the current migration crisis, which allow governments to legitimise exclusionary responses in public minds. Yet, there are harsh consequences for those who find themselves on the wrong sides of Europe's fences. In Kamala Kempadoo's words this is another reminder of the 'collateral damage' for migrants (Kempadoo 2015) that is a consequence of anti-trafficking policies that shore up the policing and fortification of borders.

Conclusion

Martha Finnemore and Kathryn Sikkink propose that at the far end of the lifecycle, common knowledge about a norm is so well established that it becomes 'taken for granted'. In many respects this seems to be the case in respect of human trafficking. From the outset one of the puzzles provoking this book was the disconnection between a well-established sense of a global problem existing and the lack of firm foundation for many of the claims made about it. Knowledge about trafficking has spread regardless of this disconnection and this chapter suggests that, as well as being the result of all the entrepreneurial and architecture-building processes that are charted through the earlier chapters, common knowledge has grown in other ways. Popular accounts, campaigns and media coverage are just some of the ways that social awareness of human trafficking as a 'bad thing' in need of governing has multiplied (Walters 2008). However the idea in the lifecycle model that common knowledge sees an end to controversy is fallacious, as dissident voices and perspectives remain. Moreover, it is vital to remain aware of two things. First is the politics of knowledge production and the ways that certain versions of an issue come to dominate popular discourses. And second is the lack of neutrality of knowledge and the role that recourse to common understandings can play in legitimating particular responses to issues. Common knowledge about human trafficking rests primarily on connections with sex, migration and crime (Milivojevic and Pickering 2013). As such it can be used to create a 'picture of pressing dangers out there' that allow governments to use 'the blackmail of security' (Walters 2008, 281) to pursue anti-migration responses. This produces collateral damage for migrants and consequences (intended and unintended) for the moral entrepreneurs, states and transnational organisations engaged in the international politics of human trafficking.

Bibliography

Anderson, B. (2007). Motherhood, Apple Pie and Slavery: Reflections on trafficking debates. *Centre on Migration, Policy and Society Working Paper* No. 48, 1–20.

Andrijasevic, R. (2007). Beautiful dead bodies: Gender, migration and representation in anti-trafficking campaigns. *Feminist Review, 86*, 24–44.

Andrijasevic, R., & Anderson, B. (2009). Anti-trafficking Campaigns: Decent, honest, truthful? *Feminist Review, 92*, 151–155.

AP (Associated Press). (2016). Hungary's Orban: EU leaders don't want to stop the migrants. 28 February 2016, http://bigstory.ap.org/article/d7fb79783f73486d957a1e3a83a00221/hungarys-orban-eu-leaders-dont-want-stop-migrants, date accessed 29 February 2016.

Aradau, C. (2004). The perverse politics of four-letter words: Risk and pity in the securitisation of human trafficking. *Millennium Journal of International Studies, 33*(2), 251–277.

Arthurs, J. (2012). Distant suffering, proper distance: Cosmopolitan ethics in the film portrayal of trafficked women. *International Journal of Media & Cultural Politics, 8*(2/3), 141–158.

Bernstein, E. (2010). Militarized humanitarianism meets Carceral Feminism: The politics of sex, rights, and freedom in contemporary anti-trafficking campaigns. *Signs, 36*(1), 45–72.

Blue Blindfold. (2016). Blue Blindfold. http://www.blueblindfold.gov.ie/website/bbf/bbfweb.nsf/page/knowthesigns-sexualexploitation-en, date accessed 17 February 2016.

Bravo, K. (2015). Interrogating the State's role in human trafficking. *Indiana International and Comparative Law Review, 25*(1), 9–31.

CATW. (2006). "Buying sex is not a sport" CATW launches campaign against promotion of prostitution during the World Cup Games in Germany. http://www.catwinternational.org/Content/Documents/Reports/CATW06newsletter.pdf, date accessed 27 February 2016.

Cooper, K., & Branford, S. (2013). *Exploitation and trafficking of women: Critiquing narratives during the London Olympics 2012*. London: CAWN—Central American Women's Network.

Dagistanli, S., & Miliojevic, S. (2013). Appropriating the rights of women: Moral panics, victims and exclusionary agendas in domestic and cross-borders sex crimes. *Women's Studies International Forum, 40*, 230–242.

Daily Telegraph. (2011). Smugglers 'Will Use Olympics'. http://www.nexis.com/results/enhdocview.do?docLinkInd=true&ersKey=23_T23529582665&format=GNBFI&startDocNo=26&resultsUrlKey=0_T23529594056&backKey=20_T23529594057&csi=8109&docNo=33, date accessed 28 February 2016.

deSisto, F. (2016). *The Central Mediterranean Route and the Italian Protection/Reception System: Between myth and reality*. Research seminar in Irish School of Ecumenics, Trinity College Dublin. 22 January 2016.

Deutsche Presse-Agentur. (2016). NATO anti-migrant smuggling mission will return people to Turkey. http://www.nexis.com.elib.tcd.ie/results/enhdocview.do?docLinkInd=true&ersKey=23_T23579116860&format=GNBFI&startDocNo=1&resultsUrlKey=0_T23579120745&backKey=20_T23579120746&csi=144245&docNo=5, date accessed 28 February 2016.

Dittmer, J. (2003). *European Re-union: Representations of Eastern Europe in NATO and EU Expansion*. PhD Thesis Florida State University.

European Parliament at a Glance. (2015). EU mounts new maritime operation to tackle Mediterranean People Traffickers. http://www.europarl.europa.eu/RegData/etudes/ATAG/2015/559489/EPRS_ATA%282015%29559489_EN.pdf, date accessed 29 February 2016.

Finnemore, M., & Sikkink, K. (1998). International norm dynamics and political change. *International Organization, 52*(4), 887–917.

FitzGerald, S. (2012). Vulnerable bodies, vulnerable borders: Extraterritoriality and human trafficking. *Feminist Legal Studies, 20*, 227–244.

FRONTEX. (2016). Migratory routes map. http://frontex.europa.eu/trends-and-routes/migratory-routes-map/, date accessed 28 February 2016.

Galusca, R. (2012). Slave hunters, brothel busters, and feminist interventions: Investigative journalists as anti-sex-trafficking humanitarians. *Feminist Formations, 24*(2), 1–24.

Half the Sky Movement. (2016). http://www.halftheskymovement.org/, date accessed 28 February 2016.

Haynes, D. (2014). The celebritization of human trafficking. *ANNALS AAPSS, 653*, 25–45.

Hochmüller, M., & Müller, M. (2014). Encountering knowledge production: The International Crisis Group and the Making of Mexico's Security Crisis. *Third World Quarterly, 35*(4), 705–712.

Huijsmans, R. (2011). Teaching (Anti)trafficking: Some reflections drawing on the Dutch Context. Paper presented at *Incorporating Human Trafficking in Academic Institutions: The European experience*. Organized by the Protection Project, John Hopkins University, Kloveniersburgwal 48, Oost-Indisch Huis, University of Amsterdam, 25–26 November 2011.

Huysmans, J. (2000). The European Union and the securitization of migration. *Journal of Common Market Studies, 38*(5), 751–777.

IOM South Africa. (2009). Human trafficking is real: Warning young Internet users. https://www.youtube.com/watch?v=kSdKKzdOclw, date accessed 17 February 2016.

IOM Tunisia. (2013). Anti-Trafficking Campaign (IOM): The story of Fatma. https://www.youtube.com/watch?v=rKoKfU4zuMM, date accessed 17 February 2016.

Kempadoo, K. (2015). The Modern-Day White (Wo)Man's Burden: Trends in anti-trafficking and anti-slavery campaigns. *Journal of Human Trafficking, 1*(1), 8–20.

Khosravi, S. (2011). *'Illegal' Traveller: An auto-ethnography of borders*. Basingstoke: Palgrave MacMillan.

Kristof, N., & DuWunn, S. (2009). *Half the sky: Turning oppression into opportunity for women worldwide*. New York: Alfred Knopf.

Mail OnLine. (2012). London set to be flooded with prostitutes during Olympics as Escort Agencies Touting 'Gold Medal' Services Cash in on Games Trade. http://www.nexis.com/auth/checkbrowser.do?ipcounter=1&cookieState=0&rand=0.6390606151685012&bhcp=1, date accessed 29 February 2016.

Mail Online. (2016). More than 100,000 migrants have already Reached Europe this Year, Official Statistics Show… A Landmark that was not Reached until July Last Year. http://www.nexis.com.elib.tcd.ie/results/enhdocview.do?docLinkInd=true&ersKey=23_T23583035815&format=GNBFI&startDocNo=0&resultsUrlKey=0_T23583035817&backKey=20_T23583035818&csi=397135&docNo=9, 29 February 2016.

Malarek, V. (2004). *The Natashas: The new global sex trade*. Toronto: Viking Books.

Milivojevic, S., & Pickering, S. (2013). Trafficking in people, 20 years on: Sex, migration and crime in the global anti-trafficking discourse and the rise of the 'Global Trafficking Complex'. *Current Issues in Criminal Justice, 25*(2), 585–604.

Morning Star. (2011, November 10). Johnson Snubs Conference on Women's Equality. *Morning Star.*

Musto, J. (2010). Carceral protectionism and multi-professional anti-trafficking human rights work in The Netherlands. *International Feminist Journal of Politics, 12*(3–4), 381–400.

Nagy, B. (2015). Securitization and Schizophrenia: Hungary's Unfortunate Departure from Reality. Paper presented at *Forced to Flee: Conflict in Syria and the Movement of People,* conference in Dublin City University, Institute for International Conflict Resolution and Reconstruction, 18 November 2015.

Nay, O. (2014). International organisations and the production of Hegemonic knowledge: How the World Bank and the OECD Helped Invent the Fragile State Concept. *Third World Quarterly, 35*(2), 210–231.

NBC News. (2015). *Hungary's latest barrier against migrants: Razor-wire train car.* http://www.nbcnews.com/storyline/europes-border-crisis/hungarys-latest-barrier-against-migrants-razor-wire-train-car-n426956, date accessed 26 February 2016.

Schuckman Matthews, E. (2015). Portraying trafficking in Lukas Moodysson's Lilya 4-Ever. *Feminist Media Studies, 15*(5), 829–844.

Soderlund, G. (2011). The rhetoric of revelation: Sex trafficking and journalistic expose. *Humanity: An International Journal of Human Rights, Humanitarianism and Development, 2*(2), 193–211.

Soderlund, G. (2013). *Sex trafficking, scandal and the transformation of journalism: 1885–1917.* Chicago, Illinois: University of Chicago Press.

The Guardian. (2016a). EU's Schengen Members Urged to Lift Border Checks to Save Passport-free Zone. http://www.theguardian.com/world/2016/mar/02/eus-schengen-members-urged-to-lift-border-checks-to-save-passport-free-zone, date accessed 2 March 2016.

The Guardian. (2016b). Double crisis deepens despair in Greece's 'Warehouse of Souls'. http://www.theguardian.com/world/2016/feb/27/greece-refugees-warehouse-of-souls-athens-eu-afghanistan, date accessed 2 March 2016.

The Observer. (2016). 10,000 Refugee Children are Missing, says Europol; The EU's Criminal Intelligence Agency Warns Pan-European Gangs are Targeting Minors for Sex Abuse and Slavery. http://www.nexis.com.elib.tcd.ie/results/enhdocview.do?docLinkInd=true&ersKey=23_T23583035815&format=GNBFI&startDocNo=26&resultsUrlKey=0_T23583116289&backKey=20_T23583116290&csi=143296&docNo=26, date accessed 29 February 2016.

The Sun. (2016). Jihadis, Voodoo Murders, Sex Trafficking...We can Stop them all if We Quit EU; Criminologist on Threat to Britain. http://www.nexis.com/results/enhdocview.do?docLinkInd=true&ersKey=23_T23647181042&format=GNBFI&startDocNo=0&resultsUrlKey=0_T23647181044&backKey=20_T23647181045&csi=234674&docNo=1, date accessed 29 February 2016.

The Times. (2011). What can be done to stop it? http://www.nexis.com/results/enhdocview.do?docLinkInd=true&ersKey=23_T23529582665&format=GNBFI&startDocNo=26&resultsUrlKey=0_T23529635189&backKey=20_T23529635190&csi=10939&docNo=30, date accessed 29 February 2016.

UNODC.GIFT.HUB. (2016). Global initiative to fight human trafficking. http://www.ungift.org/knowledgehub/en/about/unodc.html, date accessed 12 March 2016.

Vance, C. (2011). States of contradiction: Twelve ways to do nothing about trafficking while pretending to. *Social Research, 78*(3), 933–948.

Walters, W. (2008). Anti-policy and Anti-politics: Critical reflections on certain schemes to govern bad things. *European Journal of Cultural Studies, 11*(3), 267–288.

Woods, T. (2013). Surrogate selves: Notes on anti-trafficking and anti-blackness. *Social Identities, 19*(1), 120–134.

Wylie, G. (2009). Trafficking in women, networks of knowledge and the cultural construction of Europe. In J. Barkhoff & H. Eberhart (Eds.), *Networking across borders and frontiers: Demarcation and connectedness in European Culture and Society*. Berlin: Peter Lang.

Yea, S. (2015). Girls on film: Affective politics and the creation of an intimate anti-trafficking public in Singapore through film screenings. *Political Geography, 45*, 45–54.

CHAPTER 8

Conclusion: Why Trafficking and with What Consequences?

Introduction

At the beginning of this book, I set out to try to make sense of something that was puzzling me. That puzzle was the disconnection between the intensity of global interest and response to human trafficking, as compared to the shaky evidence about its nature and extent. Over the last 20 years it has become quite acceptable to regard human trafficking as a 'defining problem of the twenty-first century' (Shelley 2010, 58) and opposition to trafficking is now embedded as an international norm. Yet as Chap. 1 clarified, anti-trafficking discourses and architecture are built on problematic foundations. Amongst other problems, the statistics are dodgy and the politics surrounding defining victims are rife.

It remains important to remind readers here that I have no doubt that many people do experience abuses as they migrate or exploitation when they reach journey's end. Nor do I doubt that to some degree transnational organised criminality does flourish around the facilitation of irregular migration (McRedmond 2010). However, the concept of trafficking does not capture all the complexity of such experiences. While the Palermo Protocol definition is vague, it boils down to three elements—the recruitment and movement of a person under coercive or deceptive conditions and then their exploitation. Very few people fit easily into all three aspects of this definition. By carving out the 'innocent' trafficking victim, utterly deceived and exploited, the human agency of those who migrate is denied, as is the complexity of their stories. Similarly any discussion of the

G. Wylie, *The International Politics of Human Trafficking*,
DOI 10.1057/978-1-137-37775-3_8

structural factors by which nation-states create the conditions for exploitable migration is silenced (Bravo 2015, 31). Rather the 'folk devils' of criminal traffickers can be ascribed the blame (Dagistanli and Milivojevic 2013, 237). Why the category of human trafficking has become so ubiquitous as a way of framing the difficulties that arise in migration stories is therefore intriguing, as are the political consequences of its usage.

It was because of my own puzzlement in the face of these concerns that I decided to explore the questions of 'why human trafficking', 'why now' and 'with what consequences'? To do this I decided to use the norm lifecycle model, as first outlined by Martha Finnemore and Kathryn Sikkink. I was drawn to the model because its creators propose that it helps to explain puzzles about where norms come from, how they change, how they create change and how we can know that they make a difference in politics (Finnemore and Sikkink 1998). Engagement with the model enabled me to trace the emergence of the anti-trafficking norm, the work of its key entrepreneurial promoters, its tipping point and cascade through the international system to the end point of 'taken for grantedness'. Yet, as I followed the pathway in the model, I found that the norm lifecycle needed to be nuanced with, for example, reference to other historical and political factors, in order to account for the contemporary international politics of human trafficking.

In this short conclusion I will pull together the answers to my three guiding questions about human trafficking, while also reflecting more generally on what my exploration of the lifecycle model reveals about the construction of norms in international relations.

Why Human Trafficking and Why Now?

According to the lifecycle norms emerge as the result of the work of 'moral entrepreneurs'. These are basically people (as individuals or in NGOs or governments) driven by altruism, empathy or ideational commitment to pursue a new normative agenda in political life (Finnemore and Sikkink 1998, 899). One important point to surface in the analysis, however, is that norms generally have a prehistory. So, in relation to anti-trafficking activism, the current elaboration of the norm is shaped by the background of earlier activism that focused on the exploitation of women and children for sexual exploitation in the late nineteenth to mid twentieth century. The abolition of prostitution was a key aim of the dominant moral entrepreneurs of that first era. Consequently, sexual exploitation continues to be the exploitative end most readily associated with the term human trafficking. In addition, the vexed question of whether prostitution and sex trafficking are indistinguishable and whether 'neo-abolitionism' (advocating the criminalising of the purchase of sex) is the answer shapes today's 'norm battles' (van Kersbergen and Verbeek 2007, 218).

What this prehistory does not explain, however, is why anti-trafficking moral entrepreneurship re-emerged in the last decades in particular. Here it is important to see the issue of sex trafficking as part of the wider agenda of the increasingly active transnational women's movement of the 1970s onwards (Keck and Sikkink 1998). Using the newer openness of UN platforms to civil society participation (Reimann 2006), global women's movements shadowed the UN World Conferences on Women from Mexico (1975) to Beijing (1995). Issues relating to violence against women, broadly defined, were part of the feminist concerns permeating these conferences. Thus, by the Beijing Platform for Action in 1995, trafficking in women and 'the violence due to prostitution' were embedded in the outcomes (UN Women 2016). Feminist coalitions were therefore well placed when the opportunity to lobby around the negotiations to create the anti-trafficking Palermo Protocol arose within the UN. Despite the apparently unified appearance of the Platform for Action, it is not the case that feminist consensus existed about defining prostitution as violence or as inextricably linked to sex trafficking. Contending feminist voices stressed the agency of women who engage in what they understand as 'sex work' and the transnational movements that support the rights of these workers still continue to oppose the conflation of trafficking and prostitution. This perpetual contestation between feminist viewpoints offers another important insight into the lifecycle of norms. Norms are rarely singular or universal, but the scene of controversy over meaning and political aspirations. Yet, there is little doubt that feminist entrepreneurs have been crucial to the revival of the anti-trafficking norm, providing evidence for Janet Halley's suggestion that the last decades have seen the rise of 'governance feminism' (Halley 2006).

Moral entrepreneurship provoking anti-trafficking norm adoption is also clear to see in the work of other actors who took up the (sex) trafficking cause. Chapters of this book drew attention to the role of civil society actors such as evangelical Christians (in the USA and Northern Ireland), radical feminists (in the Republic of Ireland and the European Women's Lobby) and anti-slavery activists in norm promotion. The efficacy of their activism was often facilitated by individuals in governments whose theological or moral agendas coalesced with feminist abolitionism, as in the cases of G.W. Bush, Ambassador John Miller and Lord Morrow (in Northern Ireland). Each of these cases suggested that norm socialisation is not simply imposed on nation-states by international actors but also results from the local mores of those who are 'norm takers' (Acharya 2004).

However, moral entrepreneurship alone is not enough to explain the renewed salience of anti-trafficking activism in the late twentieth century. It is no coincidence that concerns about trafficking occurred contemporaneously with the end of the Cold War (Wylie and McRedmond 2010, 3). The fluidity of the post Cold War order stimulated the identification (or perhaps invention) of new international security agendas, including concerns over transnational organised crime and increasing migration in the context of neo-liberal globalisation. Such thinking ensured receptivity among nation-states to the border disciplining potential in new instruments like the UN Convention on Transnational Organized Crime [the umbrella document including the anti-trafficking Palermo Protocol and the Protocol against the Smuggling of Migrants by Land, Sea and Air (UN Treaty Collection 2000)]. The fact that the anti-trafficking norm can meet statist security interests has been demonstrated amply in the last two years, as EU states make recourse to the concepts of trafficking and smuggling in justifying their actions to block migrants seeking asylum arriving in Europe, on the grounds of combatting the security threat posed by organised criminality.

In answering the questions 'why trafficking and why now', what also becomes evident is that we tend to be forever circling around trafficking for sexual exploitation. There is a relative silence about trafficking for labour exploitation that also needs quizzing. Although the new Palermo definition expanded the range of exploitative ends trafficking can result in, labour issues are significantly neglected in terms of moral entrepreneurship or state responses. This book suggests that this occurs as a combination of the frisson of excitement around sexual exploitation that is not generated by more mundane work and gendered thinking underpinning conceptualisations of trafficking and smuggling, whereby expectations of men as agents of their own fates and not prone to the 'vulnerabilities' of femininity, militate against inspiring moral concern (Allais 2013). Equally too the neo-liberal economic interest of many states in cheap labour to maintain global competitiveness makes labour exploitation hard to define and decent work hard to protect.

The paragraphs above have singled out some of the dynamics that explain the rise of the human trafficking norm (or particular understandings of trafficking) as an international cause célèbre in the last 20 years. We are now at the stage of the norm lifecycle where a degree of common knowledge about the wrongs of trafficking and the need for government responses is well established in public discourses. Knowledge about trafficking is imbibed from diverse sources in popular culture, as well as campaigning materials and journalism. But the politics of norm construction, whether expressed in the interests of states, the activism of entrepreneurs or the cultural creation of hegemonic understandings, are not without their consequences.

What Are the Political and Human Consequences of the Trafficking Norm?

Normative efforts to promote the principle that nobody should be bought and sold, deceived and moved under duress, exploited by another human, seem in many ways to be entirely laudable. Opposition to human trafficking constitutes an archetypal case that speaks to our fundamental empathy for other humans and our revulsion at the idea of harm done to anyone, especially anyone innocent or vulnerable (Finnemore and Sikkink 1998). For many people the establishment of an anti-trafficking norm at least speaks of the desire to prevent such harm and establish the rights of those victimised. So, therefore, although the Palermo Protocol is a convoluted text and a crime control rather than human rights instrument, it is something for which we should at least give 'two cheers' (Gallagher 2015a). However, this assessment needs to be leavened, I think, by consideration of the other political consequences and human costs associated with the rise of anti-trafficking architecture from Palermo onwards.

Some of these have already been mentioned above. One was the reinforcement of gendered stereotypes of migrant masculinity with agency and criminality while femininity is associated with innocence and vulnerability. Another, the ability given to states to individualise the blame for trafficking onto criminals and so sway attention from the structures of global inequality and border regimes that create exploitable migration. Others include the categorisation of 'deserving' from 'undeserving' migrants, which the labels of 'trafficking victim' versus 'smuggled migrant' enable governments to do. By carving out a small group of victims (usually women and children) who might be deemed by states to be deceived, coerced, moved and exploited enough to be considered victims of trafficking, the vast majority of irregular migrants can be deemed unworthy of any rights or protections (Coghlan and Wylie 2011, 1518). The shift within transnational feminism to a more 'carceral' approach (Bernstein 2010) is also a worrisome consequence of anti-trafficking politics. Radical feminists now willingly partner states in law and order approaches to prostitution. Abolitionist feminists lobby for the criminalisation of sex buyers and the collaboration of victims in prosecutions rather than approaching the prostitution/sex work issue from a social justice or social work perspective (Skilbrei and Holmström 2013).

For me though perhaps the most heinous fallout from the embedding of the trafficking norm is the reinforcement of the 'securitization of migration' (Huysmans 2000) that states achieve by reference to trafficking discourses. This is a recurring motif throughout this book. Chapter 3 illustrated how the Palermo Protocol's drafts became evermore lengthy on border control measures. Chapter 5 suggested that feminist lobbyists across Ireland ended up using the politics of border enforcement to call for mirroring laws on both sides. Chapter 7 detailed some recent examples of the manner in which European governments refer to the criminal threat from traffickers to justify blocking entry to those seeking asylum. In a bizarre twist to this saga, even human rights activists and volunteers giving aid to the refugees traversing Europe in 2015–2016 are sometimes being prosecuted under people trafficking laws. In one example Lisbeth Zornig, Denmark's former Children's Ombudsman, was fined as a people trafficker after giving a lift within Denmark to a Syrian family. Not only does the anti-trafficking norm become a means for states to discipline the transnational mobility of people (Geiger and Pécoud 2013) but a means of disciplining citizens by 'criminalizing decency' in Lisbeth Zornig's words.

The Construction of Norms in IR

In this specific exploration of the evolution of the anti-trafficking norm, there is surely confirmation of the general claim made by constructivist scholars of IR that norms shape states' interests and identities (Katzenstein 1996) and that the study of norm entrepreneurship reveals how 'ought becomes is' in international politics (Finnemore and Sikkink 1998, 911). Even if we begin only from Palermo there is evidence of moral proselytisers agitating for an ideal and indelibly shaping the emerging international Protocol. Since then, judging by today's byzantine architecture worldwide, it is clear that nation-states have been socialised into the trafficking norm in a relatively short space of time. A multitude of regional conventions, domestic laws, policing practices, NGO services, education curricula, cultural representations and so on are all testimony to the grasp the anti-trafficking idea has acquired in just about 20 years. Opposition to trafficking is now a constitutive norm, shaping states' identities in the sense that adhering to it is a sign of legitimate state behaviour. It is also a regulative norm in terms of placing obligations on states to act in certain ways. The norm has cascaded through the international system through the persuasive power of civil but also political moral entrepreneurs, such as the United States and the European Union. The support for the norm coming from these powerful international actors also makes it in most states' interests to conform. Not only states, but also populations in general now share in a pervasive common awareness of human trafficking. After 20 years, it is taken for granted that a problem exists and must be addressed.

However, from reflection on the lifecycle of the trafficking norm it is equally clear that the construction of norms does not simply follow a straight path from entrepreneurs to tipping point, to cascade, to socialisation, to common knowledge. The story of how this particular norm comes to shape international politics needs to be read in the light of the critical literature about norms in IR, which I introduced in Chap. 2. Any rounded account of the norm lifecycle must necessarily be aware of politics 'before and after' and 'within and without'. I would also add here, on the basis of my analysis, politics moving 'upwards as well as downwards'.

With regard to 'politics before', the preponderant version of the trafficking norm needs to be read back into history to pinpoint the enduring legacy of prostitution abolitionism and the subsequent neglect of any version of the norm not concerned with sex. As for politics 'within and without', the internal instability of the norm must be acknowledged, in recognition of the deep contestation between entrepreneurs and on-going ideological disputes over definitions and policies. Understanding the willingness of governments to internalise the norm can only be accounted for by looking beyond entrepreneurial circles, recognising the material interests of states in adopting the norm as a means of managing the contradictions of globalisation. In reference to politics 'upwards and downwards', the trajectory of norm socialisation moves upwards, from domestic norm takers to regional bodies, as well as downwards from global elites to domestic politics. And crucially, at lifecycle's 'far end', the political consequences of norm establishment need to be constantly scrutinised 'after' adoption. In this case asking whether the establishment of the human trafficking norm is producing forms of international politics that do little to benefit those it seems, at first glance, designed to help.

Bibliography

Acharya, A. (2004). How ideas spread: Whose norms matter? Norm localization and institutional change in Asian regionalism. *International Organization, 58*(2), 239–275.

Allais, C. (2013). The profile less considered: The trafficking of men in South Africa. *South African Review of Sociology, 44*(1), 40–54.

Bernstein, E. (2010). Militarized humanitarianism meets Carceral Feminism: The politics of sex, rights, and freedom in contemporary anti-trafficking campaigns. *Signs, 36*(1), 45–72.

Bravo, K. (2015). Interrogating the State's role in human trafficking. *Indiana International and Comparative Law Review, 25*(1), 9–31.

Coghlan, D., & Wylie, G. (2011). Defining trafficking/Denying justice? Forced labour in Ireland and the consequences of trafficking discourse. *Journal of Ethnic and Migration Studies, 37*(9), 1513–1526.

Dagistanli, S., & Miliojevic, S. (2013). Appropriating the rights of women: Moral panics, victims and exclusionary agendas in domestic and cross-borders sex crimes. *Women's Studies International Forum, 40*, 230–242.

Finnemore, M., & Sikkink, K. (1998). International norm dynamics and political change. *International Organization, 52*(4), 887–917.

Gallagher, A. T. (2015a). Two cheers for the trafficking protocol. *Anti-Trafficking Review, 4*, 14–32.

Gallagher, A. T. (2015b). Exploitation in migration: Unacceptable but inevitable. *Journal of International Affairs, 68*(2), 55–74.

Geiger, M., & Pécoud, A. (2013). *Disciplining the transnational mobility of people.* Basingstoke: Palgrave MacMillan.

Halley, J., Kotiswaran, P., Shamir, H., & Thomas, C. (2006). From the International to the local in feminist legal responses to rape, prostitution, sex work and sex trafficking: Four studies in contemporary governance feminism. *Harvard Journal of Law and Gender, 29*, 335–423.

Huysmans, J. (2000). The European Union and the securitization of migration. *Journal of Common Market Studies, 38*(5), 751–777.

Katzenstein, P. (1996). *The Culture of National Security: Norms and Identity in World Politics.* New York: Colombia University Press.

Keck, M., & Sikkink, K. (1998). *Activists beyond borders: Advocacy Networks in International Politics.* Ithaca, New York: Cornell University Press.

McRedmond, P. (2010). Defining organized crime in the context of human trafficking. In G. W. McRedmond (Ed.), *Human trafficking in Europe: Character, causes, consequences* (pp. 181–197). Basingstoke: Palgrave MacMillan.

Reimann, K. (2006). A view from the top: International politics, norms and the worldwide growth of NGOs. *International Studies Quarterly, 50*(1), 45–68.

Shelley, L. (2010). *Human trafficking: A global perspective*. Cambridge: Cambridge University Press.

Skilbrei, M.-L., & Holmström, C. (2013). *Prostitution Policy in the Nordic Region: Ambiguous sympathies*. Farnham: Ashgate.

UN Treaty Collection. (2000). Protocol to prevent, suppress and punish trafficking in persons, especially women and children, supplementing the United Nations Convention against Transnational Organized Crime New York, 15 November 2000, United Nations Treaty Collection. https://treaties.un.org/Pages/ViewDetails.aspx?src=TREATY&mtdsg_no=XVIII-12-a&chapter=18&lang=en, date accessed 20 February 2016.

UN Women. (2016). World Conferences on Women. http://www.unwomen.org/en/how-we-work/intergovernmental-support/world-conferences-on-women, date accessed 27 March 2016.

van Kersbergen, K., & Verbeek, B. (2007). The politics of international norms: EU subsidiarity and the imperfect competence regime of the European Union. *European Journal of International Relations, 13*(2), 217–238.

Wylie, G., & McRedmond, P. (2010). *Human trafficking in Europe: Character, causes, consequences*. Basingstoke: Palgrave MacMillan.

References

Caballero-Anthony, M., & Cook, A. D. B. (2013). In C. Mely (Ed.), *Non-Traditional Security in Asia: Issues, challenges and framework for action.* Singapore: Institute of South East Asian Studies.

CATW. (2011). *Coalition against trafficking in women.* http://www.catwinternational.org/, date accessed 30 January 2015.

CdeBaca, L. (2013, July 11). *The State Department 2013 Trafficking in Persons Report: Testimony Luis CdeBaca.* http://www.state.gov/j/tip/rls/rm/2013/211833.htm, date accessed 21 February 2016.

Chuang, J. (2006a). Beyond a Snapshot: Preventing human trafficking in the global economy. *Indiana Journal of Global Legal Studies, 13*(1), 137–163.

Chuang, J. (2006b). The United States as Global Sheriff: Using unilateral sanctions to combat human trafficking. *Michigan Journal of International Law, 27*, 437–494.

Council and Parliament of the European Union. (2012). Directives Establishing Minimum Standards on the Rights, Support and Protection of Victims of Crime, and Replacing Council Framework Decision 2001/220/JH, 25 October 2012. http://eur-lex.europa.eu/legal-content/EN/TXT/PDF/?uri=CELEX:32012L0029&from=EN, date accessed 31 August 2015.

Council of the European Union. (2002). Council Framework Decision of 19 July 2002 on Combating Trafficking in Human Beings (2002/629/jha). http://eur-lex.europa.eu/legal-content/EN/TXT/PDF/?uri=CELEX:32002F0629&from=EN, date accessed 31 August 2015.

Council of the European Union. (2004). Residence Permit for Victims of Human Trafficking, EC Directive 2004/81/EC. http://eur-lex.europa.eu/legal-content/EN/TXT/HTML/?uri=URISERV:l33187&from=EN, date accessed 31 August 2015.

G. Wylie, *The International Politics of Human Trafficking*,
DOI 10.1057/978-1-137-37775-3

Council of the European Union. (2011). Directive 2011/36/EU of the European Parliament and of the Council of 5 April 2011 on Preventing and Combating Trafficking in Human Beings and Protecting its Victims, and Replacing Council Framework Decision 2002/629/JHA. http://eur-lex.europa.eu/legal-content/EN/TXT/PDF/?uri=CELEX:32011L0036&from=EN, date accessed 31 August 2015.

International Justice Mission. (n.d.). *Rescue thousands. Protect millions: Prove that justice for the poor is possible.* https://www.ijm.org/, date accessed 21 February 2016.

Iordanova, D. (2010). Making traffic visible: Adjusting the narrative. In W. I. Brown, D. Iordanova, & L. Torchin (Eds.), *Moving people, moving images: Cinema and trafficking in the New Europe* (pp. 84–117). St Andrews: St Andrews Film Studies.

Jordan, A. (2010). *Swedish Law to criminalize clients: A failed experiment in social engineering.* American University, Washington College of Law Issue Papers, 4.

Leidholdt, D. (n.d.). *Demand and the debate.* http://www.catwlac.org/en/wp-content/uploads/2013/10/Demand_and_the_Debate.pdf, date accessed 30 January 2015.

Nanu, C. (2012). Moldova: Women's rights and trafficking. In C. van den Anker & I. van Liempt (Eds.), *Human rights and migration: Trafficking for forced labour.* Palgrave MacMillan: Basingstoke.

OSCE Secretariat. (2015). *OSCE combatting trafficking in human beings.* http://www.osce.org/secretariat/trafficking, date accessed 31 August 2015.

The Guardian. (2016). *Danish Children's Rights activist fined for people trafficking.* http://www.theguardian.com/world/2016/mar/11/danish-childrens-rights-activist-lisbeth-zornig-people-trafficking, date accessed 27 March 2016.

TiP Report. (2006). *Trafficking in Persons Report, US State Department.* http://www.state.gov/j/tip/rls/tiprpt/2006/index.htm, date accessed 26 February 2016.

TiP Report. (2008). *Trafficking in Persons Report, US Department of State.* http://www.state.gov/j/tip/rls/tiprpt/2008/index.htm, date accessed 26 February 2016.

UK Parliament. (2006). Joint Committee On Human Rights. Examination of Witnesses (Questions 1–19) Ms Annie Campbell, Ms Rebecca Dudley, Ms Ann Hamilton And Ms Bronagh Andrew, 22 May 2006, http://www.publications.parliament.uk/pa/jt200506/jtselect/jtrights/245/6052202.html, date accessed 21 September 2015.

UNODC Eleventh session. (2000). *Ad Hoc Committee on the Elaboration of a Convention against Transnational Organized Crime.* October 2–27, 2000, https://www.unodc.org/unodc/en/treaties/CTOC/background/session11.html, date accessed 11 February 2016.

UNODC First Session. (1999). Ad Hoc Committee on the Elaboration of a Convention against Transnational Organized Crime, January 19–29, 1999. https://www.unodc.org/unodc/en/treaties/CTOC/background/session1.html, date accessed 11 February 2016.

Verité. (2015). *Strengthening protections against trafficking in persons in Federal and Corporate Supply Chains*. Research Sponsored by the US State Department, date accessed 11 January 2016.

Index

G. Wylie, *The International Politics of Human Trafficking*,
DOI 10.1057/978-1-137-37775-3

Printed by Printforce, the Netherlands